The British Firearms Law Handbook

The British Firearms Law Handbook

By

Laura Saunsbury, LL.B Consultant Solicitor

Honorary Solicitor and Shotgun Licensing Advisor to the Clay Pigeon Shooting Association

And

Nick Doherty, LL.B

of Lincoln's Inn and the Inner Temple, Barrister

With

Helen Dobby, LL.M

of the Middle Temple, Barrister

Incorporating the work previously published as

Gun Law

By the late

Godfrey Sandys-Winsch, Solicitor.

SWEET & MAXWELL

First Edition	1969	Godfrey Sandys-Winsch (as Gun Law)
Second Edition	1973	Godfrey Sandys-Winsch (as Gun Law)
Third Edition	1979	Godfrey Sandys-Winsch (as Gun Law)
Fourth Edition	1985	Godfrey Sandys-Winsch (as Gun Law)
Fifth Edition	1990	Godfrey Sandys-Winsch (as Gun Law)
Sixth Edition	1999	Godfrey Sandys-Winsch (as Gun Law)

Published in 2011 by Sweet & Maxwell, 100 Avenue Road, London NW3 3PF part of Thomson Reuters (Professional) UK Limited (Registered in England & Wales, Company No 1679046.
Registered Office and address for service: Aldgate House, 33 Aldgate High Street, London EC3N 1DL)

For further information on our products and services, visit *www.sweetandmaxwell.co.uk*

Typeset by Letterpart Ltd, Reigate, Surrey

Printed and bound in Great Britain by CPI Group (UK) Ltd, Croydon, CR0 4YY

No natural forests were destroyed to make this product; only farmed timber was used and re-planted.

A CIP catalogue record of this book is available for the British Library.

ISBN: 978-0-41404-498-2

Thomson Reuters and the Thomson Reuters logo are trademarks of Thomson Reuters.

Sweet & Maxwell ® is a registered trademark of Thomson Reuters (Professional) UK Limited.

Preface

Although this is the first edition of the British Firearms Law Handbook, it is in effect the Seventh edition of Gun Law, last published in July 1999, which this work incorporates. The aim of this book, and its predecessor, is simple; to help the ordinary reader understand the complexities of firearms legislation in Britain

As the late Godfrey Sandys-Winsch said of his intention to write a simple book in the Preface to his first edition of Gun Law in 1969, which follows, "it soon became apparent that the complications of the law would not allow the attainment" of that objective. Those familiar with this subject will agree with our view that the "complications of the law" have increased many times in the intervening 40 or so years.

This work is concerned with the law as it stands today, which we have attempted to explain in terms as concise and easily understood as possible given the complexities that exist in this area. We are not concerned with the various policies behind the legislation currently on the statute book, although there is certainly scope for the view that if the overriding objective was a reduction in armed crime, it has achieved little, whilst leading to the abolition of some shooting sports and causing additional inconvenience for many hundreds of thousands of other law abiding shooters. The administrative burden and cost on the police who have to license the activities of those lawful shooters is enormous.

The police rely heavily on the Home Office publication *Firearms Law, Guidance to the Police* to assist them in interpreting and administering firearms law and licensing. This was last published in 2002 and there has been talk for several years now of a new edition being produced. We had hoped the new *Guidance* would have been published in time to be reflected in this work but it remains unclear when it will finally become available and so we have been asked not to delay publication of this book. We can therefore only apologise if this work fails to incorporate changes to the *Guidance* which are published shortly afterwards. No doubt it is only a matter of time before there will be other developments requiring this edition to be updated, particularly if Parliament follows the recommendations made in late 2010 by the Home Affairs Select Committee inquiry into firearms control for consolidation and substantial amendments of the various Acts which form present firearms legislation. However, until such time as any of the Committee's recommendations become law, they fall outside the scope of this work. In the present edition the law is stated so as to include all amendments up to August 31, 2011.

We would like to express our gratitude to all those who have helped us with this work. There are many and so we apologise now if you have not been given an individual mention here. Nonetheless, we trust you know who you are and that your various contributions are appreciated. We would particularly like to thank Helen Dobby who is responsible for the updated Chs 10 to 13 relating to shooting game, poaching, protected birds and animals and the tenant's right to shoot. The well-known firearms expert David Dyson has, as usual, been a source of great knowledge and help to us in all of the areas covered by this book. We must also thank Joe Beatham of The Gunshop in East Barnet for his wisdom and advice, particularly in relation to Registered Firearms Dealers. Mike Wells, the General Secretary of the Sportsman's Association of Great Britain and Northern Ireland has been a great help and has drawn various matters to our attention which have been issues for that organisation's members.

We are of course indebted to Godfrey Sandys-Winsch for writing and periodically updating Gun Law, the predecessor to this work. We should perhaps say that our decision to give this new edition a different title is not in any way an attempt to minimise the value of his work in writing the book originally, and we trust it will not be viewed as such. Whilst "Gun Law" may have been a perfectly respectable term of art in our predecessor's day, the reality is that the political landscape and society in Britain have changed out of all recognition since the first edition of Gun Law was published over 40 years ago. Nowadays, the phrase 'gun law' is likely to have negative connotations in the minds of most individuals and to be associated with 'gun crime', a term that crops up all too often in the media. We hope the new title we have chosen will be more reflective of the subject matter of the book and its continuing aim to become once again a handy reference source for anyone who has an interest in firearms and wishes to stay on the right side of the law.

We should add that Gun Law was a book about firearms legislation in England and Wales. We have extended the work to cover Scotland, for the simple reason that the principle legislation applies there as it does further south. As Scottish readers will know, although the law in this area is the same, the practice and procedure in the Scottish Courts is quite different to that in England and Wales. We have dealt with this to a limited extent in Ch.5 relating to appeals. This is a further reason for the change of title.

Much has changed in the field of firearms law since the last edition of Gun Law was published in 1999 such that we have substantially rewritten and expanded parts of the text, and have added several new chapters. However, significant parts of the text from the Sixth Edition remain. Had we been required to write this book completely from scratch it would have been a significantly greater undertaking than it has been already, and it may well be that you would not be reading this now!

Finally we must thank barrister Sophie Chaplin for agreeing to undertake the proof reading of the manuscript. As they say, the errors that remain are all ours!

We are delighted to have been approached by the publishers to write a new edition of Gun Law as there is not to our knowledge any other comparable work currently available. In the six editions written by Godfrey Sandys-Winsch, he established a fine tradition of providing an accessible guide for anyone interested in firearms and shooting. We hope that we have taken on the mantle with a reasonable degree of success and have managed to continue this tradition, so that all who read this book will find it useful.

Laura Saunsbury,

Nick Doherty,
London, September 2011.

Preface to the First Edition

I have ventured to write this small book on a subject which, to the best of my belief, has not before had devoted to it a separate book. It seemed to me that there might be a wide need for such a book, from a father wondering whether he could allow his son to use an air gun to the police and others in authority who might not have the right answers at their fingertips.

It was my intention, when I began writing, to produce a book in simple terms and primarily for the ordinary person who handles a gun. Alas, it soon became apparent that the complications of the law would not allow the attainment of the first object. I have, nevertheless, tried to keep the text as straightforward as possible, but am conscious that in so doing I may have fallen between the virtue of simplicity on the one hand and the need for comprehensiveness on the other.

The law governing the use of guns is sometimes a strange mixture of the old and the new: there is the body of legislation passed between 1825 and 1850 and retained in the verbiage of an age when the infringement of gaming rights was so seriously regarded that a poacher might be transported overseas for 14 years; modern society has, on the other hand, been more concerned to curb the indiscriminate and illegal use of guns by its less responsible members and to protect wild life. This is not to say that poaching is no longer a problem; in many rural areas it is still prevalent, though a modern poacher is often, by background and method of operation, a very different fellow from his predecessor of 100 years ago.

The law relating to guns has been subjected to recent change as much as any other branch of the law, and this has necessarily added to the difficulties of writing. Gun licences were abolished on 13th December 1966, and shot gun certificates were introduced on 1st May 1968.

The law is stated in the book as at 1st January 1969.

Because, as I have said, this book was intended primarily for the ordinary person who handles a gun, I have not dealt with the following matters: military weapons; what may be called "vicious offences", by which I mean the use of guns by the criminal classes; the regulations affecting game dealers; the killing of birds and animals otherwise than by shooting, except occasionally for purposes of completing a passage in the text; and the law outside England and Wales.

I readily acknowledge the help which I have received, particularly on some of the more difficult points concerning game, from Oke's Game Laws, the last edition of which was published in 1912 and which I believe to be the only book extant (but not readily available) on the subject.

In conclusion, I would like to express my gratitude to the Home Office for the ready and comprehensive advice given on certain topics, and to Superintendent E Beverley and Mr A M Duffin for their most valuable help in perusing parts of the manuscript.

Godfrey Sandys-Winsch
Leasingham, Lincolnshire

Abbreviations used in this book

App: Appendix
Ch: Chapter
EFP: European firearms pass
FAC: Firearm Certificate
FEO: Firearms Enquiry Officer
fn: footnote
Guidance in this book refers to *Firearms Law, Guidance to the Police* (last published by the Home Office in 2002)
HO: Home Office
RFD: Registered Firearms Dealer
RIF: Realistic Imitation Firearm
s.1 firearm: section 1 firearm, i.e. a firearm as defined in section 1 Firearms Act 1968
SGC: Shotgun Certificate
UKPSA: United Kingdom Practical Shooting Association

The principle Acts relating to firearms legislation are referred to either by the year in which they were passed, e.g. 'the 1968 Act' or as 'FA 1968', and so on as appropriate. For a full list of the Acts of Parliament referred to in this book, and the relevant abbreviation, see the Table of Statutes.

TABLE OF CONTENTS

TABLE OF CASES

TABLE OF STATUTES

TABLE OF STATUTORY INSTRUMENTS

CHAPTER 1

Firearms and Ammunition: Definitions and General Exceptions

INTRODUCTION

It cannot be pretended that firearms law in Great Britain is either simple or **1–01** straightforward. The aim of this book is not to produce a highly technical legal textbook but rather to unravel the complexities with which this field of law is so frequently peppered and to make it as approachable to the average layman as possible. That said, there are times where it is difficult to avoid being legalistic. To understand the fundamental principles that are the foundations of firearms law in Britain we must begin with definitions of the key terms, some of which are inevitably rather technical in their nature. These definitions are, perhaps for obvious reasons, dealt with at the beginning of the book, although the reader who has an enquiry regarding a particular type of weapon or topic may find it helpful to consult the Table of Contents to identify the relevant chapter, and then revert back to this chapter where necessary.

The main body of the law regulating the use of firearms and ammunition is contained in the Firearms Acts of 1968 ('the principle Act') and 1982, as amended by the Firearms (Amendment) Acts of 1988, 1992 and 1994, plus two amending Acts of 1997. In addition, the Firearms Acts (Amendment) Regulations 1992 were made to implement European legislation. There are further relevant provisions in the Criminal Justice Act 2003, the Violent Crime Reduction Act 2006, the Criminal Justice and Immigration Act 2008 and the Crime and Security Act 2010.

1–02   The major parts of this book that deal with the words "firearm" and "ammunition" are Chs 2 to 9, 14, 15 (part) and 16 where those words frequently appear. Whilst the meanings of these words are very wide and will cover all ordinary cases, it is appropriate, at the outset, to examine their precise meanings. For certain purposes particular kinds of weapons are defined in the law. This is the case with prohibited weapons, s.1 firearms, shot guns and slaughtering instruments. These definitions are dealt with later in the relevant chapters.

As with all laws, there are exceptions, and the general rules which are set out in this chapter do not apply for the purposes of firearms being proved, nor do they apply to 'antiques', which are both dealt with at the end of this chapter. It must be appreciated that the law relating to firearms is a mixture of law and fact and that whilst the definitions given here have general application, there will always be items which for various reasons cannot easily be classified.

DEFINITION OF "FIREARM"

1–03   The word "firearm" is lengthily defined in the 1968 Act, and several ingredients of this definition must be examined with the help of a number of court decisions. The definition falls into two parts: the core of the definition, and the particular additions to it.

The core of the definition

1–04   The expression "firearm" means a lethal barrelled weapon of any description from which any shot, bullet or other missile can be discharged.[1] The words in this part of the definition mean as follows.

(a) Lethal

1–05   By dictionary definition this means: causing, sufficient or designed to cause, death. In fact a weapon does not have to be as deadly as this definition might at first sight suggest. A flare pistol, clearly not designed to cause death, is none the less lethal at short range and the intentions of the designer or manufacturer of the weapon are immaterial.[2] The least powerful type of air gun, which normally would cause only trivial injury, can nevertheless be classed as lethal because its

---

[1] Firearms Act 1968 (FA 1968) s.57(1).
[2] *Read v Donovan* [1947] 1 All E.R. 37.

pellet, fired at a particularly vulnerable point such as an eye, could cause death.[3] Attempts have been made by the Forensic Science Service and others to quantify lethality it terms of muzzle energy (2 foot pounds being suggested as 'lethal') but this has not been definitively established in English law.

(b) Barrelled

The relevant dictionary definition of "barrel" is: cylindrical body or trunk of an object; metal tube of gun. Thus, a barrel must at least be cylindrical; it would not be sufficient for the missile to be discharged along a groove or channel which was unenclosed for any part of its circumference. Despite the second part of the definition, it is suggested that the barrel may be made of any substance.

    The length of the barrel is immaterial in this context, although as we will see, for other reasons the length may affect the classification of a firearm under the legislation.[4]

1–06

(c) Weapon

The dictionary defines a "weapon" as a material thing designed or used (or usable) as an instrument for inflicting bodily harm on humans or animals.[5] It must be remembered that whilst a firearm is described as a "weapon", the Firearms Acts also refer to "prohibited weapons", a term which includes not only firearms but also certain other types of devices such as stun guns and CS gas canisters which do not fall within the definition of a "firearm", as (in those cases) they do not have a barrel. See further Ch.2.

1–07

(d) Any shot, bullet or other missile

Following the general rule for construing Acts of Parliament, the meaning of the words "or other missile" must be confined to things of the same kind as shot and bullet. This leads to the probable conclusion that the missile must be a solid object; thus a dart from an air gun would be included, but not liquid or gas.[6]

1–08

(e) Can be discharged

Here, also, the normal meaning of these words has been expanded by decisions of the courts and by legislation. The fact that a gun at the time of an offence is not capable of discharging a missile will not necessarily prevent it from fulfilling this part of the definition, as is shown by the following three cases:

1–09

---

[3] *Moore v Gooderham* [1960] 3 All E.R. 575; *R. v Thorpe* [1987] 2 All E.R. 108. 3.7 foot pounds has been known to cause death when an air weapon was fired into the side of a small child.

[4] For example; for the definition of a shot gun, as to which see Ch.4, and as to a 'small firearm', see Ch.2.

[5] An electric stunning device is a prohibited weapon (*Flack v Baldry* [1988] 1 All E.R. 673), as is an item which discharges CS or other noxious liquids or gasses: FA 1968 s.5(1)(b).

[6] For guns and ammunition discharging a noxious liquid, gas or other thing, see prohibited weapons in Ch.2.

Case (A)

1–10   This was a dummy revolver, with the shape and appearance of an ordinary revolver, with a barrel which was solid except for a hole which was drilled in 3/8ths of an inch from the muzzle. The revolving "cartridge chamber" was also solid except for shallow recesses at the ends of what would ordinarily be the cartridge chambers, and there was a vent hole for the escape of gas. In that state it was not capable of firing a bullet or other missile, but by five minutes' electric drilling the necessary parts could be made to do so sufficiently to kill a man at five feet.

The definition of "firearm" in that case described it as "any lethal firearm or other weapon of any description from which any shot, bullet, or other missile can be discharged, or any part thereof".

HELD: the dummy revolver was a firearm within that definition because: it contained everything else necessary for making a revolver except the barrel and therefore all the other parts of it, except those which required to be bored, were "component parts thereof" within the quoted definition; or, alternatively, the dummy as a whole was part of a firearm within the definition and, by adding something to it or adapting it, the dummy would be a complete revolver.[7]

Case (B)

1–11   This was a Scottish case concerning a double-barrelled pistol the barrels of which had been pierced but if the holes had been blocked up the pistol would have been capable of firing live ammunition. The court decided that the pistol was a firearm.[8]

Case (C)

1–12   This was a .38 starting pistol with a revolving chamber and of solid construction. The firing chambers had constrictions at the front ends. The barrel was solid except that at the muzzle end a hole had been drilled coming out at the top behind the front sight. By drilling the necessary parts the gun could fire bullets with lethal force.

HELD: following Case (A) above, the pistol was a firearm within the definition.[9]

It should be noted, for completeness that there is no limitation on the means of propulsion of the missile. The explosive charge is most common, and compressed air and liquid carbon dioxide are used for air weapons, but the use of other forces, e.g. springs, elastic or tension as used in a bow, is acceptable.[10]

If an item that was once a firearm has ceased to be capable of firing a shot with lethal potential, for whatever reason, it has ceased to be a 'firearm', unless it is

---

[7] *Cafferata v Wilson* [1936] 3 All E.R. 149.
[8] *Muir v Cassidy* 1953 S.L.T. (Sh. Ct.) 4.
[9] *R. v Freeman* [1970] 2 All E.R. 413. Although the effect of this decision is as stated, the main argument in the case was directed to the point as to whether the interpretation of the similar definition of "firearm" in the Firearms Act 1920 was still applicable.
[10] Although query to what extent a barrel is necessary for some of these methods?

still 'readily convertible'.[11] Bear in mind however that the law treats possession of component parts of a firearm the same as a firearm itself. So, for example, possession of a non working gun which still has the barrel intact is itself an offence. A firearm that is no longer capable of working, or being repaired so it will work, is usually referred to as a 'deactivated' firearm.

Deactivated Firearms

The Firearms (Amendment) Act 1988 provided a procedure by which a firearm can be deactivated to an approved standard. It provides that:—   **1–13**

> "a firearm shall be presumed, unless the contrary is shown, to be incapable of discharging any shot, bullet or other missile and has consequently ceased to be a firearm within the definition of that word, if—
>
> (a)   it bears an approved mark denoting that fact which has been made *either*by:
>   (i)   the Worshipful Company of Gunmakers of London or the Guardians of the Birmingham Proof House; *or*
>   (ii)   some other approved person, *and*
> (b)   the company or person making the mark has certified in writing that the work has been done in a manner approved[12] for rendering the firearm incapable of discharge.[13]"

Those considering buying a deactivated weapon are strongly advised to check that it carries the appropriate mark and is provided with the correct certificate, which will include the serial number of the weapon. It should be noted that there are two sets of specifications relating to deactivation: those issued in 1989 and those issued in 1995. The later specifications tend to be more stringent, but the 1989 specifications are still valid and apply to weapons deactivated up to 1995.[14]

Whether a firearm has been deactivated is always a question of fact for a court.   **1–14** It is possible therefore for a weapon to be held to be a firearm, despite the presumptions set out in the 1988 Act. It is unlikely in practice that the police would prosecute in circumstances where the owner had possession of the certificate and the weapon bore the approved mark, but not impossible. Conversely, the fact that a weapon has been deactivated but never submitted to the Proof House to be marked and has no deactivation certificate does not mean it has not ceased to be a firearm. The question of fact remains; has it been rendered inoperable? In these circumstances experience shows that the owner would be likely to face prosecution if there were any doubts about the item's capabilities.

---

[11] FA 1982, see Ch.9.
[12] Where the word 'approved' is used in this section it means approved by the Secretary of State for the Home Department. The approved marks and the approved manner of work may be found in "*Firearms Law: Specifications for the Adaptation of Shot Gun Magazines and the De-activation of Firearms*" obtainable from Stationery Office bookshops.
[13] Firearms (Amendment) Act 1988 (F(A)A 1988) s.8.
[14] See *Guidance* 2.12–2.16

Summary of the definition of "firearm"

1–15   In summary the following can be stated from the basic definition of 'firearm':—
the meaning of the word 'lethal' is very wide; the cheapest kind of air gun would
not ordinarily be described as a deadly weapon, but is considered 'lethal'. A
weapon can be lethal even if it can cause mortal injury only by striking at an
especially vulnerable point; and it matters not, it seems, if this can be achieved
only by using the weapon at point-blank range. The fact that the weapon was
never designed or sold for killing, or even harming, any person or animal is
irrelevant.

An interpretation of the words "can be discharged" is more difficult in the
context of firearms which need work done to them before they can be fired. It is
suggested that for these kinds of firearms three tests should be applied:

(1)   If the firearm meets the deactivation requirements of the Firearms
(Amendment) Act 1988 (see para.1–13), it is to be deemed incapable of
discharge unless it can be shown to be otherwise.

(2)   If the firearm is not caught by (1) above, the provisions of the Firearms Act
1982 relating to 'readily convertible firearms'(as set out in Ch.9) must be
examined. If the criteria of that Act are met, then the firearm is treated as a
s.1 firearm and, with the exceptions noted in Ch.9, becomes subject to the
law applying to a s.1 firearm.

(3)   If the firearm is not caught by (1) or (2) above, then the cases discussed at
paras 1–10 to 1–12 must be looked at to see whether the decisions there are
relevant. If those decisions prompt the conclusion that the firearm is one
that can be discharged, it will be treated as a firearm generally for the
purposes of the Firearms Acts.

The particular additions to the definition

1–16   After the core of the definition, set out above, the Act goes on to say—

"and includes—

(a)   any prohibited weapon, whether it is such a lethal weapon as aforesaid or not;
and

(b)   any component part of such a lethal or prohibited weapon; and

(c)   any accessory to any such weapon designed or adapted to diminish the noise
or flash caused by firing the weapon.[15]"

Two points in this part of the definition need to be noted.

(1) Prohibited weapon

1–17   The meaning of "prohibited weapon" is discussed fully in Ch.2.

---

[15] FA 1968 s.57(1).

(2) Component parts and accessories

It is clear from a reading of paras (b) and (c) of this part of the definition that a **1–18** component part or accessory is not caught by the definition unless the weapon to which it is related is itself a firearm within the definition discussed above or a prohibited weapon as described in Ch.2.[16]

There is no definition in law as to what constitutes a component part and there are no decided cases of general application to this question. It is suggested in *Firearms Law, Guidance to the Police* that the following constitute component parts which require separate certification:—

(i)   the barrel, chamber & cylinder;
(ii)   the frame, body or receiver;
(iii) the breech, block, bolt or other mechanism for containing the charge at the rear of the chamber;
(iv) any other part of the firearm upon which the pressure caused by firing the weapon impinges directly.[17]

In addition to these items we would probably add the firing pin (if a separate **1–19** item) and we suggest that an appropriate question might be—'Is it an item without which it will not operate as a lethal barrelled weapon?'

It is generally accepted that other items which form parts of a firearm such as magazines (detachable or not), sights and other 'furniture' are not considered component parts and possession of them is not controlled.[18]

It should be noted that items such as sound moderators need to be on certificate if they indeed come within s.57(1)(c) because they are accessories of a s.1 firearm. If they are accessories for a s.2 shotgun, or an air weapon, no licensing is necessary.[19] This can lead to problems—a sound moderator for a .22 rifle and a .22 air rifle are often identical. If you do not have it on your FAC, whether you are prosecuted for possession of the sound moderator may depend on what weapons you have in your possession!

DEFINITION OF "AMMUNITION"

The definition in the Firearms Act 1968 indicates that "ammunition" means: **1–20** ammunition for any firearm and includes grenades, bombs and other missiles, whether capable of use with a firearm or not, and also includes prohibited ammunition.[20] There are three points in this which require examination:

---

[16] For certain purposes the statutory definition of a shot gun specifically includes any component parts of it and any accessory to it designed or adapted to diminish the noise or flash caused by firing it (FA 1968 ss.3(1), 45(2), 57(4)). As to the general need for a firearm certificate for component parts and accessories, see para.3–06 onwards in Ch.3.
[17] *Guidance* 13.70
[18] *Guidance* 13.70
[19] *Guidance* 13.71
[20] FA 1968 s.57(2).

Ammunition for any firearm

1–21   The use of the words "any firearm" indicates that the definition includes ammunition for a firearm which does not fall within the definition of "firearm" as earlier discussed; in other words, the precise legal definition of "firearm" does not apply in this context.[21] Consequently, "ammunition" also includes blank ammunition for use in a blank firing gun.

Parts of ammunition

1–22   Unlike the definition of "firearm", there is no reference to a component part, and therefore the ingredients or component parts of a piece of ammunition are not caught by the definition. However the sale of primers, other than to those with an appropriate certificate, is restricted.[22] Simple possession of component parts of ammunition is not controlled, nor is possession of complete shotgun ammunition.[23]

Prohibited ammunition

1–23   The meaning of "prohibited ammunition" is discussed fully in Ch.2.

The Court of Appeal has decided that to constitute ammunition, it has to be capable of causing some effect, so a primed case constitutes ammunition, but a spent case does not.[24]

Beware that the ammunition that is frequently seen for sale at militaria fairs, boot sales and the like is *supposed* to have been rendered inert. Our experience shows that a small percentage has not been rendered inert and is still live! Check it carefully and if you do decide to buy it take the seller's name and address. If he is happy to provide his details he's probably confident it is inert.

Component parts of ammunition

1–24   There is no definition of this in the Acts, but those who reload their own ammunition will be aware that there are restrictions on the sale and purchase of primers. The prohibition relates to the sale or purchase of "cap-type primers for use in metallic ammunition" unless the seller is an RFD, or in business selling such ammunition, and the buyer holds a certificate "authorising him to possess a firearm of a relevant kind".[25] As with shotgun ammunition, simple possession of primers is not an offence, and neither is the possession of other component parts of ammunition.

---

[21] This view is reinforced by the fact that in Firearms Act 1937 (FA 1937) the wording of the first part of the definition was: ammunition for any firearm *as hereinafter defined*. The inference is therefore that in the FA 1968 the definition of "firearm" does not apply. Some prohibited weapons are not 'lethal barrelled weapons'.

[22] Violent Crime Reduction Act 2006 (VCRA 2006) s.35.

[23] FA 1968 s.4.

[24] *R. v Stubbings* [1990] Crim. L.R. 811.

[25] VCRA 2006 s.35.

GENERAL EXCEPTIONS TO THE CONTROL OF FIREARMS

There are two exceptions to the provisions in the Firearms Acts which take all types of firearm outside of the requirements of the Acts:— **1–25**

(1) Proving Firearms

The Firearms Act 1968 says:

> "Nothing in this Act shall apply to the proof houses of the Master, Wardens and Society of the Mystery of Gunmakers of the City of London and the Guardians of the Birmingham Proof House or the rifle range at Small Heath in Birmingham where firearms are sighted and tested, so as to interfere in any way with the operations of those two companies in proving firearms under the provisions of the Gun Barrel Proof Act 1868 or any other Acts for the time being in force, or to any person carrying firearms to or from any such proof house when being taken to such proof house for the purposes of proof or being removed therefrom after proof.[26]"

Any person can take a gun to the Proof House to have it proved, or be in possession of it for purposes connected with it being proved, and, as the above confirms, that individual will not be committing any offence by having that firearm in their possession even if they do not hold an FAC.

(2) Antique Firearms

The provisions of the Act do not apply to an antique firearm which is sold, transferred,[27] purchased, acquired[28] or possessed[29] as a curiosity or ornament.[30] **1–26**

When is a firearm an antique? The Act itself does not assist in any way. Until 1977 there was some support for the proposition that a firearm only became an antique when it was 100 years old. A decision of the High Court in that year[31] rejected that approach holding that the question of whether a firearm was an antique or not was a question of fact and degree to be left to the good sense and judgement of the magistrates (or Jury) trying each case. It was wrong, the Court said, to fix a particular age at which a firearm should be said to become an antique. In addition to the question as to whether the tribunal of fact considered the weapon to be an antique of itself, the Court indicated that factors which might properly be taken into account in deciding whether a firearm is held as an antique or not are: whether the owner is a genuine collector of old firearms; whether he possesses them as curiosities or ornaments; and whether they have peculiar value because of their age.

This decision would have helped to some extent if its criteria had not been upset by a 1980 case which laid down that a firearm manufactured in that century **1–27**

---

[26] FA 1968 s.58(1).
[27] "Transfer" is defined to include let on hire, give, lend, and part with possession (FA 1968 s.57(4)).
[28] "Acquire" is defined to mean hire, accept as a gift or borrow (FA 1968 s.57(4)).
[29] For commentary on the meaning of "possessed", see para.3–07.
[30] FA 1968 s.58(2).
[31] *Richards v Curwen* [1977] 3 All E.R. 426. The case concerned revolvers 83 and 85 years old respectively.

(i.e. from 1900 onwards) could not be an antique.[32] However, the latest Home Office Guidance to the Police, taking a more lenient view, indicates that some categories of firearms manufactured up to the Second World War may be classified as antiques.[33] Readers are referred to Appendix A at the end of the book which reproduces the key parts of the Guidance as to what may or may not be classified as an antique firearm. Bear in mind that the question of antiquity is affected by the continuous passage of time.

The second point to note is that antique firearms are only excluded from the operation of the 1968 Act when possessed or handled *as a curiosity or ornament*. Using them in any other way, for example by firing them, removes this exemption. It follows from this that the fact a weapon is capable of firing does not necessarily prevent it from being classified as an antique. However, possession of ammunition suitable for use in the weapon will be taken by the police as a strong indication that the item was not possessed as a curiosity, unless there is some other good reason to have such ammunition.

1–28   Another court case in 1977[34] established that a modern reproduction of an antique was not an antique and that the belief of the holder, even though honestly and reasonably held as to the age of the item, was irrelevant.

The Home Office Guidance[35] attempts to set out what they and the police consider to be antique weapons. They cite their motivation as being one of public safety and in order to achieve this objective base their criteria on whether either the method of loading or operating the firearm is 'obsolete', or the ammunition which would be suitable for use in the firearm is not now available. They provide a long list of 'obsolete' calibres.[36] If a pre-1939 weapon utilises an obsolete calibre the police should consider it to be an antique, as long as you don't actually have any ammunition for it, and you keep it as a curiosity. This criteria has nothing to do with whether a firearm is an antique, nor does it have any force of law. Cases often come before the courts regarding this issue, for example *R. v Kevin Schofield* Unreported March 2008 at Leeds Crown Court. Mr Schofield was charged with possession of a Lanchester sub-machine gun in 9mmP calibre made in 1940. 9mmP (9mm Parabellum, also called 9mm Luger) is probably the most common handgun ammunition available and is certainly not obsolete. The jury accepted that this working machine gun was an antique. Once the issue of antiquity has been raised, it is for the prosecution to prove that it is not an antique, and it is a question of fact for the jury, not a question of law for the judge.[37]

1–29   A firearm can change status as an antique. A person may possess it as a curiosity and then sell it to someone who wishes to use it. The second owner would require a certificate, but when he passed it on to his son who kept it as an ornament, he would not. The same applies to a single owner who, over time, changes his mind as to the reasons for which he keeps it. Guidance suggests a letter to the licensing authority to notify the change of status is sufficient.

---

[32] *Bennett v Brown* (1980) 71 Cr App. R 109, when an 1886 weapon was accepted as an antique but two others made after 1905 and 1910 respectively were not.
[33] *Guidance* Ch.8.
[34] *R. v Howells* [1977] 3 All E.R. 417.
[35] Ch.8. See App.A at the end of this book.
[36] *Guidance* App.5.
[37] *R. v Burke* 67 Cr. App. R. 220 CA.

The question of whether a firearm is an antique is not to be confused with the provisions in the Firearms Amendment Act 1997 regarding 'historic' handguns.[38] These provisions are dealt with in Ch.2. See the comments there as to the circumstances where a firearm certificate might be required for a firearm which would also qualify as an antique.

The question of antiquity applies to firearms, but is not considered to apply to ammunition. Those who wish to collect ammunition will need to obtain a certificate.

1–30

(3) 'Persons in the service of Her Majesty'

Whilst dealing with general exceptions it should be pointed out that '*Persons in the service of Her Majesty*' are exempt for all purposes from firearms controls.[39] This not only includes the armed forces (including the Territorial Army and Cadet Corps) and the police, but all those others one might think of within that description, such as the Serious Organised Crimes Agency or the Border Agency. The Channel Tunnel Act 1987 and the Regulations under it added 'Officers of the French Republic' to the list. For obvious reasons this exemption only applies to official duties and not to such employees' activities in a private capacity. This exemption obviously applies to all firearms and not just those that are prohibited by virtue of s.5, but includes all of those items within ss.1, 2 and 5.

It is under these powers that police officers can seize firearms and ammunition, as well as carry them.

1–31

---

[38] Firearms Amendment Act 1997 (FAA 1997) s.7.
[39] See FA 1968 s.54 for more precise details.

CHAPTER 2

Prohibited Weapons and Ammunition

GENERAL OVERVIEW

Let us begin by saying we would be the first to concede this is the most difficult chapter in the book to digest. (Heaven knows it was certainly the most difficult to write!) The terms "prohibited weapon" and "prohibited ammunition" are fundamental in the Firearms Acts. They cover a very wide range of different things and whether or not a particular firearm, other weapon or ammunition is deemed prohibited can have serious implications.

2–01

In very broad terms, "prohibited weapons" are handguns and automatic weapons, whilst "prohibited ammunition" is ammunition which is designed to explode, expand or ignite on or immediately before impact. However, it should be said this is a considerable over-simplification of a very complex area of law which even the most experienced lawyers or police officers can struggle to get to grips with. As will be seen shortly below, in a vain attempt to reduce violent gun crime, there have been a number of Acts of Parliament which have each in succession extended the scope of the terms "prohibited weapon" and "prohibited ammunition" to include further categories of item within their definitions. We are now left with a long and unwieldy list of categories of item, each of which in themselves requires defining.

As is also discussed later in this chapter, possession of prohibited weapons or prohibited ammunition without proper lawful authority is a serious criminal offence for which there can be very grave consequences. We have represented enough people who have inadvertently fallen foul of this area of law to know that you cannot be too careful about checking whether an item in your possession might potentially be classified as a prohibited firearm or ammunition. Therefore, whilst this does not make for easy reading, we considered it our duty to fully explore in this work the finer details of what is included in the terms "prohibited weapons" and "prohibited ammunition".

2–02

DEFINITION OF PROHIBITED WEAPONS

2–03   In general terms, "prohibited weapons" are those considered by the legislature to be so dangerous that the special authority of the Home Office is needed before their possession or use becomes lawful. In the Firearms Act 1968 as originally enacted, which remains the basis of modern firearms legislation, prohibited weapons included only automatic weapons and those discharging noxious liquids and other things. The violent incidents at Hungerford in 1987 and at Dunblane in 1996 have caused Parliament to add several other types of weapon to the listing. In addition, European legislation[1] has required Parliament to make further amendments.

The following is the current list of Prohibited weapons using the Section and subsection numbers in the Act for ease of reference:—

5(1)(a)   Any firearm which is so designed or adapted that two or more missiles can be successively discharged without repeated pressure on the trigger.[2]

5(1)(ab)   Any self-loading[3] or pump-action[4] rifled[5] gun, other than one which is chambered for .22 rim-fire cartridges.

5(1)(aba)   Any firearm which *either* has a barrel less than 30cm (about 11.8 inches) long *or* is less than 60cm (about 23.6 inches) in length overall, other than an air weapon, a muzzle-loading gun or a firearm designed as signalling apparatus.[6]

5(1)(ac)   Any self-loading or pump-action smooth-bore gun which is not an air weapon or chambered for .22 rim-fire cartridges *and either* has a barrel less than 24 inches long[7]*or* is less than 40 inches in length overall.[8]

5(1)(ad)   Any smooth-bore revolver gun[9] other than one which is chambered for 9mm rim-fire cartridges or a muzzle-loading[10] gun.

5(1)(ae)   Any rocket launcher, or any mortar, for projecting a stabilised missile, other than a launcher or mortar designed for line-throwing[11] or pyrotechnic[12] purposes, or as signalling apparatus.

---

[1] Directive 91/477/EEC which was translated into English law by the Firearms Acts (Amendment) Regulations.1992, and others, which attempt to 'harmonise' firearms legislation across the Union.

[2] This includes burst fire weapons.

[3] This means a weapon designed or adapted, so that it is automatically re-loaded (FA 1968 s.57(2A); F(A)A 1988 s.25(2)).

[4] This means a weapon so designed or adapted that it is re-loaded by the manual operation of the fore-end or forestock of the weapon (FA 1968 s.57(2A)).

[5] i.e. not smooth bored.

[6] For the purposes of subs.(1)(aba) and (1)(ac) any detachable, folding, retractable or other moveable butt-stock shall be disregarded in measuring the length of any firearm (FA 1968 s.5(8); F(A)A 1997 s.1(6)). Items in this category are often referred to as 'small firearms'.

[7] Measurement is from the muzzle to the point at which the charge is exploded (FA 1968 s.57(6)(a); F(A)A 1988 s.25(1)).

[8] See fn.7 above with regard to measuring the overall length of the gun.

[9] "Revolver" in relation to a smooth-bore gun means a gun containing a series of chambers which revolve when the gun is fired (FA 1968 s.57(2D), F(A)A 1988 s.25(2)).

[10] A muzzle-loading gun is a gun which is designed to be loaded at the muzzle end of the barrel or chamber with a loose charge and a separate ball (or other missile) (FA 1968 s.5(9); F(A)A 1997 s.1(6)).

[11] e.g. for coastguard rescue purposes.

[12] i.e. for firework displays.

5(1)(af) Any air rifle, air gun or air pistol which uses, or is designed or adapted for use with, a self-contained gas cartridge system.[13]

5(1)(b) Any weapon of whatever description designed or adapted for the discharge of any noxious liquid, gas or other thing.[14]

5(1A)(a) Any firearm which is disguised as another object.[15]

5(1A)(c) Any launcher or other projecting apparatus not falling within 5(1)(ae) above which is designed to be used with any rocket or ammunition falling within 5(1A)(b), or with ammunition which would fall within that subsection, but for it being ammunition falling within subsection 5(1)(c).[16]

The Home Office may, within limitations, add other firearms, except air weapons, to the foregoing list.[17]   **2–04**

As to 5(1)(b) above, the words "weapon of whatever description" show that the weapon need not be any sort of gun or in any way resemble a gun.[18] A dictionary definition of a weapon is "a material thing designed or used or usable as an instrument for inflicting bodily harm."

The word "noxious", meaning 'harmful or unwholesome', is thought to apply to the words "gas" and "other thing" as well as to "liquid". The words "other thing" should be interpreted, it is suggested, as meaning "any other thing of any kind", i.e. their meaning is not restricted to a thing which is of the same kind as liquid or gas.[19] Thus it appears that the last seven words in item 5(1)(b) could be written as "any noxious liquid, any noxious gas, or any noxious thing of any kind".[20] It is interesting to note that, as already stated, the most common item in practice in this category is CS gas. This is carried by police forces throughout this country for the very reason that it causes no lasting damage to the body. Is it therefore 'noxious' within the above meaning? Arguably not, but the courts have always tended to readily accept CS gas is 'noxious' and have therefore classified as a prohibited weapon any item designed for the discharge of CS gas.

As to items in 5(1)(a) above, there are three court decisions concerned with   **2–05** automatic weapons which had been modified or adapted, or were incomplete. It has been held that a sub-machine gun which had been modified to prevent it from being fired when the automatic mode was selected was not a prohibited weapon,[21] but an adaptation to the trigger mechanism of an automatic weapon making the firing of single shots easier did not prevent the weapon from being an

---

[13] Anti-Social Behaviour Act 2003 s.39(3). Although not the only type, these are predominately known as 'Brococks'.

[14] This has wide application, but by far the most common in practice are items which discharge CS gas, freely available in Europe. Electricity is a noxious thing and its discharge by means of an electric stunning device is a discharge within the meaning of that word. Such a device is a therefore a prohibited weapon (*Flack v Baldry* [1988] 1 All E.R. 673), Cattle prods are not. Likewise, weapons specially designed or adapted to discharge tranquillising darts are prohibited weapons.

[15] This is to comply with European criteria. Firearms and swords that look like umbrellas or walking sticks are common examples.

[16] See paras 2–06 and 2–07 for discussion of items falling under this category and the associated ammunition under FA 1968 s.5(1A)(b) & 5(1)(c).

[17] F(A)A 1988 s.1(4).

[18] This is demonstrated by a 'Taser' being classified as a prohibited weapon.

[19] This construction is different from that applied to the words "any shot, bullet or other missile" at para.1–04 because the words "liquid" and "gas" do not constitute a category or class of thing (*Halsbury's Laws of England*, 4th edn, Vol.44, para.877).

[20] In the absence of any court decisions on the point, this interpretation can be tentative only.

[21] *R. v Jobling* [1981] Crim L.R. 625.

automatic weapon and therefore prohibited.[22] The third case concerned a sub-machine gun lacking three parts which could easily be replaced so as to make it fire normally; the Court decided that the gun was a prohibited weapon.[23] In only the first of these decisions did the Court rule that the weapon was not prohibited. As already mentioned, it has become increasingly important to ascertain whether an item is indeed a 'prohibited' weapon as possession etc. of such weapons now carries a mandatory minimum term of five years imprisonment.

In the past attempts were sometimes made to take firearms out of the prohibited category by 'converting' them to a weapon in a lower category. Perhaps the most obvious example being to smooth bore a machine gun or rifle and thereby (under the previous legislation) removing it from s.5, or s.1, and placing into s.2, a smooth-bore gun. Parliament has attempted to stop this practice. The conversion of a prohibited weapon into a weapon not classified as prohibited may therefore now fail. A weapon which—

(i)   has at any time been a weapon of a kind described in ss.5(1)(a) to 5(1A)(a) above or in s.5(1A)(c) above, *and*

(ii)   is not a self-loading or pump-action[24] smooth-bore gun which has at any time been a weapon of the type described at (i) above by reason only of having had a barrel less than 24 inches long[25]

is to be treated as a prohibited weapon notwithstanding anything done to convert it into a different kind of weapon.[26]

DEFINITION OF PROHIBITED AMMUNITION

2–06   As with prohibited weapons, the classification of prohibited ammunition has been much widened since the earlier definition in the Firearms Act 1968 which only covered ammunition containing, or designed or adapted to contain, any noxious liquid, gas or other thing. The following is the current list of Prohibited ammunition using the Section and subsection numbers in the Act, as amended:—

5(1)(c) Any cartridge with a bullet designed to explode on or immediately before impact,[27] any ammunition containing or designed or adapted to contain any noxious thing as is mentioned in 5(1)(b) above and, if capable of being

---

[22] *R. v Pannell* (1983) 76 Crim App. R 53, CA.

[23] *R. v Clarke (Frederick)* [1986] 1 All E.R. 846. The Court also decided that, in any case, the incomplete gun constituted component parts of a prohibited weapon which fell within the definition of that kind of weapon by virtue of FA 1968 s.57(1)(b).

[24] This means a weapon so designed or adapted that it is re-loaded by the manual operation of the fore-end or forestock of the weapon (FA 1968 s.57(2A)).

[25] Measurement is from the muzzle to the point at which the charge is exploded (FA 1968 s.57(6)(a); F(A)A 1988 s.25(1)).

[26] F(A)A 1988 s.7(1).

[27] Hollow-point and soft-point bullets ('expanding ammunition') are not within this definition, they come within s.5(1A)(f).

used with a firearm of any description,[28] any grenade, bomb (or other like missile), or rocket or shell designed to explode as aforesaid.

5(1A)(b) Any rocket or ammunition not falling within items 5(1)(c) above which consists in or incorporates a missile designed to explode on or immediately before impact, and is for military use.[29]

5(1A)(c) Any launcher or other projecting apparatus not falling within 5(1)(ae) of that subsection which is designed to be used with any rocket or ammunition falling within paragraph 5(1A)(b) above or with ammunition which would fall within that paragraph but for it being ammunition falling within 5(1)(c).[30]

5(1A)(d) Any ammunition for military use which consists in or incorporates a missile designed so that a substance contained in the missile will ignite on or immediately before impact.[31]

5(1A)(e) Any ammunition for military use which consists in or incorporates a missile designed, on account of its having a jacket and hard-core, to penetrate armour plating, armour screening or body armour.

5(1A)(f) Any ammunition which incorporates a missile designed or adapted to expand on impact.[32]

5(1A)(g) Anything which is designed to be projected as a missile from any weapon and is designed to be, or has been, incorporated in—

    (i)   any ammunition falling within any of the preceding paragraphs; or

    (ii)   any ammunition which would fall within those items but for its being specified in subsection (1) of this section.

The Home Office may, by order, add specially dangerous ammunition of other descriptions to the foregoing list.[33]

It can be seen that some of these definitions are somewhat tortuous to say the least, particularly in relation to prohibited ammunition. An item may fall into more than one category of prohibition, but following the normal rules of statutory interpretation the list should be looked at as being in sequential order and you should consider which subsection an item is prohibited by first. It would be an incorrect approach to prosecute someone for having an item contrary to s.5(1)(aba) when in fact it is a fully automatic weapon covered by s.5(1)(a), although the item might actually fall into both classifications. This may clearly have an effect in relation to the level of punishment for any unlawful possession, but will also be relevant when considering the many exemptions which apply to s.5.

2–07

---

[28] i.e. including a firearm which does not fall within the definition of that term as discussed in Ch.1.

[29] Any rocket or ammunition which is designed to be capable of being used with a military weapon shall be taken to be for military use (FA 1968 s.5(7)(a)).

[30] This is intended to cover items such as rocket launch tubes fitted to aircraft. Launch rails are not included unless they provide initial guidance to the rocket. It is submitted that it does not cover items such as the spent launcher tube from a LAW 66 rocket, these are 'one use only' items and cannot be reused.

[31] References to a missile designed as described in this item will include references to any missile containing a substance that ignites on exposure to air (FA 1968 s.5(7)(b)). Napalm is an example. This does not include tracer or spotter ammunition.

[32] References to a missile expanding on impact include references to its deforming in any predictable manner on or immediately after impact (FA 1968 s.5(7)(c)).

[33] F(A)A 1988 s.1(4).

Those readers who have managed the significant achievement of remaining alert after reading the last few pages may have noticed that subs.5(1A)(c) appears listed as both a category of prohibited weapon and also a category of prohibited ammunition. This repetition was deliberate. Even the relatively uninformed reader will be aware that a wide variety of munitions has been designed and developed in recent years. Depending on your point of view, some of these rockets, grenades and similar items which are intended to be encompassed by the various subsections of s.5(1A) might themselves be considered to be prohibited weapons, or alternatively prohibited ammunition for use in such weapons. The inclusion of the words "for military use" in a number of the subsections of s.5(1A) makes it clear that items which create a similar effect but are designed for other purposes, such as for use in the film industry or large fireworks displays, will not be classified as prohibited.

In reality, items falling within the various categories of prohibited ammunition covered by s.5(1A) probably only amounts to a very small quantity of items in private hands. We therefore don't propose to dwell any further on this topic within this work. We might add that anyone who has an issue with any item potentially falling into any of these categories really does need to seek expert help and advice.

DEALINGS WITH PROHIBITED WEAPONS AND PROHIBITED AMMUNITION

2–08   Authority to deal with prohibited weapons and ammunition is usually known as a 'Section 5 authority' and is issued by the Home Office following consultation with the police. It will normally only be granted to those who can show a need to possess such items for business purposes, particularly for trading within the UK or abroad, or for other purposes such as theatrical or film hire. It is normal for such authority to be issued subject to conditions specified therein.

With the exceptions mentioned below, you will commit an offence if you have in your possession,[34] purchase, acquire,[35] manufacture, sell or transfer[36] any prohibited weapon or ammunition. These offences are considered very seriously by the Courts and most now carry a *mandatory minimum* sentence of five years.[37] The maximum is usually 10 years. These recent changes in the law can lead to what some might view as draconian penalties. For example self contained gas cartridge air weapons ('Brococks') were freely available until 2006 and had been widely sold since the early 1980's. There are doubtless many which once belonged to father or grandfather still in lofts, cellars and garages across the country. Those widows and children who inherit such items are automatically facing a minimum five year sentence, for an offence of which we would suggest most of the public is unaware. The courts do have the power to find 'exceptional circumstances' not to impose the mandatory minimum punishment, and it is to be hoped that in these cases such circumstances would be found, but it is a daunting prospect to go to court hoping that the normal rule of the law will be overturned

---

[34] For *Guidance* on the meaning of "possession", see para.3–07.

[35] "Acquire" is defined to mean hire, accept as a gift or borrow (FA 1968 s.57(4)).

[36] "Transfer" is defined to mean let on hire, give, lend or part with possession (FA 1968 s.57(4)).

[37] Criminal Justice Act 2003 s.287, inserting s.1A into the FA 1968.

in your case[38]. Brococks were banned because they were easy to convert to fire live .22 ammunition, and had gained popularity amongst criminal gangs.

If an authority from the Secretary of State is not held there are a number of other exceptions to the general rule that those items in s.5 are prohibited. This was necessary as, in addition to the sport of target shooting, there are a number of other legitimate uses for handguns in circumstances where they are the only realistic option.

EXCEPTIONS TO THE CONTROL OF PROHIBITED WEAPONS

In relation to s.5(1)(aba) ('small firearms') the exceptions are: **2–09**

(1)   When your handling of weapons or ammunition is covered by a **museum's** firearms licence.[39]

(2)   When you are killing livestock for human consumption if you are a licensed **slaughterman** you do not need a firearms certificate[40] to possess a slaughtering instrument[41] and suitable ammunition for use in any slaughter house or knackers yard, and this also applies to your employees. Further you do not need the authority of the Secretary of State to possess what would otherwise be a prohibited weapon by virtue of s.5(1)(aba), if you do not require a firearm certificate for the instrument by virtue of s.10 of the 1968 Act.[42] This would also cover 'prohibited' ammunition.

(3)   If you have a firearm certificate authorising your possession of a firearm conditioned for use in connection with the **humane killing of animals**, you do not need the authority of the Secretary of State to possess what would otherwise be a prohibited weapon by virtue of s.5(1)(aba).[43] This applies to vets,[44] huntsmen and hunt servants, hunters who may have to dispatch injured deer and the like, and RSPCA Inspectors. It might also apply to those who farm wild boar and other large animals where it would be desirable and necessary to have a handgun to dispatch large and dangerous animals at close quarters. The current *Guidance* suggests that a 2 shot .32 calibre revolver is adequate for this,[45] but with larger animals most

---

[38] A comprehensive analysis of the penalties available for possession of prohibited weapons is beyond the scope of this work, but in summary it is a five year minimum mandatory sentence (and a 10 year maximum) for all prohibited weapons except for s.5(1)(b) items [stun guns and CS gas]. Firearms disguised as other objects are subject to the mandatory five years, but some types of prohibited ammunition (including expanding) are not. We have indicated the relevant penalties for most offences in this book in the footnotes.

[39] See Ch.17 and Appendix B for this kind of licence.

[40] FA 1968 s.10.

[41] "Slaughtering instrument" is defined to mean a firearm which is specifically designed or adapted for the instantaneous slaughter of animals or for the instantaneous stunning of animals with a view to slaughtering them (FA 1968 s.57(4)).

[42] F(A)A 1997 s.2.

[43] F(A)A 1997 s.3.

[44] Vets at racecourses are the only persons who are considered appropriate to have a silencer for a handgun; not to prevent them frightening the horses, but the crowd. *Guidance* 13.36.

[45] *Guidance* 13.36.

practitioners would take the view it is wholly inadequate, both in terms of muzzle energy and the number of rounds available.

(4) If you have a firearm certificate authorising your possession of a **shot pistol** conditioned for use in connection with the **shooting of vermin**, you do not need the authority of the Secretary of State to possess what would otherwise be a prohibited weapon by virtue of s.5(1)(aba).[46] Such a shot pistol can only be in .410, or 9mm rimfire calibre.[47] This is for persons who control vermin (perhaps in confined spaces) where a shotgun would be too cumbersome.

(5) If you have a firearm certificate authorising your possession of a firearm conditioned for use in connection with the **starting of races at athletics meetings**, you do not need the authority of the Secretary of State to possess what would otherwise be a prohibited weapon by virtue of s.5(1)(aba).[48]

(6) If you have a firearm certificate authorising your possession of a firearm which is a **trophy of war.**[49] The item has to have been acquired before January 1, 1946. No ammunition will be permitted, and there is no charge for the certificate.[50] Trophies of war can be inherited, so it is possible to keep that Luger your grandfather liberated in Berlin at the end of the war, on certificate.

(7) **Firearms of Historic Interest**. The authority of the Secretary of State is not required to have a firearm in your possession, or to purchase or acquire it, where you are authorised by a firearm certificate to have in your possession or buy, acquire, sell or transfer a firearm which:—

(a) was manufactured before January 1, 1919 and

(b) such firearms were manufactured before that date and no ammunition is readily available for them,

subject to a condition that you do so only for the purpose of their being kept or exhibited as part of a collection.[51]

This provision ('a s.7(1) authority') allows collectors to keep such historic handguns at home, without ammunition. The Secretary of State has by Statutory Instrument[52] issued a list of calibres which are considered to be readily available and therefore firearms in those calibres are not permitted under this provision. Commonly available calibres such as .22 rimfire, 9mm and .45 ACP are all excluded. The relevant calibres are set out in Annex A. No sale or transfer may be made under these provisions except to a person who produces an appropriate authority to acquire the weapon.

(8) The authority of the Secretary of State is also not required to possess, buy, acquire, sell or transfer a firearm which is of:—

(a) particular rarity, aesthetic quality or technical interest, or,

(b) is of historical importance,

---

[46] F(A)A 1997 s.4.
[47] F(A)A 1997 s.4(2).
[48] F(A)A 1997 s.5.
[49] F(A)A 1997 s.6.
[50] *Guidance* 13.56.
[51] F(A)A 1997 s.7(1).
[52] F(A)A 1997 s.7(2).

if you are authorised by a firearm certificate or a visitor's firearm permit to
have it in your possession subject to a condition requiring it to be kept and
used only at a place designated by the Home Office[53];

This provision ('a s.7(3) authority') allows owners to keep and shoot
firearms which qualify at a limited number of locations in this country.
They may be used at those authorised locations, but may not be kept at
home. An entire book could be written on the criteria to be met for a
firearm to enjoy this exemption from prohibition, and there may well be
differences of opinion for example as to 'aesthetic qualities'. Rarity and
technical interest might be easier to resolve, but in all cases the police
would expect to see evidence of the claimed exemption. 'Historical
importance' would normally include the use of the firearm by a famous
person, or evidence of it being used in a famous battle.

Section 7 'has effect without prejudice to s.58(2) of the 1968 Act',[54] in
other words it does not affect the classification of a firearm as an antique,
dealt with in Ch.1. We would suggest that a large number, if not all,
firearms which meet the criteria in s.7(1) would also benefit from the
exemption relating to antiques, as long as they are held as a 'curiosity or
ornament'. Given that those held under s.7(1) cannot be fired, this is likely
to be so. Another anomaly is that under s.7(3) they can be fired, and so
would not qualify as antiques, but this provision relates to firearms of real
rarity or historical interest where one might imagine the owner would wish
to fire them only very occasionally, if at all, in order to preserve their
pristine condition!

(9) The authority of the Secretary of State is also not required to possess, buy,
     acquire, sell or transfer any firearm, weapon or ammunition which falls
     within the provisions of s.5(1)(aba), (b) or (c) which is designed or adapted
     for the purpose of tranquillising or otherwise **treating any animal** if you
     are authorised by a firearm certificate or a visitor's firearm permit to
     possess, buy or acquire it subject to a condition restricting its use to use in
     connection with the treatment of animals.[55]

     This applies to vets and those who run zoos and safari parks where there is
     a need to deal humanely with large and dangerous animals. It may also be
     appropriate for those who farm deer and wild boar.

(10) Section 9 of the Firearms Amendment Act 1997 introduced a general
     prohibition on **expanding ammunition**. Section 5(1A)(f) now prohibits the
     possession of "any ammunition which incorporates a missile designed or
     adapted to expand on impact".[56]

     This is generally considered to be 'semi jacketed soft point' or 'hollow
     point'. These types are designed to expand on impact causing a larger
     amount of the kinetic energy to stop in the body of the animal and thus
     ensuring a humane kill. Target or 'match' ammunition which sometimes
     has a small hole in the front and flat nosed 'wadcutter' ammunition do not
     fall within this definition.

---

[53] F(A)A 1997 ss.1(8), 7(3). There are now a number of such centres across the country.
[54] F(A)A 1997 s.7(4).
[55] F(A)A 1997 s.8.
[56] FA 1968 s.5A(8) and F(A)A 1997, Sch.3.

To allow for the continued use of such ammunition on animals the authority of the Secretary of State is not required to possess, buy, acquire, sell or transfer any ammunition which falls within the provisions of s.5(1A)(f), if—

(a)   you are authorised by a firearms certificate or a visitor's firearm permit[57] to possess, buy or acquire any expanding ammunition; *and*

(b)   the certificate or permit is subject to a condition restricting the use of such ammunition to use for one or more of the following purposes:

(i)   the lawful shooting of deer[58];

(ii)   the shooting of vermin[59] or, in the course of estate management, other wildlife[60];

(iii)   the humane killing of animals;

(iv)   the shooting of animals for the protection of other animals or humans.[61]

It should be noted that s.5(1A)(f) covers the missiles themselves, so shooters who reload have to include the number of bullet heads in their possession in their total to ensure that they are within the limit of their allowance for that calibre on their certificate. This is a common mistake as non expanding (i.e. s.1) bullet heads do not count towards your total. Expanding ammunition can only be sold or transferred to those with appropriate authority.[62].

Those who run slaughter houses and have an exemption under s.10 of the 1968 Act have a similar exemption for expanding ammunition.[63]

(11)   When you carry on the business of a firearms dealer, you or your employees may have in your possession, buy, acquire, sell or transfer any expanding ammunition or the missile for any such ammunition in the ordinary course of that business.[64]

(12)   the authority of the Secretary of State shall not be required by virtue of subs.(1A) of s.5 of this Act for any person to have in his possession, or to purchase, acquire, sell or transfer, any prohibited weapon or ammunition if he is authorised by a certificate under this Act to possess, purchase or acquire that weapon or ammunition subject to a condition that he does so only for the purpose of its being kept or exhibited as **part of a collection**.[65] Similar provisions are made for collectors recognised in other EU countries.[66] There are restrictions upon the transfer of such items by the certificate holder[67]. Essentially they can only be transferred to other individuals or museums authorised to acquire and possess them as part of a collection.

---

[57] For visitors' firearm permits, see Ch.7. All references to being exempt from prohibition in this Ch. regarding holders of a firearm certificate apply equally to those who hold a visitor's firearm permit, F(A)A 1997 s.1(8).

[58] For the shooting of deer, see Chs 10 and 12.

[59] There is no statutory definition of "vermin".

[60] For the protection of wildlife generally, see Ch.12.

[61] FA 1968 s.5A(4).

[62] FA 1968 s.5A(6).

[63] FA 1968 5A(5).

[64] FA 1968 s.5A(7).

[65] FA 1968 s.5A(1).

[66] FA 1968 s.5A(3).

[67] FA 1968 subss.5A(2&3)

CHAPTER 3

The Licensing of Section One Firearms and Ammunition

DEFINITION OF SECTION 1 FIREARM

The term "section 1 firearms" (hereafter referred to as "s.1 firearms") is **3–01** commonly applied to those guns which are caught by the definition in s.1 of the Firearms Act 1968 and which, in general, require a firearm certificate for lawful possession or use.

These firearms are mainly defined by exception,[1] but include one type of gun which can be positively identified. Rules made by the Home Office have declared certain kinds of air weapons to be specially dangerous. These are—

(1) An air rifle or air gun capable of discharging a missile so that the missile has, on discharge from the muzzle, kinetic energy exceeding 12 ft.lb., except a weapon as described below.
(2) An air pistol discharging a missile as above but with a kinetic energy exceeding 6 ft.lb., except a weapon as described below.

---

[1] FA 1968 s.1(3).

The exceptions from items (1) and (2) above are weapons designed for use only under water.

(3) An air rifle, air gun or air pistol which is disguised as another object.[2]
Air weapons include weapons powered by compressed carbon dioxide.[3]

3–02   In total, s.1 firearms consist of—

(A) Air weapons declared to be specially dangerous as above.
(B) All other kinds of firearms[4] except—
    (a) air weapons not declared to be specially dangerous as above; and
    (b) smooth-bore guns[5] (not being air guns) which—
        (i) have barrels not less than 24 inches long[6] and do not have any barrel with a bore exceeding 2 inches; *and*
        (ii) *either* have no magazine *or* have a non-detachable magazine incapable of holding more than two cartridges; *and*
        (iii) are not revolver guns.[7]

The effect of para.B(b) is that a shotgun with a magazine capable of holding more than two cartridges will be classified as a s.1 firearm rather than as a s.2 shotgun. The exemption in (ii) above for limited capacity magazines does not apply unless the magazine—

(a) bears an approved[8] mark denoting that it so limited; *and*
(b) that mark has been made, and the adaptation certified in writing as having been carried out in an approved[9] manner, by the Worshipful Company of Gunmakers of London, the Birmingham Proof House or by another approved[10] person.[11]

3–03   In other words a 2 shot capacity magazine shotgun does not qualify as a s.2 shotgun unless the magazine has the appropriate stamp from the proof house. If not it will be classified as a s.1 firearm (for which you need an FAC) even if the magazine is in fact 2 shot only.
A weapon which—

---

[2] Firearms (Dangerous Air Weapons) Rules 1969 (SI 1969/47). Item (3) was added to the list on July 1, 1993 by amending rules. Note that air weapons within item (3) are declared to be specially dangerous irrespective of their kinetic energy performance.

[3] F(A)A 1997 s.48.

[4] For the full scope of meaning of the term "firearm", see paras 1–03 to 1–09.

[5] For shot guns generally see Ch.4.

[6] Measurement is from the muzzle to the point at which the charge is exploded (FA 1968 s.57(6)(a)).

[7] FA 1968 ss.1(1)(a), (3)(a); F(A)A 1988 s.2(1), (2). "Revolver gun" in relation to a smooth-bore gun means a gun containing a series of chambers which revolve when the gun is fired (FA 1968 s.57(2B)).

[8] "Approved" means approved by the Secretary of State for the Home Department. The approved marks and the approved manner of adaptation may be found in "Firearms Law: Specifications for the Adaptation of Shot Gun Magazines and the De-activation of Firearms" obtainable from Stationery Office bookshops.

[9] As above.

[10] As above.

[11] FA 1968 ss.1(3A), 58(1); F(A)A 1988 s.2(3).

(1)   has at any time since July 1, 1989[12] been a weapon of a kind described at items (A) and (B) above, *or*

(2)   would at any time before that date have been treated as a Section 1 firearm if the present legislation had then been in force,

shall, if it has or at any time has had, a rifled barrel less than 24 inches long,[13] be treated as a s.1 firearm notwithstanding anything done to convert it into a shot gun or an air weapon.[14] But, for the foregoing purposes, the shortening of a barrel by a registered firearms dealer[15] solely to replace part of it so as to produce a barrel not less than 24 inches long shall be disregarded.[16]

Air Weapons

Air rifles below 12 foot pounds and air pistols below 6 foot pounds do not require a certificate and can be freely held, although there are now age limits as to possession and purchase, see Ch.14.[17] Be aware however that the owner and user of an air weapon obviously cannot tell the power of the weapon from firing it. This can only be determined with a chronograph which measures the muzzle velocity. Almost all firearms dealers own such a device and will check your air weapon and give you a certificate with the results for a modest fee. We thoroughly recommend that this is done when an air weapon is acquired and perhaps at three yearly intervals thereafter. We may sound paranoid, but most police forces now have air weapons checked if they come to their notice and there are a large number of prosecutions every year of persons whose air weapon (unbeknownst to them) developed 14 foot pounds. They are then in possession of a s.1 firearm without a certificate, an offence which attracts up to five years imprisonment as a maximum, and there are guidelines suggesting the penalty should usually be a custodial sentence! Being able to produce a certificate to show you had the air weapon's power tested might avoid a prosecution, and in any event, even if the certificate proves to be inaccurate, it might reduce the penalty to a conditional discharge. Possession of a firearm is an offence of 'strict liability', in other words what the owner thought about the weapon is irrelevant. You have been warned.

3–04

As stated above, 'air weapons' includes those powered by compressed carbon dioxide.[18] Guns used for paint balling games are not normally considered to be controlled under the Firearms Acts. Air weapons disguised as another object are deemed to be 'specially dangerous'[19] and so a firearm certificate would be required.

---

[12] The date on which F(A)A 1988 s.2 came into force (Firearms (Amendment) Act 1988 (Commencement No 2) Order 1989 (SI 1989/853), art.3(a) and Sch. Pt I).

[13] Measurement is from the muzzle to the point at which the charge is exploded FA 1968 s.57(6)(a).

[14] F(A)A 1988 s.7(2). "Air weapons" are defined as air rifles, air guns and air pistols (FA 1968 ss.1(3)(b), 57(4)).

[15] As to the registration of firearms dealers, see Ch.16.

[16] F(A)A 1988 s.7(3).

[17] Readers in Scotland should however be aware there are currently proposals under the Scotland Bill 2011 for the Scottish Parliament to be given devolved powers with a view to enabling them to tighten the controls on air weapons in Scotland. At the time of going to press this has not yet received Royal Assent.

[18] F(A)A 1997 s.48.

[19] Firearms (Dangerous Air Weapons) Rules 1969 r.2(b).

DEFINITION OF SECTION 1 AMMUNITION

3–05   This classification is totally defined by exception. Section 1 applies to any ammunition for a firearm[20] except:

(a)   Cartridges containing five or more shot, none of which exceeds 0.36 of an inch in diameter.

(b)   Ammunition for an air gun, air rifle or air pistol.

(c)   Blank cartridges not more than one inch in diameter.[21]

It should be mentioned here that the sale or purchase of primers for metallic ammunition must be to or by a person who holds a relevant certificate authorising possession of ammunition or a firearm 'of a relevant kind'. This does not include blanks, primers for shotgun ammunition, or rimfire ammunition. RFD's, those who trade in such components and others who do not need a certificate are exempt from this requirement.[22] This places primers in a similar position to shotgun ammunition, simple possession is not an offence, but a certificate is needed to purchase. Others can purchase on your behalf by presenting your certificate and a suitable letter.

WHEN DO I NEED A FIREARM CERTIFICATE?

3–06   Subject to the many exceptions mentioned below, you need a firearm certificate if you purchase, hire, accept as a gift, borrow or have in your possession a s.1 firearm or s.1 ammunition.[23]

Before dealing with the specific exceptions below, three matters of general application need to be noted.

The proving of firearms and the handling of antique firearms, which are described more fully in Ch.1, do not require firearm certificates.

As detailed in Ch.1, the definition of a firearm includes its component parts and accessories for diminishing noise or flash which therefore implies that these need a certificate as much as the firearm itself.

3–07   The extent of the meaning of the word "*possession*" in the requirement to hold a certificate has long been an important and contentious subject in this area of law and it may be helpful here to attempt some explanation of the word in this context. The law itself admits that it has not yet been able to evolve a satisfactory definition of the term. For example it is now decided that the word has a slightly

---

[20] For the full scope of meaning of the term "firearm" see Ch.1.

[21] FA 1968 s.1(4). The one inch measurement is to be made immediately in front of the rim or cannelure of the base of the cartridge (FA 1968 s.1(4)(c)).

[22] VCRA 2006 s.35.

[23] FA 1968 ss.1(1), 57(4), The maximum punishment for non-compliance, on summary conviction, is imprisonment for six months or a fine of the prescribed amount (currently £5,000) or both; or, on indictment, five years' imprisonment, or an unlimited fine, or both, unless the offence is committed in an aggravated form within the meaning of FA 1968 s.4(4) when the maximum term is seven years (FA 1968 s.51(1), (2) and Sch.6, Pt I). For special provisions about buying firearms in a country which is a Member State of the European Community, see F(A)A 1988 s.18A and Ch.7.

different (and less draconian) meaning when considered in relation to controlled drugs than it does in relation to firearms! However, cases decided in the last 35 years have produced some guidance.

The words should be construed in a popular and not a narrow sense; a person has possession of an object, not only when carrying it, but also when the object is in some place, e.g. a building or a vehicle, over which that person has control, unless he does not realise that the object is, or may be, in that place.[24] Even control of the place where the object is may not be necessary; in a case concerning the need for a firearm certificate it was decided that the owner of firearms kept at his mother's flat in a different part of the country might still possess the firearms even though he did not have physical custody of them.[25]

In a further case it was decided, perhaps predictably, that a person, whose only interest in a firearm was to convey it from one person to another, nonetheless had possession of it during that time.[26] In another case the court decided that the fact that the accused did not know that what he possessed was a firearm was immaterial; the offence is an absolute one.[27] **3–08**

The latest court cases on the question of possession have introduced a new concept of dual possession. C had left two of his shot guns with T for safekeeping while C and T went on holiday together and for later cleaning by T. The court held that during that period C had "proprietary possession" of the guns and T had "custodial possession".[28] Further, if you are aware that you have possession of a bag, even though you could not reasonably have known it contained a firearm, you are guilty[29]. This would be 'custodial possession'. In a drugs case you would at least have to believe that the bag contained a controlled drug, even if not the correct one. This anomaly has been pointed out to the courts who have made it clear that in relation to firearms the law will remain as it is for reasons of public policy, and this line of authorities will not be reopened,[30] so possession of a firearm (or component parts) without the correct certificate is an absolute offence.

EXCEPTIONS FROM THE NEED TO HOLD A FIREARM CERTIFICATE.

The specific cases in which a firearm certificate is not needed for a s.1 firearm are as follows:— **3–09**

(1) Firearms dealers

---

[24] *Lockyer v Gibb* [1966] 2 All E.R. 653; *Warner v Metropolitan Police Commissioner* [1968] 2 All E.R. 356.

[25] *Sullivan v Earl of Caithness* [1976] 1 All E.R. 844.

[26] *Woodage v Moss* [1974] 1 All E.R. 584. Note that if the person conveying the firearm had been a carrier in business as such or a registered firearms dealer in business as such, or acting as an employee of either, he would not have needed a firearm certificate—see items (1) and (2) at para.3–09.

[27] *R. v Hussain* [1981] 1 W.L.R. 416. The weapon in question was an 8 inch metal tube with a striker pin activated by a spring, capable of firing .32 cartridges.

[28] *Hall v Cotton* [1986] 3 All E.R. 332. Whilst the point at issue concerning possession was possession by T, who held no shot gun certificate, it is evident that the Court was of the view that there was concurrent possession by C.

[29] *R. v Steele* [1993] Crim. L. R. 298 CA.

[30] *R. v Vann & Davis* [1996] Cr. L. R. 52 CA.

The purchase, hiring, accepting as a gift, borrowing or possessing, in the ordinary course of business, of a firearm by a person carrying on the business of a firearms dealer, and registered as such, or by an employee of such a person.[31] See Ch.16 for further details.

(2) **Auctioneers, carriers and warehousemen**

The possession,[32] in the ordinary course of business, of a firearm by a person carrying on the business of an auctioneer,[33] carrier or warehouseman, or by an employee of such a person.[34]

The Police and the Home Office do not consider this exception to cover the carriage or sale of prohibited weapons (despite the wording of s.9, and the fact that the relevant part of the 1968 Act is headed 'Special exemptions from section 1 to 5'!) on the basis that a 'certificate' can only be granted in respect of firearms within s.1, or for s.2 shotguns, and not for items within s.5. Some carriers are now granted authority by the Home Office to carry prohibited firearms and ammunition. This will now include expanding ammunition.

(3) **Slaughtering instruments**[35]

(a) The possession by a licensed slaughterer[36] of a slaughtering instrument in any slaughterhouse or knacker's yard in which he is employed.[37]

(b) The possession[38] of slaughtering instruments[39] and ammunition for them for the purpose of storing them in safe custody at a slaughterhouse of knacker's yard by—

(i) the proprietor of that slaughterhouse or knacker's yard; or

(ii) a person appointed by the proprietor to take charge of those slaughtering instruments and ammunition for the purpose of such storage.[40]

3–10　　(4) **Ships and signalling apparatus**

---

[31] FA 1968 ss.8(1), 57(4). As to firearms dealers and their registration, see Ch.16. This exception applies notwithstanding that the firearm was in the possession of or bought or acquired by the dealer or his employee at a place which is not the dealer's place of business or where he is not registered as such (FA 1968 s.8(1A)).

[32] Note that possession only is covered by this exemption, and not a purchase, hiring, accepting as a gift or borrowing.

[33] Auctioneers require a police permit to cover the sale by auction of firearms. See Ch.6 regarding Police Permits.

[34] FA 1968 s.9(1). Failure to take reasonable precautions for the safe custody of a firearm by persons of these descriptions, or to report forthwith any loss or theft to the police, is an offence. The maximum punishment is six months' imprisonment, or a fine at level 5 on the standard scale (currently £5,000), or both (F(A)A 1988 s.14).

[35] See more detail in Ch.2.

[36] i.e. licensed under the Welfare of Animals (Slaughter or Killing) Regulations.1995 (SI 1995/731) or Slaughterhouses Act 1974 s.39 which was superseded by the 1995 Regulations.

[37] FA 1968 s.10(1).

[38] Note that possession only is covered by this exemption. A free certificate will be issued for the purchase or acquisition of a slaughtering instrument and ammunition (FA 1968 s.32(3)(c)).

[39] A slaughtering instrument is defined as a firearm which is specially designed or adapted for the instantaneous slaughter of animals or for the instantaneous stunning of animals with a view to slaughtering them (FA 1968 s.57(4)).

[40] FA 1968 s.10(2).

(a)   The possession[41] of a firearm on board a ship,[42] or the possession of signalling apparatus on board an aircraft or at an aerodrome, as part of the equipment of the ship, aircraft or aerodrome.[43]

(b)   The removal of signalling apparatus, which is part of the equipment of an aircraft, from one aircraft to another at an aerodrome, or from or to an aircraft at an aerodrome to or from a place appointed for the storage of the apparatus in safe custody at that aerodrome; and the keeping of such apparatus at such a place.[44]

(c)   If a permit from a constable[45] is held for the purpose, the removal of a firearm from or to a ship or signalling apparatus from or to an aircraft or aerodrome to or from such a place and for such purpose as is given in the permit.[46]

(5)   **Carrying firearms for others**

The carrying of a firearm belonging to another person, who holds a firearm certificate, under instructions from, and for the use of, that person and for sporting purposes only.[47]

This covers gun bearers and the like when the certificate holder is shooting game. Although the Act does not specify this, the police would normally expect the certificate holder to be present, or at least nearby. The bearer is not permitted to use the guns.

(6)   **Rifle clubs and muzzle-loading pistol clubs**   3–11

The possession[48] by a member of a rifle club[49] or a muzzle-loading pistol club[50] approved by the Home Office of a rifle or a muzzle-loading pistol[51] (as the case may be) when engaged as a member of the club in target shooting.[52] Such approval may restrict the types of weapons to be used at the club, may be given subject to conditions, may at any time be varied or withdrawn, and shall endure for six years (unless withdrawn earlier) from its grant or renewal.[53]

---

[41] Note that possession only is covered by this exemption, and not a purchase, hiring, accepting as a gift or borrowing.

[42] The word "ship" includes hovercraft (Hovercraft (Application of Enactments) Order 1972 (SI 1972/971) art.4, Sch.1 Pt A).

[43] FA 1968 s.13(1)(a).

[44] FA 1968 s.13(1)(b).

[45] As well as police constables, including special police constables, "constable" includes others holding that office, e.g. harbour constables. The hallmark of a constable is his attestation as such before, usually, a Magistrate.

[46] FA 1968 s.13(1)(c).

[47] FA 1968 ss.11(1). The shooting of rats in a barn is not shooting for sporting purposes only (*Morton v Chaney* [1960] 3 All E.R. 632). The Judge had obviously not tried it!

[48] Note that possession only is covered.

[49] A rifle club includes a miniature rifle club (F(A)A 1988 s.15(10)).

[50] A muzzle-loading pistol club means a club where muzzle-loading pistols are used for target shooting (F(A)A 1988 s.15(12)).

[51] A muzzle-loading pistol is defined as a pistol designed to be loaded at the muzzle end of the barrel or chamber with a loose charge and a separate ball (or other missile) (F(A)A 1988 s.15(11), (12)).

[52] F(A)A 1988 s.15(1), (11).

[53] F(A)A 1988 s.15(4), (5), (11).

A free firearm certificate will be given to a responsible officer of the club for the rifles and pistols used there by members for target shooting.[54]The Home Office publishes guidance for clubs seeking approval.[55]

Constables,[56] and those defined in the Firearms Act 1968 as "civilian officers",[57] are given wide powers to inspect club premises and records to see whether the terms of an approval have been met.[58]

This exemption applies to all full members of an approved club, not just at club premises, but also for example where a member of a club takes a firearm to another club 'when engaged as a member of the club in connection with target shooting'.[59] This exemption applies not only to 'club guns' (i.e. those held by the club Secretary on the club's firearm certificate) but to weapons owned by other members of the club.

As one would expect, the police, who administer club approval on behalf of the Home Office, require approved clubs to be properly and democratically run by responsible persons. Note however that there is no requirement in law for the officers of a club to be certificate holders themselves, although if the club itself has a certificate this will usually be held by the Secretary who will have to meet all the usual criteria for grant of a firearms certificate. Details of the approval criteria are beyond the scope of this work, but are set out in the *Guidance* and are available from all police firearms licensing departments.

3–12   Approved clubs exist for the purpose of target shooting, no other shooting sport can be involved. Members of the public who wish to acquire firearms for target shooting will inevitably have to join a HO approved club in order to demonstrate that they have a 'good reason' for each of the target weapons they wish to own. Unless a person is an existing member of another approved club, all clubs will require them to serve a probationary membership, usually six months, before granting them full membership and enabling them to apply for a firearms certificate. They will have had to demonstrate safe gun handling and an appropriate attitude to firearms generally. Clubs should, and do, refuse to make people full members if they are considered unsuitable. Sadly, there are well known tragic examples where members of clubs have gone on to commit murder with licensed weapons. A contrasting example is Barry George, also known as Barry Bulsara, the gentleman who was eventually acquitted of murdering Jill Dando, who was turned down by the club he had attempted to join[60] after four visits, as he was not considered a suitable person to possess firearms.

---

[54] The certificate may also be varied or renewed without charge, but these provisions may be limited or negatived by the terms of approval of the club (FA 1968 s.32(2), (2A).

[55] F(A)A 1988 s.15(3), (11).

[56] As well as police constables, including special police constables, "constable" includes others holding that office, e.g. harbour constables. The hallmark of a constable is his attestation as such before, usually, a Magistrate.

[57] A civilian officer is, broadly speaking, a civilian employed by a police authority. The full definition is in FA 1968 s.57(4). This is designed to include firearms enquiry officers, many of whom are retired police officers who have been re-employed as civilian staff.

[58] F(A)A 1988 s.15(7), (8), (10), (11). Obstruction of these officers in performing their duties is an offence carrying a maximum punishment of a fine at level 3 on the standard scale (currently £1,000) (F(A)A 1988 s.15(9), (11)).

[59] F(A)A 1988 s.15(1).

[60] Kensington Rifle & Pistol Club.

There are a number of anomalies relating to the Home Office approval of clubs. There is, for example, no definition in law of a 'rifle', so can an approved club purchase for the use of its members a 'carbine' (which is also not defined, except to say that 'rifle includes carbine'[61])? A recent attempt by the Metropolitan Police to prosecute a club secretary for acquiring a 'long-barrelled pistol' on a club FAC failed on this basis.[62] Perhaps partly as a result of that case and other issues which have arisen recently, Assistant Chief Constable Adrian Whiting of Dorset Police has suggested in his report into the Cumbria shootings by Derrick Bird in 2010 that consideration should be given to allowing Home Office approved clubs to be able to use all s.1 firearms.[63] This would have the advantage of clubs being approved for large capacity shotguns as well as long barrelled pistols.

Currently 'Practical Shotgun' shooting, which involves the use of large magazine capacity 'section 1 shotguns' is not covered by the s.15 exemption. Such activities obviously do not use a 'rifle' or a 'muzzle-loading pistol' but are considered by the Home Office to be a 'good reason' for an applicant to have such a shotgun. It will generally be sufficient for the applicant to state that he or she has membership of the UK Practical Shooting Association, or of a club affiliated thereto. It would appear that these clubs do not need to be Home Office 'approved', indeed the Association of Chief Police Officers (ACPO) argue that they cannot be, as they do not shoot either of the approved type of weapon.

(7) **Cadet corps**   3–13
   (a) The possession[64] by members of a cadet corps approved by the Home Office[65] while engaged as corps members in, or in connection with, drill or target practice;
   (b) The possession[66] by such members of prohibited weapons or prohibited ammunition[67] when engaged in target practice on service premises[68];
   (c) The possession[69] by persons providing instruction to such members while engaged as in (a) or (b) above.[70]
(8) **Persons supervised by members of the armed forces**

---

[61] FA 1968 s.57 (4).

[62] *R. v Michael Wells* Unreported November 2010 at Kingston Crown Court (Judge Dodgson and a Jury).

[63] The report is available at *http://www.dorset.police.uk/Default.aspx?page=626* ACC Whiting was commissioned to write this report in his capacity as Chair of the Association of Chief Police Officers Firearms & Explosives Licensing Working Group (ACPO FELWG), although he has since retired from that post.

[64] Note that possession only is covered, and not purchase, hiring, accepting as a gift or borrowing for which a certificate will have to be obtained by a responsible officer of the corps.

[65] The Home Office has given a general approval to all "recognised units" of the Combined Cadet Force, Sea Cadet Corps, Army Cadet Force and Air Training Corps.

[66] As per fn.64 above.

[67] For the meanings of "prohibited weapons" and "prohibited ammunition", see Ch.2.

[68] "Service premises" means any premises, including any ship or aircraft, used for any purpose of any of the naval, military or air forces of Her Majesty (F(A)A 1988 s.16A(3)). "Premises" includes any land (FA 1968 s.57(4)), and "land" includes land covered with water (IA 1978 s.5 and Sch.1).

[69] As per fn.64 above.

[70] FA 1968 s.54(4)–(6).

The possession on service premises[71] of a firearm by a person under the supervision of a member of the armed forces,[72] but excluding a person engaged in providing security protection on those premises.[73]

3–14   (9)   **Miniature rifle ranges and shooting galleries**

(a)   The purchase, hiring, accepting as a gift, borrowing or possessing of a miniature rifle[74] not exceeding .23 calibre by a person conducting or carrying on a miniature rifle range (whether for a rifle club or otherwise) or a shooting gallery at which in either case no firearms are used other than non-dangerous air weapons[75] or miniature rifles not exceeding .23 calibre.[76]

(b)   The use by any person at any rifle range or shooting gallery described in item (9)(a) above of the miniature rifles there described and ammunition for them.[77]

Despite the wording, this is taken to mean .22 rimfire, and not, for example, .223 centre fire. A number of shooting clubs have a miniature rifle range 'exemption' which permits any member of the public to take part, whether a club member or not, but this is really to permit shooting galleries at fairgrounds and the like to operate. Although this is as an 'exemption' from the Act in relation to small bore rifles, no paperwork is required. It is a matter of fact as to whether you are operating such a rifle range. The National Small Bore Rifle Association and the Showman's Guild do issue certificates to those who operate such ranges, but they have no force of law. Although any person is permitted to shoot, it would still be an offence if you were a prohibited person (see Ch.5) or were under age (see Ch.14).

(10)   **Theatrical performances**

The possession[78] by a person taking part in a theatrical performance or any rehearsal thereof, or in the production of a film, of a firearm during, and for the purpose of, that performance, rehearsal or production.[79]

3–15   (11)   **Athletics Meetings**

The possession[80] of a firearm by any person at an athletic meeting for the purpose of starting races at that meeting.[81]

(12)   **Police permits**

---

[71] As per fn.68 above.

[72] "Armed forces" are defined as any of the naval, military or air forces of Her Majesty (FA 1988, s.16A(3)).

[73] F(A)A 1988 s.16A(1), (2).

[74] The term "miniature rifle" is not defined in the Firearms Acts. It includes non-dangerous air weapons (for which see para.3–04) and rimfire rifles up to .22" may be used at the rifle range or shooting gallery without a firearms certificate.

[75] For these weapons, see para.3–04.

[76] FA 1968 ss.11(4), 57(4).

[77] FA 1968 s.11(4).

[78] Note that possession only is covered by this exemption, and not a purchase, hiring, accepting as a gift or borrowing.

[79] FA 1968 s.12(1). This exemption may be taken to apply equally to television productions and rehearsals.

[80] Note that possession only is covered by this exemption, and not a purchase, hiring, accepting as a gift or borrowing.

[81] FA 1968 s.11(2). Though clearly intended to permit the use of starting pistols, s.11(2) in fact allows the use of any firearm to start races.

The possession,[82] in accordance with the terms of the permit, of a firearm by any person who holds a police permit.[83]

(13) **Military and police forces**

The possession[84] by certain Crown servants,[85] members of visiting military forces[86] and by police officers of a firearm in their capacities as such servants, members or officers. See Ch.1 for more detail.

(14) **Museums**   3–16

The possession, purchase, hiring, accepting as a gift or borrowing of firearms by a museum within the terms of a museum firearms licence.[87] Full details are contained in Ch.17.

(15) **Borrowed rifles**

The borrowing by a person aged 17[88] or more of a rifle[89] from the occupier of private premises[90] and the use of the rifle there in the presence of[91] the occupier or his employee if the occupier or his employee in whose presence the rifle is used holds a firearm certificate for the rifle, and the borrower's possession and use complies with any relevant conditions in that certificate.[92]

In this case a person borrowing a rifle may also, without holding a firearm certificate, purchase or acquire[93] ammunition for use in the rifle and may possess both during the period of the borrowing if—

(a) the lender's firearm certificate authorises possession by the lender of the ammunition held by the borrower; *and*

(b) any conditions about ammunition in the lender's certificate are met by the borrower.[94]

This provision corrected the situation where visitors to estates were previously lent a rifle and ammunition for some stalking and were usually in illegal possession of them. Either the certificate holder or his servant, usually a gamekeeper, has to be present.

(16) **Visitors' permits**   3–17

---

[82] Note that possession only is covered by this exemption, and not a purchase, hiring, accepting as a gift or borrowing.

[83] FA 1968 s.7(1). As to police permits, see Ch.6.

[84] Possession only is covered by this exemption. In some of these cases a purchase, hiring, accepting as a gift or borrowing may be done without a certificate; in other cases a free certificate will be given.

[85] Principally, these will be members of the three Armed forces. Others, such as customs officers, may be included.

[86] FA 1968 s.54; Visiting Forces and International Headquarters (Application of Law) Order 1965.

[87] FA 1968 s.57(4); F(A)A 1988 ss.19, 25(1) and Sch, para.1(2).

[88] A person attains a particular age expressed in years at the beginning of the relevant anniversary of the date of his birth (Family Law Reform Act 1969 s.9(1)). Thus, a person becomes 17 at the midnight immediately preceding his 17th birthday.

[89] "Rifle" is defined to include a carbine (FA 1968 s.57(4)).

[90] The term "private premises" is not defined in the Firearms Acts, though the word "premises" includes any land (FA 1968 s.57(4); F(A)A 1988 s.25(1)), and "land" includes land covered with water (Interpretation Act 1978 s.5 and Sch.1). Contrasting the term with "public place", discussed in Ch.15 at para.15-05, it is suggested that it means any land, water or buildings other than those to which the public are admitted with or without payment.

[91] It remains for the courts to decide how near the borrower must be to the occupier or employee for this condition to be fulfilled.

[92] F(A)A 1988 s.16(1).

[93] "Acquire" is defined to mean hire, accept as a gift or borrow (FA 1968 s.57(4), F(A)A 1988 s.25(1)).

[94] F(A)A 1988 s.16(2).

The possession[95] of firearms by a holder of a visitor's firearm permit.[96] Full details are contained in Ch.7.

(17) **Firearms for export**

The purchase of firearms for export purposes. The conditions under which this may be done are as follows:

    (i)   the firearms must be bought from a registered firearms dealer[97]; *and*

    (ii)   the buyer shall not have been in Great Britain[98] for more than 30 days[99] in the preceding 12 months; *and*

    (iii) the firearms are to be bought for the purpose only of being exported from Great Britain without first coming into the buyer's possession.[100]

As with s.1 firearms, there are numerous cases in which a firearm certificate is not needed for the handling of s.1 ammunition. The cases are those in which under the exemptions at paras 3–09 to 3–17 a certificate is not needed for a s.1 firearm.[101] A certificate is also unnecessary for firearms or ammunition or signalling apparatus which are part of the equipment of a ship or aircraft,[102] nor for blank cartridges as they are not s.1 ammunition.

If your circumstances do not fall within one of the exceptions above and you wish to have possession of one or more firearms, you need to obtain a firearms certificate.

HOW DO I GET A FIREARM CERTIFICATE?

3–18   In Great Britain all firearm and shotgun certificates are issued by the police. What follows is a general guide to obtaining a certificate, although as circumstances vary enormously, we have probably not covered every eventuality! So what do you have to do is:—

Complete a set of forms which is obtainable from your local police. It is now usually possible to ask for the 'pack', and it is quite a pack, via email on the website of your local police force. If this is not for you it should be possible to obtain the pack at your local police station, although most forces have now centralised this function. The application must be made to the chief officer of

---

[95] Note that possession only is covered by this exemption, and not a purchase, hiring, accepting as a gift or borrowing.

[96] F(A)A 1988 s.17(1), (1A).

[97] As to the registration of firearms dealers, see Ch.16.

[98] "Great Britain" means England, Wales and Scotland, and excludes the Channel Islands and the Isle of Man.

[99] i.e. a continuous period of 30 days, or an accumulated period of 30 days composed of two or more shorter periods.

[100] F(A)A 1988 s.18(1). The 1988 Act imposes certain duties on firearms dealers selling firearms under these provisions (s.18(2)–(4)), and these may be found in Ch.16. Further conditions are imposed in relation to firearms falling within Category B for the purposes of Annex I to the European Community Directive 91/477/EEC (FA 1968 s.18(1A)–(6); Firearms Acts (Amendment) Regulations 1992 (SI 1992/2823) reg.8).

[101] FA 1968 ss.7(1), 8(1), 9(1), 10, 11(1)–(4), 54, 57(4); F(A)A 1988 ss.15, 17(1), 18(1), 19 and Sch.

[102] FA 1968 s.13(1)(a), (b).

police for the police area in which you 'reside'.[103] For those with more than one address, it is advisable to apply from the address where you intend to store the guns as this will be inspected to check your security. A fee is payable at the time of application,[104] which is refunded if you are refused.

The application form includes declarations by two referees to the effect that your personal details given on the form are true. Each referee must also endorse one of the four photographs to accompany the application with a declaration that it is a current true likeness of the applicant.[105] Your application cannot be considered by the police until they have received references from the two referees.[106]

3–19

To be qualified to act as a referee, a person must not be a member of your immediate family, a serving police officer, a police employee or a registered firearms dealer,[107] and must be resident in Great Britain,[108] have known you personally for at least two years, and be of good character.[109] If you are applying for weapons for target shooting one of your referees must be an official (usually the Secretary) of the Home Office approved club of which you are a member, membership of such a club being essential in order to establish good reason for the target shooting guns. Your other referee, as well as complying with the conditions above, by contrast cannot be a member of any target shooting club. This is presumably on the basis either that members of such clubs can't be trusted to be impartial, or that referees should only have a limited knowledge of the person and their handling of firearms about whom they are giving a reference! This provision was brought in after the tragedy at Dunblane, but perhaps the reader can see that not only does it have some potentially unfortunate consequences, it may not achieve its intended purpose, whatever that was?

It is very important when completing the forms to be as honest and accurate as possible. This may seem obvious, but as an example, it is a reason to refuse a certificate that you have lied about your previous convictions. As the explanatory notes on the application form make clear, you are expected to disclose all convictions, no matter how old or how minor the offence, and whether or not the conviction was in Great Britain or abroad. A common mistake is to presume that this does not include motoring offences. You are unlikely to be refused a certificate because you have a 10 year old speeding conviction, or if you were cautioned for shoplifting when you were 15 (and you're now 45), but you might

---

[103] FA 1968 s.26(1). An applicant cannot be said to reside at a property which he has let (*Burditt v Joslin* [1981] 3 All E.R. 203; *The Times*, February 13, 1981).

[104] Currently it is £50 for a first application and £40 for renewal, and if you have 'co-terminous' firearm and shotgun certificates there is a slight saving.

[105] Firearms Rules 1998 (SI 1998/1941) r.3(1)-(3), Sch.1 Pt I.

[106] Firearms Rules 1998 r.4(2). A form is provided for this purpose (Firearms Rules 1998, Sch.1 Pt III).

[107] An exception is that a referee can be an RFD where he is also the Secretary of your target shooting club.

[108] "Great Britain" means England, Wales and Scotland, and excludes the Channel Islands and the Isle of Man.

[109] Firearms Rules 1998 r.(3). No referees are necessary for an application to vary a certificate.

be if you fail to declare those convictions on the form![110] It is an offence to give false information in order to obtain a certificate.[111]

'GOOD REASON' FOR REQUIRING FIREARMS

3–20   You must include on the application form details of the firearms and ammunition in your possession (if it is a renewal) and of those you wish to acquire[112] and your reasons for acquiring each of those other firearms. The reasons given must be applicable to each firearm which you wish to possess. The number of firearms to be covered by the certificate will be limited by the reasons for which they are required. Genuine collectors of firearms and ammunition, including those capable of use, will be regarded by the police as having a good reason for their possession.[113]

It is very important to state the 'good reason' for requiring each firearm as fully as possible, it is a common ground for refusal where insufficient detail has been given. For example, a certificate for a sporting rifle, or one for vermin control, would not be granted unless you could show that you have, or are likely to have, some opportunity of using it for those purposes. You will be expected to provide evidence that you have permission to shoot over land where quarry suitable for the particular weapon is present. Unless the land is already known to police as suitable for shooting over they will want to check that it will be safe. They keep records of land and if necessary make enquiries with other forces to check that this is so. In addition to demonstrating good reason in principle the firearms you intend to acquire have to be suitable for the stated purpose in terms of power and range. This can sometimes be a matter of opinion, and whilst most forces take a reasonable approach to such questions, be prepared to argue your point of view, particularly if your application is out of the ordinary. For shooting deer there are additional requirements, see Ch.12.

3–21   As already stated, for target shooting you will need to be a full member of a club and you will need to demonstrate access to ranges suitable for the use of the firearm(s) you are applying for; most ranges have muzzle velocity limits. There are several other more specialist examples of good reason to possess firearms, such as the humane killing of animals, or for a Trophy of War, but in each case you have to establish that good reason.

The initial enquiries will be conducted by a Firearms Enquiry Officer (FEO) who will check your background, the information you have given, and will contact your referees to verify what they say about you, and that they are who they say they are. You will be visited by the FEO to inspect your security arrangements and to see your home circumstances. When those checks are completed your file will be passed to the Firearms Licensing Manager who will review it and decide whether your application should be granted in whole, or perhaps in part if you have applied for a number of weapons, or refused. Don't be

---

[110] The Rehabilitation of Offenders Act 1974 does not apply to firearm and shotgun certificate applications; therefore all convictions must be disclosed even if they would be regarded as 'spent' for most other purposes.

[111] FA 1968 ss.28A(7), 29(3), 51(1), (2) and Sch.6 Pt I. The maximum punishment is six months' imprisonment or a fine at level 5 on the standard scale (currently £5,000), or both.

[112] Firearms Rules 1998, Sch.1 Pt I.

[113] As to antique firearms and firearms of historic interest see paras 1–26 and 2–09 respectively.

surprised to find that everyone you deal with is in fact a civilian, although they may well once have been serving police officers who have now retired.

This process of assessing the application applies equally on a renewal as it does on a first application, albeit the enquiries made on renewal may not be quite as thorough as when the original application was considered. Do bear in mind that the requirement to demonstrate good reason is ongoing and therefore even if the police previously granted authority to acquire or possess a particular firearm they may not be prepared to renew that authority if they are no longer satisfied you have a good reason to possess it. This may arise where the police form the view you have used the firearm in question only very infrequently.

WHEN SHOULD A FIREARM CERTIFICATE BE GRANTED—THE TEST

The police must grant a certificate when they are satisfied that the applicant—   **3–22**

(1)   is fit to be entrusted with a s.1 firearm. Reasons for revocation of a certificate are defined as 'the holder is of intemperate habits or unsound mind, or is otherwise unfitted to be entrusted with a firearm'.[114] Clearly the police wouldn't grant a certificate in the first place if they felt the applicant came within this description; *and*

(2)   has not been prohibited by the 1968 Firearms Act from possessing a s.1 firearm. This arises when he has been given certain punishments by the courts[115]; *and*

(3)   has a good reason for having possession of or acquiring the firearms and ammunition which are the subject of the application; *and*

(4)   can, in all the circumstances, be permitted to have the firearm and ammunition in his possession without danger to the public safety or to the peace.[116]

Note that this test is slightly different to the test to be applied for a shotgun certificate—see Ch.4.

As can been seen, there are a number of criteria that have to be met, and there are a number of decided cases on the test. These are considered in more detail in Ch.5. If the police refuse your application for a certificate, or they subsequently revoke it, they will have to justify their decision to a Crown Court if you choose to appeal.

---

[114] FA 1968 s.30A(2)(a).
[115] See Prohibition in Ch.5
[116] FA 1968 s.27(1).

CONDITIONS IMPOSED UPON FIREARM CERTIFICATES

3–23   The certificate will be issued subject to a number of conditions.[117] Five will be imposed in all cases, and others[118] may be added by the police. The five 'prescribed' conditions are:

(1)   That the holder must, on receipt of the certificate, sign it in ink with his usual signature.

(2)   That the holder must within seven days inform the chief officer of police by whom the certificate was granted of the theft, loss or destruction in Great Britain[119] of the certificate. (There is also a requirement to report a loss or destruction outside Great Britain within 14 days[120] by means of registered post, or the nearest local equivalent.)

(3)   That any change in the permanent address of the certificate holder shall be notified without undue delay to the chief officer of police by whom the certificate was granted.

(4)   That the firearms and ammunition to which the certificate relates must at all times (except in the circumstances described in (5) below) be stored securely so as to prevent, so far as is reasonably practicable, access to them by unauthorised persons.

(5)   That, where a firearm or ammunition to which the certificate relates—
   (a)   is in use[121]; *or*
   (b)   the certificate holder has the firearm with him for the purpose of cleaning, repairing or testing, or for some other purpose connected with its use, transfer[122] or sale; *or*
   (c)   is in transit to or from a place in connection with its use for any of the purposes at (b) above,

   reasonable precautions must be taken for the safe custody of the firearm or ammunition.[123] For further details of these security requirements, see Ch.8.

3–24   Any of the conditions, except those five just mentioned, may be varied by the police at any time, and they may require you to send them the certificate for alteration within 21 days.[124] You may yourself apply to the police for it to be

---

[117] Failure to comply with a condition is an offence for which the maximum punishment on summary conviction is 6 months' imprisonment, or a fine at level 5 on the standard scale (currently £5,000), or both (FA 1968 s.1(2), 51(1), (2) and Sch.6 Pt I).

[118] For example, that the firearms and ammunition shall only be used for certain purposes or on certain land.

[119] "Great Britain" means England, Wales and Scotland, and excludes the Channel Islands and the Isle of Man.

[120] FA(A) 1997 s.35(3)

[121] In a case decided under the earlier Firearms Rules of 1969, which referred to "actual use", it was held that live ammunition concealed in the back of an unattended car for about half an hour was not in actual use nor kept in a secure place with a view to preventing access to it by unauthorised persons (*Marsh v Chief Constable of Avon & Somerset, The Independent, May 8, 1987, DC*).

[122] "Transfer" is defined to include let on hire, give, lend and part with possession (FA 1968 s.57(4)).

[123] Firearms Rules 1998 r.3(4). Further conditions can be imposed in the case of specialised weapons and ammunition, such as humane killers, shot pistols and starting pistols, restricting their use to their special purposes (Firearms Rules 1998, r.3(5)).

[124] FA 1968 s.29(1).

altered.[125] You should, for example, do this if the quantity or description of the firearms in your possession varies during the lifetime of a certificate, or if you want to hold or buy more ammunition than is authorised by the certificate.

It appears that there is no right of appeal against the conditions attached to a firearm certificate by the police.[126] As the police are a public body and are required to act reasonably, the imposition of a totally unreasonable condition could however still be subject to challenge in the High Court, see Ch.5.

If you apply for a firearm certificate for a rifle or muzzle-loading pistol[127] (not being a prohibited weapon)[128] and the police are satisfied that your only reason for having it is for target shooting, the certificate will be given (or renewed) subject to the following conditions, in addition to any others—

(1)   that it is to be used only for target shooting; and
(2)   that you must be a member of an approved rifle club or muzzle-loading pistol club[129] (as the case may be) named in the certificate.[130]

There are many other conditions which are routinely added to certificates, for example to allow the possession of expanding ammunition, or a condition as to when solid slug ammunition for a shotgun may be used, etc. A firearm certificate is a legal document that allows possession of firearms and ammunition. If you do not abide by the conditions you will be committing a criminal offence. It is therefore important to check your certificate and any conditions attached to it upon receipt to ensure it allows you do what you require, if not go back to the police. We also recommend that you keep an up to date copy of your certificate separate from the original. It can be extremely useful if you should lose your certificate, or even if it is taken by or submitted to the police for any reason.   **3–25**

WHAT ELSE SHOULD I KNOW ABOUT FIREARM CERTIFICATES?

When granted the certificate will specify particulars of the firearms already possessed and of those authorised by the certificate to be acquired,[131] and will give authority for the possession and acquisition of stated amounts of ammunition. On later purchases of firearms or ammunition, particulars are to be entered in the certificate by the seller. A photograph of the holder of the certificate will be affixed to it.   **3–26**

---

[125] FA 1968 s.29(2). The usual application form is used for this purpose (Firearms Rules 1998 r.3(1) and Sch.1 Pt I).

[126] This is the view of the Home Office which they say has been supported by the courts, but has been disputed. No express right of appeal regarding conditions has been given by the Firearms Acts.

[127] A muzzle-loading pistol is defined as a pistol designed to be loaded at the muzzle end of the barrel or chamber with a loose charge and a separate ball (or other missile) (F(A)A 1988 s.15(11), (12)).

[128] For the meaning of "prohibited weapon", see Ch.2.

[129] A muzzle-loading pistol club means a club where muzzle-loading pistols are used for target shooting (F(A)A 1988 s.15(12)).

[130] F(A)A 1997 s.44. For approval of clubs, see para.3–11.

[131] FA 1968 s.27(2); F(A)A 1988 s.9; Firearms Rules 1998 r.3(6), Sch.1 Pt II. The exchange by a person with a firearms dealer of one firearm for another, even though similar, is not covered by that person's certificate unless it has been previously varied by the police to authorise the acquisition of the second firearm (*Wilson v Coombe Law Society's Gazette*, October 26, 1988 at p.44).

The certificate will last for five years, unless previously revoked by the police[132] or cancelled by the Court,[133] and may be renewed every five years[134] by completing a further application form.[135]

Arrangements may be made for your firearm certificate and shot gun certificate to be co-terminous,[136] i.e. falling due for renewal on the same date even if they were originally granted on different dates. In the long run this will obviously save time for both you and the police.

In addition to the fees payable for the grant and renewal of firearm certificates, there is a fee payable for a variation to a certificate. In some circumstances there is no fee, for example in relation to a Trophy of War. The police will be able to advise you.

3–27   If you wish to change a firearm in your possession for a similar one, say in the same calibre, it is necessary to obtain a 'one for one' variation. You cannot simply dispose of one firearm and replace it, because each 'acquisition' requires a fresh authority. There is no charge for this type of variation.

The holder of a firearm (or shotgun) certificate in the UK is entitled to also have issued to them a *European Firearms Pass*. For further details see Ch.7.

3–28   When carrying firearms or ammunition you must produce your certificate to a constable, if asked to do so.[137] If you fail to do so, or fail to permit the constable to read the certificate, or to show him that you are entitled to hold the firearm or ammunition without a certificate, the constable may seize and detain the firearm or ammunition and may require you to give him at once your name and address.[138] Similar provisions apply to the production of a visitor's European firearms pass.[139] Although this is the law, in the current climate there is a good chance that rather than simply being required to give your name and address, you will also be arrested on suspicion of unlawful possession of a firearm and/or ammunition. So make sure you carry your certificate, or at least a good copy of it, with you. The police should accept a good copy from people behaving lawfully with firearms. The Countryside Alliance recommend that you carry a copy in circumstances where there is a risk the original could be lost or damaged.

---

[132] As to revocation, and appeal against it, see Ch.5.

[133] The Court has power to cancel a certificate on conviction in relation to most firearms offences (although not those relating to air weapons) or for any other offence for which a term of imprisonment was imposed. This also applies where a person is bound over to keep the peace. The court also has a discretion to order forfeiture and destruction of any firearms possessed by the offender. (FA 1968 s. 52).

[134] The five-year period applies to certificates granted or renewed after January 1, 1995 (FA 1968 s.28A(1); Firearms (Period of Certificate) Order 1994 (SI 1994/2614); Firearms (Amendment) Rules 1994 (SI 1994/3022)). The period may be further revised by order of the Home Office (FA 1968 s.28A(3).

[135] FA 1968 s.28A(1); Firearms Rules 1998 r.3(1) and Sch.1 Pt I. The rules which govern the grant or refusal of the first certificate (see above) also apply on a renewal (FA 1968 s.28A(2)).

[136] F(A)A 1988 s.11.

[137] FA 1968 s.48(1). As well as police constables, including special police constables, "constable" includes others holding that office, e.g. harbour constables. The hallmark of a constable is his attestation as such before, usually, a Magistrate.

[138] FA 1968 s.48(2). If you refuse to give your name and address or give them incorrectly, you will be liable upon summary conviction to a maximum fine at level 3 on the standard scale (currently £1,000) (FA 1968 s.48(3), 51(1), (2) and Sch.6 Pt I). Furthermore, you may be arrested without warrant if you make such a refusal, or if the constable suspects you of giving a false name or address or of "intending to abscond" (FA 1968 s.50(3)).

[139] FA 1968 s.48(1A), (2), (3).

If you should be unwise enough to make a statement which is false in any material particular for the purpose of obtaining a certificate, or having it renewed or varied, whether for yourself or somebody else, you will be liable to prosecution.[140] Not surprisingly, it is also an offence[141] if, with a view to purchasing or acquiring, or procuring the repair, test or proof of, a s.1 firearm or ammunition, you produce a false firearm certificate or such a certificate in which any false entry has been made, or impersonate a person to whom such a certificate has been granted or knowingly or recklessly make a statement false in any material particular.[142]

SECTION 1 AMMUNITION

You will be limited in quantity as to the amount of s.1 ammunition you can purchase and possess in each calibre. Bear in mind that for each calibre you will be given one limit as to the maximum quantity authorised to be possessed at any one time, and a second somewhat lower limit as to the maximum quantity authorised to be purchased or acquired at any one time. These limits will be clearly set out on your certificate. The limits set should be reasonable for your proposed use and to allow you to take advantage of the opportunity, within reasonable limits, to be able to 'bulk purchase'. If you feel the limits imposed are inadequate for your purposes, and can justify that to your licensing department, you can apply for a variation of your certificate to increase your authorised limits.

3–29

It is important to stay within your limits in each calibre as you are committing the criminal offence of unlawful possession if you exceed it. As stated elsewhere, bear in mind that the limit includes not only complete rounds of ammunition, but in the case of expanding ammunition, the bullet heads as well. Re-loaders beware!

TRANSFER, DE-ACTIVATION AND LOSS OR DESTRUCTION OF SECTION 1 FIREARMS AND AMMUNITION

The Firearms Act 1968 has imposed a number of restrictions on the handling of these types of firearms and ammunition, as follows:

3–30

---

[140] FA 1968 s.28A(7), 29(3), 51(1),(2) and Sch.6 Pt 1. The maximum punishment is six months imprisonment or a fine of the prescribed sum (currently £5,000).

[141] The maximum punishment on summary conviction is imprisonment for six months or a fine of the prescribed sum (currently £5,000), or both; or, on indictment, five years' imprisonment, or an unlimited fine, or both (FA 1968 s.3(5), 51(1), (2) and Sch.6 Pt I).

[142] FA 1968 s.3(5).

(1)   You must not[143] sell or transfer[144] to any other person in the United
       Kingdom[145] these firearms and ammunition except in the following cases:
       (a)   When "the other person" is a registered firearms dealer.
       (b)   When "the other person" produces a firearm certificate authorising
              him to buy or acquire[146] the firearm[147] or ammunition, or shows that
              he is entitled[148] to buy or acquire them without holding such a
              certificate.[149]
       (c)   A person may part with the possession of a firearm or ammunition,
              otherwise than in pursuance of a contract for sale or hire or by way of
              gift or loan, to another person who shows that he is entitled to have
              possession of them without holding a firearm certificate.[150]
       (d)   When a firearm or ammunition is delivered by a carrier or
              warehouseman, or by an employee of either, in the ordinary course of
              his business or employment as such.[151]

(2)   You must not[152] by way of trade or business, unless you are a registered
       firearms dealer, manufacture, sell, transfer,[153] repair, test, prove, expose for
       sale or transfer, or possess for sale, transfer, repair, test or proof, any s.1
       firearms or ammunition.

(3)   You must not sell or transfer *any* firearm or ammunition to any person
       whom you know, or have reasonable ground for believing, to be drunk or of
       unsound mind,[154] or to have been sentenced to certain punishments[155] by
       the Courts.[156]

---

[143] FA 1968 s.3(2). The maximum punishment on summary conviction is imprisonment for six
months or a fine of the prescribed sum (currently £5,000), or both; or, on indictment, five years'
imprisonment, or an unlimited fine, or both (FA 1968 s.51(1), (2), Sch.6 Pt I).

[144] "Transfer" is defined to include let on hire, give, lend and part with possession (FA 1968 s.57(4)).
The case of *Hall v Cotton* [1986] 3 All E.R. 332 confirms that the leaving of a firearm with another
person for safekeeping and cleaning is caught by this definition.

[145] "United Kingdom" means England, Wales, Scotland and Northern Ireland, and excludes the
Channel Islands and the Isle of Man.

[146] "Acquire" is defined to mean hire, accept as a gift or borrow (FA 1968 s.57(4), F(A)A 1988
s.25(1)).

[147] A firearm certificate does not authorise the purchase or acquisition of a firearm bought or
borrowed by way of exchanging it with another firearm unless the certificate specifically authorised
that purchase or acquisition (*Wilson v Coombe Law Society's Gazette*, October 26, 1988 at p.44).

[148] For the cases where a person would be so entitled, see paras 3–09 to 3–17.

[149] FA 1968 s.3(2).

[150] FA 1968 s.3(2), 8(2)(a).

[151] FA 1968 s.3(2), 9(4).

[152] FA 1968 s.3(1). The maximum summary punishment is six months' imprisonment or a fine of the
prescribed sum (currently £5,000), or both. On indictment, the maximum is five years' imprisonment,
or an unlimited fine, or both (FA 1968 s.51(1), (2) and Sch.6, Pt I).

[153] "Transfer" is defined to include let on hire, give, lend and part with possession (FA 1968 s.57(4)).

[154] FA 1968 s.25. The maximum punishment on summary conviction is three months' imprisonment,
or a fine at level 3 on the standard scale (currently £1,000), or both (FA 1968 s.51(1), (2) and Sch.6, Pt
I).

[155] This is a reference to prohibited persons, for which see the end of Ch.5.

[156] FA 1968 s.21(1), (3), (5). The maximum summary punishment is six months' imprisonment or a
fine of the prescribed sum (currently £5,000), or both. On indictment, the maximum is three years'
imprisonment, or an unlimited fine, or both (FA 1968 s.51(1), (2) and Sch.6 Pt I). This includes air
weapons.

In addition to the foregoing restrictions, the Firearms (Amendment) Act of 1997 has added further provisions[157] about some of the dealings with s.1 firearms and ammunition which are discussed above. As will be seen from the next paragraph, the most significant is the requirement that where one or both parties to the transfer of s.1 firearms or ammunition is the holder of a firearm certificate, all such transfers must now take place on a face to face basis.[158]

3–31

If, in Great Britain,[159] you sell, let on hire, lend or give a s.1 firearm or s.1 ammunition to another person who is neither a registered firearms dealer[160] nor a person who is entitled to buy or acquire the firearm or ammunition without holding a firearm certificate[161] or a visitor's firearm permit[162]—

(a) the transferee must produce to you the certificate or permit which entitles him to buy or acquire the firearm or ammunition;
(b) you must comply with any instructions in the certificate or permit produced; and
(c) you must hand the firearm or ammunition to the transferee who must receive it in person.[163]

The Firearms (Amendment) Act of 1997 also imposed greater obligations to give notice to the police of certain transactions involving s.1 firearms than had previously existed. In each of the following circumstances you will need to give notice to the chief police officer who granted your certificate or permit;

3–32

(1) If you sell, let on hire, lend or give any s.1 firearm for which you hold a firearm certificate or a visitor's permit. If you are the transferee in such a transaction, and hold such a certificate or permit relating to the firearm, the same requirements about giving notice will apply.[164]
(2) If you de-activate,[165] destroy or lose (by theft or otherwise) a firearm to which a firearm certificate or a visitor's permit relates, and you were the last certificate or permit holder in possession of it.[166]

---

[157] These provisions replace and extend those formerly contained in FA 1968 s.42.

[158] 'Dealer to Dealer' transactions need not be face to face.

[159] "Great Britain" means England, Wales and Scotland, and excludes the Channel Islands and the Isle of Man.

[160] As to the registration of firearms dealers, see Ch.16.

[161] For persons who are so entitled, see paras 3–09 to 3–17.

[162] See Ch.7 for provisions about these permits.

[163] F(A)A 1997 s.32(1)(a), (2). Failure to comply with these requirements is an offence with a maximum punishment on summary conviction of six months' imprisonment or a fine of the statutory maximum (currently £5,000), or both; or, on indictment, five years' imprisonment or an unlimited fine, or both (F(A)A 1997 ss.32(3), 36(a)).

[164] F(A)A 1997 s.33(1)-(3) contains the provisions for such transactions within Great Britain and F(A)A 1997 ss.35(1),(5),(6) the corresponding provisions for such transactions outside Great Britain. Note, however, that where the sale or other transaction takes place outside Great Britain, notice must be given in relation to "any firearm", and is not confined solely to s.1 firearms.

[165] A firearm is said to be de-activated if it would, by virtue of F(A)A 1988 s.8 (for which see para.1–13), be presumed to be rendered incapable of discharging any shot, bullet or other missile (F(A)A 1997 s.34(5)).

[166] F(A)A 1997 s.34(1), (3) contains the provisions for such events within Great Britain and F(A)A 1997 ss.35(3)(a)-(6) the corresponding provisions for such events outside Great Britain.

(3)   When s.1 ammunition is lost (by theft or otherwise), and that ammunition is covered by a firearm certificate or a visitor's permit, and you were the last certificate or permit holder in possession of it.[167]

3–33   All such notices must give a description of the firearm (including any identification number) or ammunition, and state the nature of the transaction, or otherwise "state the nature of the event", i.e. deactivation, destruction or loss. Where it is a transfer, the notice must in addition include the name and address of the other party to the transaction. In relation to the lending of s.1 firearms, do not allow yourself to get caught out by the exemption from the need to notify the transfer of a shotgun lasting less than 72 hours. That exemption relates solely to shotguns, and the loan of a s.1 firearm, must always be notified to the police, however short the period of the loan.

The time limit for giving notice, and the method by which that notice should be sent, is determined by whether the transfer or other event took place within or outside Great Britain. If the transfer or other event occurred within Great Britain then notice must be given within seven days, the notice to be sent by registered post or recorded delivery service. Where the transfer or other event took place outside Great Britain, the notice must be given within 14 days by registered post or recorded delivery service, or if sent from outside the United Kingdom,[168] must be sent by such means as most closely correspond to registered post or recorded delivery service.

3–34   In all such circumstances, it is an offence if you fail without reasonable excuse to give notice of the transfer or other event within the requisite timescale and by the specified method.[169] That said, whilst notification of any transfer should strictly be sent by registered post or recorded delivery service, in the modern age of electronic communications most police forces have for some time now accepted notification by email. This practice has very recently been given legal approval by the Firearms (Electronic Communications) Order 2011, which permits certificate holders and firearms dealers to notify the police of transactions and other matters by email.[170] We would recommend that you always request a reply to confirm receipt of your email, and that you print and retain copies of such emailed notifications, at least until such time as you receive a reply from the police.

There are special restrictions on the handling of s.1 firearms and ammunition by young people under 18; these are considered in Ch.14. Further regulations are contained in the Firearms Act of 1968 about the holding of firearms and

---

[167] F(A)A 1997 ss.34(2), (3) contains the provisions for such events within Great Britain and F(A)A 1997 ss.35(3)(b)-(6) the corresponding provisions for such events outside Great Britain.

[168] "United Kingdom" means England, Wales, Scotland and Northern Ireland, and excludes the Channel Islands and the Isle of Man.

[169] In all such cases the maximum punishment on summary conviction is six months' imprisonment or a fine of the statutory maximum (currently £5,000), or both; or, on indictment, five years' imprisonment or an unlimited fine, or both (F(A)A 1997 s.36(a)).

[170] Emailed notifications must be sent to the email address published for this purpose by the police in your area. Check with them first what address you should use. This order also permits the police to send notices by email to certificate holders and firearms dealers, subject to you first having given your consent.

ammunition by persons given certain punishments by the courts ("prohibition").[171] For details of the criminal use of firearms, such as using firearms to endanger life, to injure property, to resist or prevent arrest[172] or with intent to commit an indictable offence[173]; possessing firearms with intent to cause belief that unlawful violence will be used,[174] and various others, see Ch.15.There is also an offence of taking in pawn firearms and ammunition.[175]

WORK ON SECTION 1 FIREARMS AND AMMUNITION

You will commit an offence[176] if you undertake the repair, test or proof of a Section 1 firearm or ammunition for any other person in the United Kingdom[177] unless—

 3–35

(a)   "the other person" is a registered firearms dealer[178]; *or*
(b)   "the other person" produces, or causes to be produced, a firearm certificate authorising him to have possession of the firearm or ammunition, or shows that he is entitled[179] to have possession of it without holding such a certificate.

You must not repair, prove or test *any* firearm or ammunition for any person whom you know, or have reasonable ground for believing, to be drunk or of unsound mind,[180] or to have been sentenced to certain punishments[181] by the Courts.[182]

None of this prevents you from working on your own guns, subject to notifying the police if you change the status of a firearm, as already indicated.

 3–36

---

[171]   FA 1968 s.21.See Ch.5 for the process of applying to court for the removal of such a prohibition.

[172]   FA 1968 s.16, 17.

[173]   FA 1968 s.18.

[174]   FA 1968 s.16A.

[175]   FA 1968 s.3(6).

[176]   The maximum punishment on summary conviction is imprisonment for six months or a fine of the prescribed sum (currently £5,000), or both; or, on indictment, five years' imprisonment, or an unlimited fine, or both (FA 1968 s.3(3), 51(1), (2) and Sch.6 Pt I).

[177]   "United Kingdom" means England, Wales, Scotland and Northern Ireland, and excludes the Channel Islands and the Isle of Man.

[178]   You would then be acting as their servant in accordance with s.8 of the Act. As to the registration of firearms dealers, see Ch.16.

[179]   For the cases where a person would be so entitled, see the exceptions, paras 3–09 to 3–17 onwards.

[180]   FA 1968 s.25.The maximum punishment on summary conviction is.3 months' imprisonment, or a fine at level 3 on the standard scale (currently £1,000), or both (FA 1968 s.51(1), (2) and Sch.6 Pt I).

[181]   This is a reference to prohibited persons, see prohibition in Ch.5.

[182]   FA 1968 s.21(5).This includes air weapons. The maximum summary punishment is six months' imprisonment or a fine of the prescribed sum (currently £5,000), or both. On indictment, the maximum is three years' imprisonment, or an unlimited fine, or both (FA 1968 s.51(1), (2) and Sch.6 Pt I).

Unless you are a registered firearms dealer,[183] you must not convert into a firearm anything which, though having the appearance of being a firearm,[184] is so constructed as to be incapable of discharging any missile through any barrel.[185]

It is an offence to shorten the barrel of a s.1 firearm which is a smooth-bore gun[186] to a length of less than 24 inches[187] unless the barrel has a bore exceeding two inches. But a registered firearms dealer[188] may do so for the sole purpose of replacing a defective part of it so as to produce a barrel not less than 24 inches long.[189]

---

[183] As to the registration of firearms dealers, see Ch.16.

[184] For imitation firearms, see Ch.9.

[185] FA 1968 s.4(3). The maximum punishment on summary conviction is imprisonment for six months or a fine of the prescribed sum (currently £5,000), or both; or, on indictment, seven years' imprisonment, or an unlimited fine, or both (FA 1968 s.51(1), (2) and Sch.6 Pt I). For a procedure for certifying that a firearm is incapable in this way, see Deactivation at para1–13.

[186] This will be a smooth-bore gun *not* falling within the description given in item (B)(b) in para.3–02.

[187] Measurement is from the muzzle to the point at which the charge is exploded (FA 1968 s.57(6)(a)).

[188] As to the registration of firearms dealers, see Ch.16.

[189] F(A)A 1988 s.6. The maximum punishments for this offence are: on summary conviction, six months' imprisonment, or the statutory maximum fine (currently £5,000), or both; on indictment, five years' imprisonment, or an unlimited fine, or both (F(A)A 1988 s.6(1)).

CHAPTER 4

Shot Guns and their Ammunition

DEFINITIONS

The Firearms (Amendment) Act of 1988, substituting a new definition of "shot gun" for that formerly supplied by the 1968 Firearms Act, defines that term to mean: **4–01**

A smooth-bore gun (not being an air gun)[1] which—

(a) has a barrel not less than 24 inches long[2] and does not have any barrel with a bore exceeding two inches in diameter; and

(b) either has no magazine or has a non-detachable magazine incapable of holding more than two cartridges; and

(c) is not a revolver gun.[3]

As to paragraph (b) above, a gun which has been adapted to have a non-detachable magazine will not fall within the definition unless the conditions concerning approved marks which are detailed in items (a) and (b) at para.3–02 are fulfilled.[4]

In short summary a 'shotgun' is a smooth bored gun, either single or double barrelled, with barrels at least 24" long. It may be pump action or self loading (but not a revolver), but if so it must have a magazine capacity limited to two **4–02**

---

[1] The term "air gun" is not defined by the Firearms Acts.

[2] This length is measured from the muzzle to the point at which the charge is exploded on firing (FA 1968 s.57(6)(a); F(A)A 1988 s.25(1)).

[3] FA 1968 s.1(3)(a); F(A)A 1988 s.2(1), (2). "Revolver gun" means a gun containing a series of chambers which revolve when the gun is fired (FA 1968 s.57(2B); F(A)A 1988 s.25(2)).

[4] FA 1968 ss.1(3A), 58(1); F(A)A 1988 s.2(1), (3).

shots. This is in addition to the round in the chamber. If such a gun has a greater magazine capacity it falls within section 1 and must be held on a firearm certificate. If it has a barrel less than 24" long it is in s.1. If it were to have a large capacity magazine *and* a barrel shorter than 24", then it becomes a prohibited weapon.[5] If a gun falls within the ordinary definition of a shotgun then it is described as a 'section 2 shotgun' (hereafter referred to as 's.2 shotgun') and can be held on a shotgun certificate.

No definition of shot gun ammunition is provided by the Firearms Acts. As we have seen, ordinary shot gun ammunition[6] is excluded from the kinds of ammunition which are classified as s.1 ammunition and therefore does not require separate certification.

WHEN DO I NEED A SHOT GUN CERTIFICATE?

4–03   Shot gun certificates were introduced in 1968 to counter the increasing use of shot guns for criminal purposes. Briefly, the intention was to control the use of shot guns by means of certificates similarly to, but less strictly than, the ways in which rifles and hand guns had been controlled by firearm certificates for many years; shot gun ammunition is not, however, controlled by certificates.[7]

You will commit an offence[8] if you have in your possession[9] or purchase or acquire[10] a shot gun without holding a shot gun certificate,[11] but a certificate is not needed for the possession of component parts of a shot gun, nor in the following cases:—[12]

(1)   If you use a shot gun at a time and place approved for shooting at artificial targets by the chief officer of police for the area in which that place is situated.[13]

(2)   If you hold a firearm certificate issued in Northern Ireland which authorises you to possess a shot gun.[14]

---

[5] This is if it is a pump-action or semi-automatic gun. Large capacity lever action or bolt action shotguns remain in s.1.

[6] Item (a) at para.3–05 is more than 5 shot, none larger than .36 of an inch.

[7] Though production of a certificate is needed to buy shot gun ammunition.

[8] The maximum punishment on summary conviction is imprisonment for six months, or the statutory maximum fine (currently £5,000), or both or, on indictment, five years' imprisonment or an unlimited fine, or both (FA 1968 ss.2(1), 51(1), (2) and Sch.6 Pt I).

[9] For some guidance on the meaning of "possession", see para.3–07.

[10] "Acquire" is defined to mean hire, accept as a gift or borrow (FA 1968 s.57(4)).

[11] FA 1968 s.2(1).

[12] See also paras 1–25 and 1 26 for two general exceptions to the need for a shot gun certificate.

[13] FA 1968 s.11(6). It is important to note that the exception only operates whilst a gun is being used in this way at the approved time and place and will not cover the possession of a gun immediately before or after such a use.

[14] FA 1968 s.15.

(3)   If you borrow a shot gun from the occupier of private premises[15]and use it on those premises in the presence[16] of the occupier.[17]

(4)   If you are able to bring your case within any one of the exceptions applying to firearm certificates (see Ch.3 at paras 3–09 to 3–17). In the case of the exception regarding the person for whom a shot gun is carried, they will require a shot gun certificate instead of a firearm certificate.

(5)   If you hold a visitor's shot gun permit.[18]

The meaning of the term "occupier" at para.(3) above is worthy of consideration as this exemption from the requirement to hold a shotgun certificate is quite widely used. "Occupier" is not defined in the Firearms Acts but the *Guidance* suggests that the definition given in s.27 of the Wildlife & Countryside Act 1981 should usually be adopted. This is wider than you might expect as it provides that "occupier" in relation to any land other than the foreshore, includes any person having any right of hunting, shooting, fishing or taking game on that land.   **4–04**

HOW DO I GET A SHOT GUN CERTIFICATE?

Firearms Rules regulating applications for shot gun certificates came into force on September 1, 1998. For general observations about making applications for a firearm certificate, which apply equally to applications for a shotgun certificate, see paras 3–18 onwards.   **4–05**

Your reasons for having the gun are not required to be given on your application. This appears to be a strange omission since, as mentioned below, the absence of a good reason will entitle the police to refuse the certificate. Despite this omission, satisfactory reasons will be needed by the police. That said, the threshold to demonstrate good reason for having a shotgun certificate is generally somewhat lower than the corresponding requirement to demonstrate good reason for having a firearm certificate.

The certificate will list particulars of the shot guns to be covered by it and provide for entries to be made when a gun is transferred (including the identification numbers if known).[19]

---

[15] The term "private premises" is not defined in the Firearms Acts, though the word "premises" includes any land (FA 1968 s.57(4)), and "land" includes land covered with water (Interpretation Act 1978 s.5 and Sch.1). Contrasting the term with "public place", discussed in Ch.15 para.15–05. It is suggested that it means any land, water or buildings other than those to which the public are admitted with or without payment.

[16] It remains for the Courts to decide how near to you the occupier must be when you are using a gun. Meanwhile, it is suggested that if the occupier is at your side or perhaps in the same shoot as yourself the condition is fulfilled, but not otherwise. Further 'occupier' ought to include the occupier's agents, such as a gamekeeper.

[17] FA 1968 s.11(5).

[18] FA 1968 ss.7(1), 8(1), 9(1), 11(1), (2), 12(1), 13(1), 54, 57(4); F(A)A 1988 ss.16(1), 17(1), 18(1), 19, 25(1). As to visitors' shot gun permits, see Ch.7.

[19] FA 1968 s.28(2A); Firearms Rules 1998 r.5(6) and Sch.2 Pt II.

4–06   Except in the cases mentioned below, where the police cannot issue a certificate, a certificate will be issued to you if the police are satisfied that you can be permitted to possess a shot gun without danger to the public safety or to the peace.[20]

This criterion has been judicially considered on four occasions. In a 1974 case[21] it was held that it was right to refuse a certificate if there was a danger of the gun being misused in such a way that good order is disturbed, and poaching with the gun was cited as an example of that, but in 1978 a court decided that it was wrong to refuse a certificate on the grounds of a previous poaching conviction.[22]

Despite the difficulty of reconciling these two decisions, clearer guidance in general terms has emerged from them and from two later court decisions in 1980[23] and 1989,[24] as follows:

(i)   It is not necessary, in order to justify a refusal or revocation, for there to be a possibility of dangerous misuse.[25]

(ii)   The police must give individual consideration to each case.[26]

(iii)   It is right for the police to take account of the applicant's irresponsibility in other activities,[27] but if he has committed offences which do not involve the slightest risk or likelihood of the use of a shot gun, there are no grounds for refusal.[28]

4–07   The cases in which the police cannot issue a shotgun certificate are if—

(a)   they have reason to believe that you are prohibited by the Firearms Act 1968 from possessing a shot gun[29]; or

(b)   they are satisfied that you do not have a good reason for possessing, purchasing or acquiring[30] a shot gun.[31]

You will be regarded, in particular,[32] as having a good reason if the gun is intended to be used for sporting or competition purposes or for shooting vermin.

---

[20] FA 1968 s.28(1); F(A)A 1988 s.3(1).

[21] *Ackers v Taylor* [1974] 1 All E.R. 771.

[22] *R. v Wakefield Crown Court Ex p. Oldfield* [1978] Crim L.R. 164.

[23] *Luke v Little* 1980 SLT (Sh Ct) 138; a case in which the applicant had been convicted three times for drunken driving.

[24] *Spencer Stewart v Chief Constable of Kent* [1989] Cr App. R 307; [1989] COD 372.

[25] *R. v Wakefield Crown Court Ex p. Oldfield* [1978] Crim L.R. 164.

[26] *R. v Wakefield Crown Court Ex p. Oldfield* [1978] Crim L.R. 164.

[27] *Luke v Little* 1980 SLT (Sh Ct) 138; a case in which the applicant had been convicted three times for drunken driving.

[28] *Spencer Stewart v Chief Constable of Kent* [1989] Cr App. R 307; [1989] COD 372.

[29] This generally arises when you have been sentenced by a court to various punishments other than a fine. For full details see 'Prohibition' in Ch.5. In addition, if you are under 17, you are prohibited from possessing a shot gun in many cases; for details see Ch.14.

[30] "Acquire" is defined to mean hire, accept as a gift or borrow (FA 1968 s.57(4)).

[31] FA 1968 s.28(1A); F(A)A 1988 s.3(1).

[32] The use of the words "in particular" indicates that the purposes mentioned are to be accepted as good reasons and that other purposes may be so accepted.

An application is not to be refused by virtue of item (b) merely because you intend neither to use the gun yourself nor to lend it for anyone else to use.[33]

Special provision is made about good reasons for youngsters under 18.[34] Although in a different terminology, this duplicates the provision made in relation to firearm certificates, for which see Ch.14.

Arrangements may be made for shot gun certificates and firearm certificates to be co-terminous.[35]

WHAT ELSE SHOULD I KNOW ABOUT SHOT GUN CERTIFICATES?

A fundamental difference between a shotgun certificate and a firearms certificate is that once granted a shotgun certificate authorises acquisition and possession of an unlimited number of shotguns, subject to them being entered onto the certificate and their acquisition notified to police in the approved manner.[36] No notification or entry on the certificate is required however if the loan or hire is for 72 hours or less.[37] The seller should enter the gun onto the buyer's certificate if it is a 'private' sale.   **4–08**

Shot gun certificates will be issued subject to six conditions. Unlike firearm certificates, the police may not add further conditions.[38] The six conditions are:

(1)   The conditions listed in items (1) to (5) in para.3–23, except that conditions (4) and (5) apply solely to the shotguns themselves and cannot be applied to shot gun ammunition.

(2)   That, where a shot gun disguised as another object is possessed, purchased or acquired[39] for the purpose only of a collection, it shall be used for that purpose only.[40] Failure to comply with any condition is an offence.[41]

A shot gun certificate will give the descriptions of the shot guns to which it relates (including, if known, the identification numbers of the guns), the makers' names and the gauge or calibre of the guns. A photograph of the holder will be affixed to it. The certificate will also provide for entries to be made in it recording details of any sale or other transfer of a shot gun to the certificate holder.[42]   **4–09**

---

[33] FA 1968 s.28(1B); F(A)A 1988 s.3(1). Work that one out! Presumably this would apply where the gun is an heirloom or has some other sentimental value.

[34] FA 1968 s.28(1C). For the general rules applying to youngsters, see Ch.14.

[35] F(A)A 1988 s.11. See para.3–26 for further information,

[36] Usually by recorded delivery and within seven days of the transaction. F(A)A 1997 s.33.

[37] F(A)A 1997 s.32. All transfers of firearms and shotguns must be in person except between RED's. See paras 3–30 to 3–34 for further details.

[38] FA 1968 s.28(2)(a).

[39] "Acquire" is defined to mean hire, accept as a gift or borrow (FA 1968 s.57(4)).

[40] Firearms Rules 1998, r.5(4), (5).

[41] The maximum punishment on summary conviction is imprisonment for 6 months, or a fine at level 5 on the standard scale (currently £5,000), or both (FA 1968 ss.2(2), 51(1), (2) and Sch.6 Pt I).

[42] FA 1968 s.28(2A); F(A)A 1988 s.3(2); Firearms Rules 1998 r.5(6) and Sch.2 Pt II. For the requirements imposed on a transferor of a shot gun to a certificate holder, see paras 3–30 to 3–34.

The certificate will last for five years,[43] unless previously revoked by the police or cancelled by the Court,[44] and may be renewed every five years for the same period by completing another application form.[45] A renewal may be refused for the same reasons as the grant of the original certificate may be refused.[46]

Fees are payable for the grant and renewal of a certificate, and a lower fee is charged for the replacement of a certificate which has been lost or destroyed.[47]

4–10   The police may revoke your shot gun certificate if they are satisfied that you are prohibited by the Firearms Act 1968 from possessing your gun[48] or that you cannot be permitted to possess it without danger to the public safety or to the peace.[49] You may appeal to the Crown Court against a revocation.[50]

The rules which are applicable in the case of firearm certificates to cancellations, appeals,[51] surrenders on revocation or cancellation, false statements to obtain certificates, production of false certificates and impersonation, and production of certificates to the police apply equally to shot gun certificates.[52]

TRANSFER, DE-ACTIVATION AND LOSS OR DESTRUCTION OF SHOT GUNS AND THEIR AMMUNITION

4–11   Many of the restrictions on transferring s.1 firearms and their ammunition, which were considered at paras 3–30 to 3–34, apply, some with modifications, to the transfer of shot guns and their ammunition. These restrictions and modifications are:—

(a)   The sale or other transfer of firearms generally, but this does not apply to shot gun ammunition. The certificate required to be produced in the case of shot guns is a shot gun certificate.[53]

---

[43] The five-year period applies to certificates granted or renewed after January 1, 1995. Formerly, the period was three years (FA 1968 ss.26(3), (3A), (3B), 28A(1)); Firearms (Period of Certificate) Order 1994; Firearms (Amendment) Rules 1994.The period may be further revised by Home Office order (FA 1968 s.28A(3)).

[44] See notes to 3–26 for the cases in which a certificate can be cancelled by a court.

[45] FA 1968 s.28A(1); Firearms Rules 1998 r.5(1) and Sch.2 Pt I. The same form is used for original applications and for renewals. In the latter case, the application is to be accompanied by the certificate to be renewed, if it is available.

[46] FA 1968 s.28(1), (1A).

[47] FA 1968 s.32(1), as amended by the Firearms (Variation of Fees) Order 1994 (SI 1994/2615).

[48] This generally arises when you have been sentenced by a court to various punishments other than a fine. For full details see prohibition in Ch.5. In addition, if you are under 17, you are prohibited from possessing a shot gun in many cases; for details see Ch.14.

[49] FA 1968 s.30C(1). For a discussion about this danger, see para.4–05. Strangely, the police are given no power to revoke if you cease to have a good reason for having the shotgun; despite it being grounds for refusing the certificate in the first instance. Also, a firearm certificate may be revoked on this basis: see Ch.5

[50] FA 1968 ss.30C(2), 44. For further details about appeals, see Ch 5

[51] Except that there can be no variation by the police of a shot gun certificate and thus no question of an appeal against such a variation arising.

[52] FA 1968 ss.3(5), 28A(6), (7), 30C(2), 30D(1), 44(1), 48, 52, 58(5); F(A)A 1988 s.12. As to these rules, see Ch.5.

[53] FA 1968 s.3(2). See paras 3–30 to 3–34 for details.

(b)   The sale, transfer and other dealings with firearms and ammunition by way of trade or business, but this does not apply to shot gun ammunition.[54] It does, however, apply to component parts of shot guns and accessories for diminishing their noise or flash.[55]

(c)   The sale or other transfer of firearms and ammunition to persons who are drunk or of unsound mind.[56]

(d)   The sale or transfer of firearms or ammunition to, or the repair, testing or proof for, persons prohibited from possessing firearms or ammunition.[57]

(e)   In addition to the exceptions noted in item (1) at para.3–30, it is also permissible to return to a person a shot gun which another person has lawfully undertaken to repair, test or prove for that person.[58]

As with s.1 firearms and their ammunition, the Firearms (Amendment) Act 1997 has added provisions requiring notice to be given to the police about some kinds of transfer of shot guns and about their de-activation, loss or destruction. These provisions[59] are very similar to those in paras 3–30 to 3–34 and will not be repeated in full here. It is sufficient, for the purpose of applying those to shotguns, to make the following adjustments—   **4–12**

(a)   for references to lending, substitute references to lending for more than 72 hours;

(b)   for references to firearms, substitute references to shot guns;

(c)   for references to firearm certificates, substitute references to shot gun certificates;

(d)   for references to visitors' firearm permits, substitute references to visitors' shot gun permits.[60]

SHOTGUN AMMUNITION

In relation to the possession and storage of shotgun ammunition, there are a couple of important distinctions as compared with s.1 ammunition. Firstly, there is no obligation to store shotgun ammunition securely in the way that there is with s.1 ammunition, although it is still recommended that reasonable precautions are taken.[61] Secondly, whilst s.1 ammunition cannot legally be possessed without holding a firearm certificate, there is no corresponding requirement to have a shotgun certificate in order to possess shotgun ammunition. However, restrictions   **4–13**

---

[54] FA 1968 s.3(1). See paras 3–30 to 3–34 for details.
[55] FA 1968 ss.3(1), 57(4).
[56] FA 1968 s.25. See paras 3–30 to 3–34 for details.
[57] FA 1968 s.21(5).
[58] FA 1968 s.8(2)(b).
[59] These provisions replace and extend those formerly contained in F(A)A 1988 s.4.
[60] F(A)A 1977 ss.32–35. Failure to comply with the requirements about notices relating to shot guns is an offence with a maximum punishment on summary conviction of 6 months' imprisonment, or a fine at level 5 on the standard scale (currently £5,000), or both (F(A)A 1997 s.36(b)).
[61] For further guidance on storage see Ch.8 on Security of Firearms.

do apply to the sale and purchase of ammunition which is not s.1 ammunition[62] *and* which is capable of being used in a shot gun *or* in a smooth-bore gun to which that section applies.[63]

You will commit an offence[64] if you sell any such ammunition to a person in the United Kingdom[65] who is neither a registered firearms dealer[66] nor a person who sells it by way of trade or business, unless that other person—

(a)   produces a firearm or shot gun certificate which authorises him to possess a shot gun or a smooth-bore gun to which s.1 applies; or

(b)   shows that he is entitled[67] to possess such a gun without holding such a certificate; or

(c)   produces such a certificate which authorises another person to possess such a gun, together with that person's written authority to buy the ammunition on his behalf.[68]

There are special restrictions on the handling of shot guns and their ammunition by young people under the age of 17; these are considered in Ch.14.

WORK ON SHOT GUNS AND THEIR AMMUNITION

4–14   All of the restrictions about carrying out work on s.1 firearms and their ammunition, which were considered at paras 3–35 and 3–36, apply to shot guns and their ammunition, but with one exception and one modification:

(a)   The restrictions on shortening shot gun barrels, which are described at para.3–36, do not apply, but for similar restrictions on shot guns which are not s.1 firearms, see below.

(b)   In the case of item (b) at para.3–36, the certificate to be produced will be a shot gun certificate.[69]

---

[62] See para.3–05 for what constitutes s.1 ammunition.

[63] For smooth-bore guns within this description, see paras 4–01 and 4–02.

[64] The offence is punishable on summary conviction by a maximum of six months' imprisonment, or a fine at level 5 on the standard scale (currently £5,000), or both (F(A)A 1988 s.5(3)).

[65] "United Kingdom" means England, Wales, Scotland and Northern Ireland, and excludes the Channel Islands and the Isle of Man.

[66] As to the registration of firearms dealers, see Ch.16.

[67] For the cases where he would be so entitled, see paras 3–09 to 3–17.

[68] F(A)A 1988 s.5(1), (2).

[69] FA 1968 ss.3(1), (3), 4(3), 25.

It is an offence[70] to shorten the barrel of a shot gun to a length of less than 24 inches[71]; but a registered firearms dealer[72] may do so for the sole purpose of replacing a defective part of the barrel so as to produce a barrel of not less than that length.[73]

PURCHASES IN THE EUROPEAN COMMUNITY

Regulations made to implement the European Council's Directive 91/477/EEC contain detailed provisions about buying shot guns and their ammunition in other Member States of the European Community.[74] The holder of a Firearm or Shotgun Certificate in the UK is entitled to also have issued to them a *European Firearms Pass*. For further details see Ch.7.

4–15

---

[70] The maximum punishment on summary conviction is imprisonment for 6 months, or a fine of the prescribed sum (currently £5,000), or both; or, on indictment, seven years' imprisonment, or an unlimited fine, or both (FA 1968, s.4(1), 51(1), (2) and Sch.6 Pt I).

[71] This length is measured from the muzzle to the point at which the charge is exploded on firing (FA 1968 s.57(6)(a); F(A)A 1988 s.25(1)).

[72] As to the registration of firearms dealers, see Ch.16.

[73] FA 1968 s.4(1), (2).

[74] Details of the provisions may be found in the Firearms Acts (Amendment) Regulations 1992 regs 5 and 9, which inserted ss.18A, 32A, 32B and 32C into FA 1968.

CHAPTER 5

Refusal, Revocation and Appeal

INTRODUCTION

This chapter deals with both Firearm and Shotgun certificates as following the 1988 Act the criteria for obtaining a certificate is very similar, save that the 'good reason' for requiring shotguns is less onerous than that for firearms. Firearms law is the same across Great Britain (but not Northern Ireland) and what is said here will generally apply to Scotland as it does to England & Wales. Scottish readers and lawyers may wish to consider the judgement in a Scottish case[1] to be aware of some differences in the procedure relating to appeals north of the border. The appeal process also covers the certificate of registration as a firearms dealer (RFD). Where there are differences, they are identified, but in general the following applies to both types of certificate and an RFD:—

5–01

REFUSAL AND REVOCATION

The police are entitled to refuse to grant or renew, or to revoke, your certificate in the following five instances:

5–02

---

[1] *Luke v Little* (1980) S.L.T. 138.

(1)   If they have reason to believe that you are of intemperate habits or unsound mind or are otherwise unfitted to be entrusted with a firearm.[2]

(2)   If they have reason to believe that you can no longer be permitted to have the firearm or ammunition to which the certificate relates in your possession without danger to the public safety or to the peace.[3]

(3)   If they are satisfied that you are prohibited by the Firearms Act 1968 from possessing firearms.[4]

(4)   If they are satisfied that you do not have, or no longer have, a good reason[5] for possessing, or for buying or acquiring,[6] the firearm or ammunition which you are authorised by the certificate to possess, purchase or acquire.[7]

(5)   If you fail to comply with a notice from the police requiring you to deliver the certificate to them for variation of its conditions.[8]

5–03   In relation to an RFD the police can further refuse to register, or de-register you, if they are satisfied that you will not engage in business to 'a substantial extent' or 'as an essential part of another trade, business or profession'[9]. The Firearms Act 1968 now provides for the partial revocation of certificates. The police may partially revoke your firearm certificate if satisfied that you no longer have a good reason for possessing, buying or acquiring[10] the s.1 firearm or ammunition to which the partial revocation relates.[11] A shotgun certificate cannot be partially revoked.

If your certificate is revoked for any of the reasons given in items (1) to (4) above, the police may by written notice require you to surrender to them forthwith the certificate and any firearms and ammunition in your possession by virtue of it.[12] Failure to do so is an offence.[13]

5–04   If your firearm certificate is revoked for the reason given in item (5) above, or is partially revoked, the police notice will require the surrender of the certificate alone (so it can be varied), and failure to do so within 21 days from the date of the notice is an offence.[14]

---

[2] FA 1968 s.30A(1), (2)(a).

[3] FA 1968 s.30A(1), (2)(b), s.30C(1) and s.34 (2) for RFD's. For a commentary on the meaning of "danger to the public safety or to the peace", see paras 5–11 to 5–14 and also 4–06.

[4] FA 1968 s.30A(1), (3) and s.30C(1) . This arises if you have been given certain punishments by the courts; see prohibition at para.5–22.

[5] As a ground for revocation, this only applies to firearms certificates and bizarrely not to shotgun certificates, despite the requirement to demonstrate good reason to acquire a shotgun certificate in the first place. For a commentary about "good reason", see para.3–20. This applies to firearms, but see the comments as to 'good reason' in relation to shotguns at para.4–07.

[6] "Acquire" is defined to mean hire, accept as a gift or borrow (FA 1968 s.57(4), F(A)A 1988 s.25(1)).

[7] FA 1968 s.30A(1), (4).

[8] FA 1968 s.30A(1), (5). This applies only to firearms certificates and not shot gun certificates.

[9] FA 1968 s.34(1A).

[10] "Acquire" is defined to mean hire, accept as a gift or borrow (FA 1968 s.57(4), F(A)A 1988 s.25(1)).

[11] FA 1968 s.30B(1), (2).

[12] F(A)A 1988 s.12(1); FA 1968 s.30D(5).

[13] The maximum punishment on summary conviction is three months' imprisonment, or a fine at level 4 on the standard scale (currently £2,500), or both (F(A)A 1988 s.12(2)).

[14] FA 1968 s.30D(1)-(3), (5). In a case of partial revocation, the police will amend the certificate and return it to you. The maximum punishment on summary conviction is a fine at level 3 on the standard scale (currently £1,000) (FA 1968 s.51(1), (2), Sch.6 Pt I).

If you appeal against either of these types of revocation (i.e. change of condition or partial revocation), the requirement to surrender is suspended if you appeal, unless the appeal is abandoned or dismissed when the 21-day period will instead run from the date of such abandonment or dismissal.[15]

Whatever the reasons for the refusal or revocation, the police "must give reasons for their decision".[16] It is expected this will normally be in writing as part of the revocation notice and this letter is an important document which you should keep. Firearms licensing departments should always have the possibility of an appeal in mind and set out clearly in the letter the precise grounds on which they are refusing or revoking. A failure to do so may be the subject of criticism by the court and may give rise to costs implications. The letter should advise you as to your right of appeal and will usually indicate the relevant Crown Court. The police are also required to notify you in writing when varying a condition of an FAC, and when requiring you to surrender an FAC or SGC, or firearms and ammunition where your certificate has been revoked by them or cancelled by order of the court. The same applies to notices served on an RFD notifying an intention to remove from the register or requiring them to surrender their certificate of registration[17]. You are well advised to keep all such correspondence from the police.

Within 21 days from receiving the decision of the police to revoke, you may appeal to your local Crown Court (or the Sheriff in Scotland), when the Court may consider any evidence or other matter whether or not it was available when the police decision to revoke was made.[18] We would advise you to notify the police as soon as possible that you intend to appeal. However most police forces do not attempt to enforce this time limit strictly as if a certificate holder is 'out of time' in lodging an appeal, all he would need to do would be to make a fresh application and, when that is refused, appeal. That would be a waste of everybody's time! These are sometimes referred to as 'Section 44 Appeals' as that is the relevant section of the 1968 Act. If you have any dealings with the Crown Court about your appeal you will probably need to make this clear, or they will think you are appealing a criminal conviction or sentence from a Magistrates Court, which is a different procedure.

5–05

In most cases the police are not keen on seizing the weapons themselves (unless they are suggesting they are exhibits in a serious criminal allegation) and are usually content to allow your firearms and ammunition to be held by an RFD or another certificate holder nominated by you. If you successfully appeal against the revocation, the firearms and ammunition will be returned to you. If the appeal is dismissed, the Court can make an order for their disposal. If no appeal is made, or an appeal is abandoned, the firearms and ammunition will be disposed of in such a manner as may be agreed between you and the police. In default of agreement, the police may decide on the method of disposal; but their decision must be notified to you and may itself be appealed against to the Crown Court. The Court may either dismiss your appeal[19] or make its own order for disposal.[20]

---

[15] FA 1968 s.30D(4).
[16] See *Guidance* 10.53 re firearms certificates and also 11.20 re shotgun certificates which is similarly worded.
[17] For all these notices see variously FA 1968 ss.29(1), 30A, 52(2)(b), 38(6) and 38(8).
[18] FA 1968 s.44(1), (3), Sch.5 Pt I para.2. There is also a right of appeal against a partial revocation.
[19] In which case the police decision on disposal stands.

5–06   If you are unfortunate enough to be convicted of certain offences or be given certain punishments[21] by a Court, the Court may cancel your firearms certificate (or shot gun certificate) and order any firearm or ammunition found in your possession[22] to be forfeited or disposed of. You must then, under threat of a further penalty,[23] surrender the certificate to the police within 21 days from the date of a notice from them to that effect. Firearms and ammunition so forfeited may be seized and detained by the police who can, if the Court so orders, destroy or otherwise dispose of them.[24]

It should be noted that there is no provision in the Acts to appeal against a decision of the police to impose a condition on an FAC or RFD. However it would be possible to challenge such a condition by way of 'judicial review' if it were totally unreasonable to have imposed such a condition in the circumstances.

THE PROCESS OF APPEAL

5–07   An appeal to the Crown Court in England & Wales is heard by a Judge or Recorder sitting together with two Magistrates, and to the Sheriff in Scotland.[25] They sit to exercise an administrative function left over from Quarter Sessions. When you notify the police that you intend to appeal they should provide you with the evidence they have as to why they have refused or revoked your certificate. If this has not been done by the time the matter comes before the court for a preliminary hearing the court may well order the police to serve their evidence within a given time. The Court cannot order the Appellant (the certificate holder) to serve their evidence in advance, but it is preferable that the Court have an opportunity to consider the evidence from both sides in writing before the hearing. It is important to bear in mind that that there are effectively no

---

[20] FA 1968 s.44; F(A)A 1988 s.12(3)-(5). You should consult a solicitor if you are considering an appeal of either kind.

[21] The offences are any under the Firearms Act 1968 or the Firearms (Amendment) Acts of 1988 and 1997, except an offence under s.22(3) of the former Act, or offences relating specifically to air weapons. The punishments are, briefly: imprisonment; detention in a young offender institution; detention in a detention centre or in a young offender institution in Scotland; an order to enter into a recognizance to keep the peace or to be of good behaviour, a condition of which is that the offender shall not possess, use or carry a firearm; and probation with a requirement that the offender shall not possess, use or carry a firearm (FA 1968 s.52(1); F(A)A 1988 s.25(5); F(A)A 1997 s.50(4)).

[22] The time of this finding is not specified. It is suggested that this must be at, or very shortly after, the commission of the offence for which one of the punishments in note 21 above has been given.

[23] The maximum fine on summary conviction is at level 3 on the standard scale (currently £1,000) (FA 1968 s.51(1), (2) and Sch.6 Pt I).

[24] FA 1968 s.52(2)-(4). The statements in this paragraph are qualified in the following cases:

(a) In the case of air weapon offences and in the case of the offence of giving a shot gun or ammunition to a person under 15 (see Ch.14), the court's power to order forfeiture or disposal extends to guns and ammunition in respect of which the offence was committed as well as to those found in the convicted persons' possession.

(b) In the case of air weapon offences, in the case of illegal possession of a shot gun by a person under 15, and in the case of any shot gun or ammunition in respect of which the offence of giving them to a person under 15 is committed, there is no power given to the police by the Act (though they may otherwise have it) to seize and detain either kind of gun or, subsequently, on the court's order, to destroy or otherwise dispose of them (FA 1968 ss.51(3), 52(2)-(4), 57(3), 58(4) and Sch.6 Pt I and Pt II, paras 7–9).

[25] See FA 1968 Sch.5 Pt II for the provisions relating to appeal.

rules of evidence in this type of hearing[26]. Obviously the court has to follow the rules of natural justice, and where it is relevant, has to apply the Human Rights Act, but 'hearsay' for example is permissible. It should also be noted that the hearing is not concerned with whether the police were correct or not in their decision, the question for the court is are *they* satisfied, on the evidence *now* available that the Appellant can be granted his certificate. In almost all cases the Court will be concerned with issues 1 and 2—set out at para.5–02—are they 'satisfied' that you are of intemperate habits or unsound mind or are otherwise unfitted to be entrusted with a firearm,[27] or are they 'satisfied' that you can no longer be permitted to have the firearm or ammunition to which the certificate relates in your possession without danger to the public safety or to the peace.[28] The only other reason to refuse or revoke which often comes before the courts is the question as to whether a certificate holder (or applicant) has shown a good reason for requiring a particular firearm. Again the court would have to be 'satisfied' on the Appellant's evidence that he did have a good reason. If a certificate is refused or revoked because the holder is prohibited under the Act it is difficult to imagine any basis of appeal! We put 'satisfied' in inverted commas because this is a slightly different test to that usually found in the courts. We would suggest that it equates to 'satisfied on the balance of probabilities'. The court can refuse the appeal, or grant it, in whole or in part.

THE HEARING

At the hearing the barrister representing the police (the 'Respondents' as they will be referred to by the court) will open the case (explain what it is about) to the court and will then call the evidence that the police rely on in objecting to you having your certificate. This evidence will either be 'live' by having the witnesses in the witness box, or by tendering written statements. The Appellant is entitled to request the attendance of those witnesses whose evidence is not accepted so they can be cross examined. The court may also wish to ask questions of the witnesses.

    In most cases one of the witnesses the police will rely upon will be the person who made the decision to refuse or revoke. The practise varies amongst different forces and this can be anyone from a Sergeant or Inspector, or a Firearms Licensing Manager (usually a civilian employee), up to a Deputy Chief Constable. Whoever it is they will probably list the various factors which they took into account in reaching their decision. If you are the Appellant you will want to give careful consideration to the reasons given. For example:—

1.   Are the facts on which the objections are based correct? If not they will need to be challenged by cross examining the witnesses who state those facts.

5–08

---

[26] *Kavanagh v Chief Constable of Devon & Cornwall* [1974] 1 Q.B. 624. See the Judgement of Lord Denning.

[27] FA 1968 s.30A(1), (2)(a).

[28] FA 1968 s.30A(1), (2)(b). For a commentary on the meaning of "danger to the public safety or to the peace", see paras 5–11 to 5–14 and also 4–06.

2.   Even if the facts are accepted, has the person making the decision to refuse/revoke taken an unreasonable view of the facts, or reached a decision which is not justified on the facts? Bear in mind however, as stated above, it is for the court to reach their own decision on the facts and the case, it does not matter if the police and their decision maker got it wrong. There may be many reasons for this, the police may not have a seen an important witness give evidence (as the court will) or they may not have had evidence from a witness that the Appellant has called to court.

3.   Is there now other evidence available to the court (which was not considered by the police) which puts the whole matter in a different light? When the police exercise their functions under the Firearms Acts they are engaging in a 'paper based exercise'. One important piece of evidence which they rarely consider is what the Appellant has to say about the matter. In a lot of cases the Appellant is not even interviewed by police to give their version of events, unless there was a criminal investigation. Further there may be witnesses who come to court to give evidence on behalf of the Appellant who the police were not aware of, or who they chose not to take a statement from.

5–09   It follows from the above that careful thought has to be given to the evidence that can be called on your behalf when considering an appeal. In addition to any witnesses who deal with the facts of any alleged incident which gave rise to the revocation (for example), are there character witnesses who can speak of the good behaviour of the Appellant or testify to his suitability and safe handling of firearms?

THE ISSUES TO BE CONSIDERED BY THE COURTS

5–10   What are the courts (and the police in the first instance) looking for when considering whether they are satisfied that a person can be permitted to possess firearms within the framework of the law? This book cannot cover every issue that will arise in these appeals, but a large majority of these cases will cover the below.

FITNESS TO BE ENTRUSTED WITH A FIREARM

5–11   The issue of fitness to be entrusted with a firearm is closely linked with the other criterion of whether the Appellant can be permitted to possess firearms, or shot guns, without danger to public safety or to the peace, the same facts often being relied on to justify concerns about both issues. The leading case on the question of danger to public safety or the peace makes it clear that what the police, and so any court on appeal, should consider is whether there is a danger arising out of the possession or potential use, or misuse, of the firearm or shot gun.[29]

Not surprisingly you are considered to be 'unfit to be entrusted with a firearm' if you are prohibited under s.21 of the Act because you have received a sentence

---

[29] *Ackers v Taylor* [1974] 1 All E.R. 771. See also para 4–06.

of imprisonment of more than a certain length. Depending on the offence for which you were convicted you may still be considered unfit even if the prohibition were no longer to be in force. See para.5–22 below ('Prohibition under s.21') for the circumstances where such a prohibition applies and when you may be able to ask a court for it to be lifted.

The police will also consider any other previous convictions carefully before granting a certificate, whether they gave rise to a prohibition or not. The Rehabilitation of Offender Act 1974 does not apply, you have to disclose all convictions, however minor and however old. Having said that common sense ought to prevail, and usually does. A woman in her 40s who now leads an industrious life will not be prevented from having a firearm certificate because of a shoplifting conviction when she was 15.[30] Conversely, someone with a conviction for armed robbery is unlikely to be granted a certificate, however old the conviction. These examples are fairly obvious, but the courts have reached decisions which are perhaps sometimes less so. A woman of good character was refused a certificate because her husband had two ancient drugs convictions, but perhaps more importantly was believed to still associate with drug users.[31] Another example where certificates have been revoked is where it comes to police attention that the son of a perfectly law abiding certificate holder is a member of a violent 'street gang'. If the boy lives at home police may have concerns about potential access to firearms. This is a difficult example as no blame can be attached to the father!

INTEMPERATE HABITS

Drug use or excessive alcohol abuse may be a reason for refusal. Bear in mind the police have the right to consult your doctor. A recurring theme in these cases is those who have been convicted of drinking and driving, particularly more than once.[32] A revocation on the basis of one conviction has been upheld, and may be justified particularly if you have a bad attitude to the offence.[33] In most cases however the police will be looking for a pattern of behaviour which demonstrates loss of temper or control, or other irresponsibility. Those who have volatile relationships, particularly where there are repeated allegations of domestic violence, even if they haven't resulted in convictions, may find this is put forward as an objection. The usual concern is the availability of firearms in the home when a person might lose their temper. This will also apply to applicants who display prejudicial attitudes of a racist, anti religious or homophobic nature, particularly when often expressed and in violent terms.

5–12

---

[30] *Spencer-Stewart v Chief Constable of Kent* 1989 Cr. App. R. 307. Handling stolen goods conviction not likely to suggest a shotgun certificate should be revoked on the basis of future danger involving firearms.

[31] *Dabek v Chief Constable of Devon & Cornwall* 1991 155 J.P. 55

[32] *Chief Constable of Essex v Germain* (1991) *The Times*, April 15, 1991. It demonstrates irresponsibility with a dangerous item, a bit like a gun. See also *Luke v Little* (1980) S.L.T. 138

[33] *Lubbock v Chief Constable of Lothian and Borders Police* Unreported June 18, 2001 at Jedburgh Sheriff Court.

UNSOUND MIND

5–13   This may also seem obvious as an objection, but it doesn't only cover those who are mentally ill in the sense that when affected by their illness they present a danger to the public. In recent years police forces have refused certificates to those who have in the past suffered from depression of any form. Given some of the recent tragedies involving firearms a conservative approach to this issue on the part of the police and the courts is perhaps not entirely surprising. Concerns include suicidal thoughts and tendencies as well as danger to others. If your GP is willing to say such problems are no longer present this will help. In some cases it may be necessary to instruct a consultant psychiatrist to prepare a report confirming that the applicant is perfectly well and in their professional opinion can safely be entrusted with firearms.[34]

BREACH OF SECURITY CONDITIONS

5–14   The security of firearms and ammunition is dealt with in Ch.8. Breaches of these rules, particularly where such a breach has led to the loss or theft of firearms or ammunition in circumstances where the certificate holder had not taken reasonable precautions for their safekeeping is almost certain to result in the revocation of your certificate. Do not leave items subject to certification in your car! The precautions have to be reasonable in the circumstances.

It will be understood that the above four issues, although dealt with separately, can all be examples of where there could be a danger 'to the public safety or to the peace' to use the words of the Act,[35] if the circumstances were found to be proved.

LACK OF CO-OPERATION WITH THE LICENSING AUTHORITY

5–15   Certificate holders and those who apply for them are expected to co-operate with the police, not only in providing the necessary information for the original application and any renewal or variation, but also on an on-going basis. A failure to co-operate may form the basis of a revocation decision or refusal to renew, or at least support other reasons. Maintaining good communication with your licensing department is therefore well advised. This includes notifying transfers and acquisitions of weapons on a timely basis, and similarly notifying any change of address without delay. At its extreme, making threatening and abusive phone calls to your licensing enquiry officer is a very good way to get your ticket pulled, as is refusing to allow him to inspect your weapons or security arrangements! The certificate holder may feel there are good reasons for such obstructive behaviour, but it is best avoided. If a certificate holder has genuine reasons for not keeping appointments or not responding to correspondence and messages, or has a legitimate complaint about the actions of the licensing

---

[34] See *Guidance*12.9
[35] FA 1968 s.27(1)(c) for firearms and s.28(1) for shot guns.

department, these should be explained clearly and calmly, if necessary to the relevant force public standards department. This can be a sensitive area and you may wish to involve a solicitor at an early stage if you have serious concerns.

LACK OF GOOD REASON

This really only applies to Firearms certificates; as to good reasons for having **5–16** shotguns, see the comments at para.4–07. 'Good reason' applies to each firearm you require, and to each type of ammunition. The application form will ask you to state your reasons for requiring each weapon you wish to have and there is a space to give a brief reason, for example, 'vermin control' or 'target shooting'. In most cases this will be self evident to the police as being good reasons because of other information they will already have; details of land over which you have permission to shoot vermin, or your shooting club, to keep with the above examples. Where they do not have such supporting information they will probably ask for further details. This is likely to be covered when the enquiry officer comes to inspect your security arrangements. At the end of the day the question of good reason is a question of fact in the particular circumstances of the applicant and it is difficult to set any hard and fast rules, or to cover all the likely examples of a 'good reason'. Your local enquiry officer may well rely on Ch.13 of the *Guidance* in determining whether you have established good reason for a particular gun and in unusual cases you would be well advised to consult it yourself before discussing the matter with the police.

Some principles need to be borne in mind:—   **5–17**

1.   When considering 'good reason' the police should look firstly "from the standpoint of the applicant, rather than from that of a possible objector.[36] However, simply wishing to own a particular gun for it's own sake is not sufficient; it is the reasons for which you want to use it that are important.
2.   Good reason is not limited to 'need'. It is for the individual to decide what type of weapon they wish to use for a particular purpose and as long as the gun is a reasonable choice for that purpose the certificate should be granted. The police cannot say to the applicant "you don't need that gun for that use", that is not the test; the test is "do you have a good reason for that gun". If so, you should have it.
3.   Since good reason relates to the use of the gun the police will want to be satisfied that you will not only have the opportunity to use it, but are likely do so. A failure to demonstrate regular use may result in refusal. At renewal the police may look at the amount of ammunition purchased in the previous period to ensure that all of the guns on the certificate have been used. If guns are for target shooting the club secretary is required to notify the police of any member who has not shot at least once during each year.
4.   Good reason has to be demonstrated for each weapon on your certificate. This can lead to questions from the police if you have 2 or more weapons which are similar to each other. For example, "Why do you need three .22 rifles?". There can be many answers to questions such as this; "I am a keen

---

[36]   *Anderson v Neilans* (1940) and *Joy v Chief Constable of Dumfries & Galloway* (1966) are cited as authority for this proposition in para.10.28 of the *Guidance,* but both appear to be unreported cases.

target shooting competitor and I need one or more spare guns in case of a malfunction", or "I prefer a lighter gun at that shoot as there is always a lot of walking". Guns may have different capabilities or work better in different conditions, and so on.

5–18   There will always be cases where the police and the shooter will not agree as to whether there is a good reason, which may end up in court as the subject of an appeal. To avoid time and expense it is advisable to give the police as much information as you can, together with any supporting documentation, when you make the application.

The most common subject areas for appeals relating to good reason are the following:—

'duplicate guns' as mentioned in point 4. above. In practice, the more often you actually go out shooting the more likely the police are to accept multiple ownership of similar guns.

'Land'. With most hunting, rough shooting and vermin destruction, the police will want to be satisfied that you have the opportunity to shoot over land on which it is safe to use that particular type of firearm. You will be expected to provide written evidence that you have permission to shoot on some suitable land, although this does not limit you to that property, subject to any conditions on your certificate. The police should keep records of land over which shooting is conducted in their area and which is considered to be safe and suitable. If the land you nominate is not within their knowledge they may well wish to obtain further information from the land owner (or his agent) or inspect it themselves. If the police do inspect it they may ask the applicant to be present to demonstrate their knowledge of any particular dangers or difficulties that may be present. The presence of occupied buildings, public footpaths and the like on or near the land will be taken into account. Depending on the circumstances they may restrict shooting on given land to particular calibres, or for example only shooting from a high seat, or precluding shooting when the ground is frozen. The responsibility for shooting safely rests with the shooter in all cases, and causing accidents to, or complaints from, members of the public is likely to lead to revocation! The police will also wish to be satisfied that the type of animal you wish to hunt or exterminate is present on the land in some numbers, or causes a particular problem there.

5–19   'Quarry'. A detailed analysis of the types of firearms and ammunition which are most suitable to kill a particular species of animal would result in a book larger than this one, and will not be attempted here. The Home Office have issued guidance[37] as to what they consider to be appropriate calibres for given quarry. This is guidance, not law, and if the applicant feels that a different calibre or type of weapon would be more suitable, they should argue it. No doubt the police will need some convincing and evidence from an experienced gamekeeper (for example) who agrees with

---

[37] See *Guidance* Ch.13.

you might well be helpful. In some cases the law does prescribe the minimum calibre to be used, such as .243 on most deer[38] and restrictions on some other wildlife[39] control.

'Overseas use'. The law allows the acquisition of rifles for use abroad, in particular for 'big game' in larger calibres than would be considered suitable for any animal found in the United Kingdom. The police will want to be satisfied that you will make trips abroad for such purposes, although these trips may not be very frequent for obvious reasons. In some cases you may be also permitted to use the same large calibre rifle for some types of deer, or wild boar in Great Britain. It should be noted that it is not possible to permit possession of expanding ammunition solely for use abroad because of the wording of the exemption in s.5(4)(b)(ii)—"concerned with the management of any estate" has been held to mean "any estate in Great Britain",[40] and therefore it is not a good reason to have the ammunition in this country. You will normally be permitted to possess a small amount of non-expanding ammunition to zero the rifle.

'Target shooting'. As already stated, you are required to be a member of a target shooting club, whether it is for rifle or muzzle loading pistol, as appropriate.[41] Approved clubs only cover rifles and muzzle loading pistols at present, which can cause some anomalies. Current police policy is that an individual can have a long barrelled pistol for target shooting, but a club cannot, as clubs cannot be approved for this type of weapon. If that is correct, how does the individual show 'good reason' for the long barrelled pistol? See para.3–12 for further information. In all cases the police will wish to ensure that you have the opportunity to use a range which has a range safety certificate that covers the type of weapon you wish to use.

5–20

'Practical shotgun'. A large magazine capacity semi automatic or pump action shotgun comes under s.1 of the Act. These can be used for practical shotgun, usually shooting at steel plates from different positions. This activity is not covered by 'approved clubs' but is nonetheless a discipline recognised by the police. The police usually require such weapons to either be used on a range with a safety certificate, or on a course of fire supervised by a qualified member of the UKPSA.

'Collectors'. Creating a collection of either firearms or ammunition is considered to be a good reason for the purposes of the Act. Collections of firearms are sometimes subject to a condition that they are not to be fired, and in any event you may not be permitted to possess ammunition for the guns in the collection. The good reason is being a 'bone fide collector' and so the police will probably wish to see evidence of membership of a relevant collector's society, or perhaps of a long standing academic interest in the subject.

Other examples of 'good reason' to possess firearms will relate to slaughtering instruments, trophies of war, controlling races, theatrical use, signalling apparatus and many others. Those who fall into these specialist categories are likely to be

5–21

---

[38] The Deer Acts, see further Ch.12.
[39] Wildlife & Countryside Act 1981, see Ch.12.
[40] *Lacey v Comm. Met. Police* (2000) Unreported, CO/0699/2000.
[41] F(A)A 1997 s.44.

aware of their particular requirements and will be able to satisfy the good reason test. Pistols for humane dispatch, as permitted under the 1997 Act[42] have caused some debate in recent years. The Home Office[43] suggest that such pistols should be in .32 calibre and should be restricted to 2 shots. This calibre is considered by most users to be totally unsuitable for use on larger animals, including large deer and wild boar; it might result in an 'inhumane' dispatch! Further the limitation of 2 shots can also render the weapon inadequate, particularly when dealing with more than one animal. There is no guidance as to how the pistol ought to be restricted. Parliament chose to say 'firearm' and not for example to specify 'revolver' or 'self loading pistol'. It is relatively easy to restrict a revolver to 2 shots by blocking up all but 2 of the chambers in the cylinder, but with a magazine fed gun the usual method is to limit the magazine to two shots. It could be argued that this creates a 3 shot gun (as you could put one in the chamber as well) but for health and safety reasons most deer stalkers (for example) would not consider it appropriate to go stalking carrying a pistol with a round in the chamber. In any event, if it is a condition of your certificate that you have a 2 shot pistol for this purpose, you commit the offence of breaching your license conditions if you load it with more than 2 shots. If you can show good reason for needing a larger calibre, or an unrestricted gun you should be granted one. There have been several successful appeals on this subject.[44]

With all of the above issues (not just good reason) it is good practice for the police to ask for further information if they have doubts. Do ask for any concerns that have been expressed to be put in writing (email is sufficient) so that you can deal with them. Ask for time to obtain further information if it is necessary, before they make a final decision. This would be important if you wished to get evidence from a doctor for example.

PROHIBITED PERSONS—APPLICATIONS TO REMOVE A PROHIBITION UNDER SECTION 21

5–22   As we have seen, it is not possible for the police to grant a certificate to a person who is prohibited under the Act from possessing firearms. This will apply for life if a person received a sentence of imprisonment of three years or more, and the prohibition is for five years from the date of release from prison if the person received a sentence of between three months and three years.[45] This applies to all forms of custodial sentence, including partly suspended sentences, but it does not

---

[42] s.3, and see also the comments regarding humane dispatch at (3) at para.2–09.

[43] *Guidance*13.36.

[44] For example *Toufexis v Commissioner of Metropolitan Police* Unreported, April 2010, Wood Green Crown Court. In another recent unreported case the court specifically rejected the argument mentioned above that a pistol with a magazine restricted to 2 shots amounted in reality to a 3 shot pistol on the basis that an extra round could be put in the chamber, *R. v Michael Wells*, Kingston Crown Court, September 23, 2011.

[45] FA 1968 s.21. It can also apply to persons on license in some circumstances. The cases in which you may be so prohibited from using a firearm fall into two categories. First, when you have been sentenced by a court to various custodial penalties; details are in FA 1968 s.21(1)–(3) and are, briefly: (1) imprisonment, custody for life, preventive detention, corrective training, detention in a young offenders' institution, youth custody, and young offenders discharged on licence. In some cases offenders are prohibited from possessing firearms for life, in others for five years from release, and, in the last case, for the duration of the licence; (2) recognizance to keep the peace or to be of good

apply to a wholly suspended sentence (no date of release), and it does not apply to any type of community order. The prisoner should be asked to sign an acknowledgement of this restriction on release, if it applies to them. It is important to understand that this prohibition applies to all firearms, not just those subject to licensing. For example, a person subject to a prohibition will commit an offence by having in their possession a standard air weapon, or blank ammunition, neither of which normally require a license, but are still 'firearms' and 'ammunition' in law.

A person who is subject to a prohibition may apply to the Crown Court (Sheriff in Scotland) for the area where they reside to have that prohibition removed, and if the application is granted the prohibition shall no longer apply to that person.[46] This type of appeal is heard by a Crown Court judge.[47] The court will want to see evidence that the applicant is now a reformed character who has 'gone straight' and lead an industrious life in the intervening years. There will normally have been a number of years gone by since release from prison, during which no further offences have been committed. If possession of firearms is now required for work or the like, the application is perhaps more likely to be granted than if a person wished to shoot purely for sport, although this is certainly not a rule of law. The factors outlined above regarding 'fitness to possess firearms' are also likely to be relevant here.

THE COSTS OF APPEAL

Legal aid is not available for any type of firearms licensing appeal to the Crown Court or the Sheriff's Court, and even if the Appellant wins is unlikely to recover their costs from the police as the police are 'only performing a public function'.[48] To recover costs the Appellant would have to show that the police either wasted costs, or acted in a wholly improper manner in coming to the original decision, which is the subject of the appeal. In relation to applications for removal of a prohibition, there are no circumstances in which you can ever expect to recover your costs as it is your criminal conviction that led to you being prohibited in the first place.

Most of the national shooting organisations have member insurance schemes, some of which may cover the legal expenses of an appeal against revocation or refusal by the police. However, the scope of cover varies and, even if it is available, do bear in mind the insurers will have quite strict criteria as to the circumstances in which they will agree to fund the legal costs of a licensing appeal. It is usually an absolute requirement that any potential claim for legal costs cover must be notified to the insurers before commencing proceedings, so do not wait until you have won your appeal to contact the insurers as they may then refuse to pay out your legal costs! In any event, readers who are minded to appeal would be well advised to contact the General Secretary of their respective

5–23

---

behaviour, and probation, when made subject, in each case, to a condition that such firearms shall not be possessed, used or carried. The prohibition lasts for the duration of the punishment.

[46] FA 1968 s.21(6) and Sch.3.

[47] Practice seems to vary as to whether this type of application is heard by a Judge alone or sitting with two Magistrates.

[48] *Chief Constable of Derbyshire v Newton & Goodman* (1998) and other cases cited therein.

organisation before proceeding. The major shooting organisations[49] are usually able to give sensible preliminary advice on such matters to their members. Failing funding being available by way of insurance the shooter either has to fund personally the legal costs of their appeal, or represent themselves.

5–24   A final warning on costs; readers should be mindful that if you proceed with an appeal and are unsuccessful, not only will you end up having to bear your own legal costs but there is also a distinct possibility you may be ordered to pay a substantial contribution towards the police's legal costs in defending your appeal.

Nonetheless, in most cases it would be advisable to at least consult a solicitor. Sometimes early intervention from a solicitor can lead to the issue being resolved with the police by negotiation and without going to the full extent and cost of a contested appeal hearing.

---

[49] Such as The Sportsman's Association of Great Britain & Northern Ireland, The Clay Pigeon Shooting Association, The Country Land and Business Association, The National Rifle Association, The National Small-bore Rifle Association, The British Association for Shooting and Conservation, The Gun Trade Association, The British Deer Society, The National Gamekeepers Organisation, The United Kingdom Practical Shooting Association, The Shooters Rights Association, The Muzzle Loaders' Association of Great Britain, The Countryside Alliance, The St. Hubert's Club of Great Britain, The Sealed Knot and several others of which the reader may be a member. Nearly all of these organisations have websites and all make a positive contribution to the many types of shooting sports pursued in Great Britain.

CHAPTER 6

Police Permits

See Ch.7 for Visitors Permits. 6–01

A **police permit** allows the holder to have in his possession[1] firearms and ammunition without holding a firearm certificate or a shot gun certificate.[2] Another form of police permit allows an auctioneer to sell by auction, expose for sale by auction and have in his possession for sale by auction firearms and ammunition without holding a certificate of either kind.[3]

Permits are obtainable from the chief officer of police for the police area where the applicant resides or, as the case may be, for the area where the auction is to be held.[4]

A general permit will only be granted in special cases where it may not be 6–02 necessary or desirable to issue a firearm certificate or a shot gun certificate and, in general, the duration of the permit will be short. A permit will, for example, be appropriate to authorise possession of firearms or ammunition by a person who has been refused a certificate, or has had it revoked, until he is able to dispose of them; or by a relative or executor of a deceased person or a receiver of a bankrupt's estate when firearms or ammunition form part of the property of the deceased person or bankrupt.

One circumstance where it is sometimes appropriate to request a permit is where an applicant for renewal of their firearm or shotgun certificate has put in their application in good time, but there has been a delay by the police in issuing the certificate. As we have seen, in these circumstances the continued possession of firearms or ammunition past the expiry date of the certificate is a criminal offence. It should be said that if the delay in issuing the new certificate was entirely that of the police, and there were no other problems regarding the application, it would probably amount to an 'abuse of the process of the court' for the police to prosecute in these circumstances. What they should concentrate their efforts on is sending you the certificate! However to remain within the law the applicant should ask the police for a permit to cover their firearms (and shotguns)

---

[1] A purchase or other form of acquisition cannot be covered by a permit.

[2] FA 1968 s.7(1). For these two kinds of certificate, see Chs 3 and 4 respectively.

[3] FA 1968 s.9(2). See also item (2) at para.3–09 for the possession of firearms and ammunition by auctioneers and their employees. A third form of permit (prescribed by the Firearms Rules 1989 r.9(3) and Sch.4 Pt V) is available for handling firearms and signalling apparatus in connection with ships and aircraft; see, further, item (4)(c) at para.3–09. Forms for each kind of permit are prescribed by the Firearms Rules 1998 r.9 and Sch 4.

[4] FA 1968 ss.7(1), 9(2). An applicant cannot be said to reside at a property which he has let (*Burditt v Joslin* [1981] 3 All E.R. 203; *The Times*, February 13, 1981).

and ammunition until the certificates can be reissued. In practice such a request is likely to result in the certificate being sent to you without further delay.[5]

6–03   There are two general forms of permit and two special forms for auctioneers, in each case one being for shot guns and the other for s.1 firearms and their ammunition. The latter, like a firearm certificate, gives full particulars of each firearm or type of ammunition; a shot gun permit describes each shot gun in the same way as a shot gun certificate.[6] All permits are likely to be issued subject to some or all of the following conditions[7]:

(1)   The person to whom the permit is granted shall inform the chief officer of police at once of the name and address of any person, except a registered firearms dealer,[8] purchasing or acquiring any of the firearms or ammunition listed in the permit.

(2)   Reasonable precautions shall be taken to ensure the safe custody of the firearms and ammunition, and any loss or theft shall be reported at once to the chief officer of police.

(3)   The permit shall be returned to the chief officer of police on or before the date on which it expires.

6–04   You should consult your local police firearms licensing department if you feel that the circumstances of your case call for the issue of a permit. No fee is payable, and there is no right of appeal against refusal by the police to grant a permit or against any of its conditions.

The use of a firearm or ammunition by a permit holder otherwise than in accordance with the terms and conditions of his permit will be an offence.[9] An offence is also committed if you knowingly or recklessly make a statement which is false in any material particular for the purpose of procuring, whether for yourself or for another person, the grant of a permit.[10]

---

[5] The *Guidance* makes it clear that the police should not use permits routinely to deal with delays in the reissue of certificates.

[6] Firearms Rules 1998 r.9(1), (2) and Sch.4. Neither the FA 1968 nor the Firearms Rules 1998 stipulate the duration of a permit, thus leaving that aspect to the police to decide in the light of the circumstances. A new permit can be sought on expiry. No forms of application for permits are prescribed, though police forms are available.

[7] The Firearms Rules 1969 (now revoked) prescribed the conditions to which permits would be subject. The 1998 Rules do not do so but allow for unspecified conditions to be imposed. The three conditions listed in the text are recommended in the *Guidance*. There is evidently no bar to further conditions being added. Additionally, permits will bear a footnote requesting holders to report the loss of the permit to the local police at once.

[8] As to the registration of firearms dealers, see Ch.16.

[9] FA 1968 ss.1(1), 2(1), 3(1)(b), 7(1), 9(2).

[10] FA 1968 s.7(2), 9(3), 13(2). The maximum punishments upon summary conviction are 6 months' imprisonment, or a fine at level 5 on the standard scale (currently £5,000), or both (FA 1968 s.51(1), (2) and Sch.6 Pt I).

CHAPTER 7

Visitors' Permits and European Firearms Passes

VISITORS' PERMITS

The provision of the Firearms Acts allow the grant by the police to visitors to this country of permits for those kinds of firearms for which a firearm or shot gun certificate would otherwise be required.

A **visitor's firearm permit** will permit the possession of s.1 firearms[1] and the possession, purchase or acquisition[2] of such ammunition for firearms as is specified in the permit. A **visitor's shot gun permit** will permit the possession, purchase or acquisition of shot guns but, unless one of a number of conditions is met, a permit authorising the purchase or acquisition of shot guns with a magazine will not be granted.[3]

Applications for both kinds of permit may be made on behalf of a visitor by a person (called "the sponsor") resident[4] in Great Britain[5] to his local chief officer of police.[6] The police may[7] grant a permit if satisfied that—

(1)   the person named in the application is visiting or intending to visit Great Britain; *and*

7–01

7–02

---

[1] For the definitions of s.1 firearms and ammunition, see Ch.3.
[2] "Acquire" is defined to mean hire, accept as a gift or borrow (FA 1968 s.57(4), F(A)A 1988 s.25(1)).
[3] F(A)A 1988 s.17(1), (1A); Firearms Rules 1998 r.8(2), (3) and Sch 3 Pts II and III. For the definition of "shot guns", see Ch.4.
[4] FA 1968 s.26(1). An applicant cannot be said to reside at a property which he has let (*Burditt v Joslin* [1981] 3 All E.R. 203).
[5] "Great Britain" means England, Wales and Scotland, and excludes the Channel Islands and the Isle of Man.
[6] Firearms Rules 1998 r.8.
[7] The police are not required to grant a permit even if satisfied on the matters at items (1) and (2) in the text; nor if there is no bar to a grant under the provisions in the following paragraph. There is no right of appeal against refusal to issue a permit.

(2)   the person has a good reason[8] for possessing, purchasing or acquiring the firearms or ammunition for which the application is made while visiting Great Britain.[9]

But a permit will be refused if the police have reason to believe—

(a)   that the person's possession of the weapons or ammunition in question would represent a danger to the public safety or to the peace[10]; *or*
(b)   that the person is prohibited by the Firearms Act 1968 from possessing those weapons or ammunition.[11]

7–03   A permit will also be refused unless (briefly):

(i)   the applicant can produce a valid European firearms pass relating to the firearm; *or*
(ii)   the applicant can prove that the visitor is not entitled to be issued with such a pass; *or*
(iii) the applicant can show that the visitor requires the permit exclusively as a collector of firearms or is a body concerned in the cultural or historical aspects of weapons.[12]

7–04   You will note that obtaining a Visitors Permit if you reside in another EU country could be more onerous than if you come from elsewhere. If the applicant does hold an EFP the original needs to be sent to the police so it can be endorsed appropriately. You would be well advised to send all applications for Visitors Permits to the sponsor's local police at least two months before the proposed trip.
       A permit will be in force for the period stated in it which cannot exceed one year.[13]
       Home Office rules[14] prescribe the form of permits, and conditions may be applied to them. A permit will specify the number and description of firearms to which it relates (including identification numbers if known) and the quantities of ammunition to be purchased, acquired and held at any one time.[15] Conditions may be varied by written notice from the police to the permit holder; but no shot gun permit can have a condition imposed, initially or on variation, which restricts the premises where the shot gun or guns may be used.[16]

7–05   A single application may be made for the grant of a permit of either kind for a maximum of 20 permits for the visitors named in the application (this is called a

---

[8] For some considerations which may be relevant to "good reason", see paras 3–20 and 5–16 to 5–21.
[9] F(A)A 1988 s.17(2).
[10] For an analysis of this criterion, see paras 5–11 to 5–14 and also 4–06.
[11] F(A)A 1988 s.17(3).
[12] F(A)A 1988 s.17(3A).
[13] F(A)A 1988 s.17(6).
[14] See the Firearms Rules 1998 r.8 and Sch.3.
[15] F(A)A 1988 s.17(1).
[16] F(A)A 1988 s.17(5). Apart from this provision, the police are free to impose such conditions as they think fit. *Firearms Law: Guidance to the Police* (2002) recommends conditions similar to those imposed on police permits (see Ch.6); others, relevant to the occasions or locations of use, may be added.

"group application"). The application must satisfy the police that the visitors' purpose in possessing the weapons in question while visiting Great Britain[17] is—

(1)   using them for sporting purposes on the same private premises[18]during the same period[19]; *or*
(2)   participating in the same competition or other event or the same series of competitions or other events.[20]

A fee of £12 is payable on the grant of a visitor's permit. In the case of a group application, when six or more permits are granted the fee will be £60 for all the permits.[21]   **7–06**

You will commit an offence if you knowingly or recklessly make a statement which is false in any material particular for the purpose of obtaining a permit, or if you fail to comply with any condition in a permit.[22]

There is no right of appeal against a refusal by the police to grant a visitor's permit or against any conditions of the permit.

EUROPEAN FIREARMS PASS

The holder of a firearm (or shotgun) certificate in Great Britain is entitled to have issued to them, free of charge, a European Firearms Pass ('EFP'), sometimes referred to as a 'European Weapons Pass'. This pass can have included upon it any or all of the weapons which are included on the holder's firearm or shotgun certificate. This enables the holder to take their weapons with them to other European Union countries. This system follows the EU Directive on Control of the acquisition and possession of firearms,[23] and the police cannot refuse to issue an EFP to a certificate holder. All weapons are broadly categorised in accordance with European rules and some categories are restricted in some countries. In general term the four categories are as follows:—   **7–07**

A.   Military missiles and fully automatic firearms. Firearms disguised as other objects. Explosive, armour piercing etc. ammunition.
B.   All pistols and other small firearms with a barrel of less than 30 cm or an overall length of 60 cm, except for single shot .22 pistols over 28 cm. All

---

[17] "Great Britain" means England, Wales and Scotland, and excludes the Channel Islands and the Isle of Man.

[18] The term "private premises" is not defined in the Firearms Acts, though the word "premises" includes any land (FA 1968 s.57(4); F(A)A 1988 s.25(1)), and "land" includes land covered with water (IA 1978 s.5 and Sch.1). Contrasting the term with "public place", discussed in Ch.15 at para.15–05, it is suggested that it means any land, water or buildings other than those to which the public are admitted with or without payment.

[19] e.g. for a game shoot.

[20] F(A)A 1988 s.17(7). The provisions mentioned earlier concerning refusal of permits, their validity and duration and the form of permits will apply to group applications and permits issued under them.

[21] F(A)A 1988 s.17(8). It follows that, when five or less permits are granted, the fee will be £12 for each. These fees may be varied, or abolished altogether, by order made by the Home Office (FA 1968 s.43, F(A)A 1988 s.17(9)).

[22] The maximum punishment on summary conviction is six months' imprisonment, or a fine at level 5 on the standard scale (currently £5,000), or both (F(A)A 1988 s.17(10)).

[23] EC Weapons Directive (91/477/EEC)

semi automatic rifles and smooth bore guns which have a magazine + chamber capacity of more than 3 rounds, or a detachable magazine, which includes guns that can be readily converted to fit this category. Smooth bore guns with a barrel length of less than 24". Repeating (pump action, lever action and bolt action) smooth bore guns and smooth bore revolver guns with a barrel less than 24".

C.   Repeating (as above) and other manually operated and single shot rifles. Repeating and other manually loaded smooth bore guns with a barrel over 24". Semi-automatic rifles and smooth bore guns where the total capacity is 3 shots or less, do not have a detachable magazine, and if a smooth bore gun have a barrel at least 24" long. Weapons in Category C must not 'resemble' fully automatic weapons.

D.   Any shotgun without a magazine, i.e. one round per barrel.

7–08   An EFP also entitles the holder to carry suitable ammunition for the weapons in question. An EFP does not permit the purchase of weapons in other EU countries, but it will certainly be accepted as evidence of your good standing in most countries and will probably enable the holder to purchase ammunition if they wish, although given the number of countries now in the Union it is beyond the scope of this work to give precise details for all countries.

The EFP contains space[24] for Member States to indicate prior authorisation to carry specified firearms to their country. Some countries will require this and others will not, and those who intend to travel need to check before doing so. This is however subject to this caveat:—prior authorisation is not *in principle* required for firearms in categories C and D to be carried with a view to engaging in hunting, and it is not required for firearms in categories B, C and D when the purpose of the trip is to take part in target shooting. This is subject to the holder being in possession of an EFP *and* being able to establish the reasons for their trip. When travelling in Europe it is therefore wise to carry a letter from your host club or hunt indicating that you have been invited. In addition, you will always be expected to have with you some proof of identification—don't leave your passport in the hotel! Member States can 'opt out' of the whole or part of this regime[25] and deem it necessary to have prior authorisation for all, or some, categories of weapons. Readers may not be surprised to learn that the United Kingdom has given such notice and European visitors to the UK (as set out above) must not only be in possession of an appropriate EFP, but must also have acquired in advance a Visitors Firearm or Shotgun Permit, as appropriate.

PURCHASES IN THE EUROPEAN COMMUNITY

7–09   Regulations made to implement the European Council's Directive 91/477/EEC contain detailed provisions about buying s.1 firearms and their ammunition in other Member States of the European Community.[26] This is commonly known as

---

[24] In the fifth section.

[25] By giving notice under art.8(3) of the Directive.

[26] Details of the provisions may be found in the Firearms Acts (Amendment) Regulations 1992 regs 5 and 9, which inserted ss.18A, 32A, 32B and 32C in FA 1968.

an **'Article 7 authority'** and permits the holder to purchase a firearm in another (usually specified) EU country, subject to a number of conditions:—

The holder does not have a certificate for the firearm under UK law.
The firearm falls within Category B of the EU Directive.
That the holder does not propose to bring the firearm into Great Britain[27].

The police will obviously wish to satisfy themselves that the applicant for an Article 7 Authority is a fit person, but they do not have to be a British certificate holder. Further this Authority permits the purchase of items such as pistols ('small firearms') and self loading rifles which are not permitted in Great Britain. This procedure is a way of getting a 'certificate of good standing' from your local police for those who wish to purchase and use firearms in other EU countries. Although it is not the concern of the British police, you may well find that the local authorities in the country of purchase will wish to be satisfied that proper arrangements have been made for storage of the weapons (with a firearms dealer for example) when not in use.

---

[27] Firearms Act 1968 S32A(2).

CHAPTER 8

Security of Firearms

INTRODUCTION

All firearms and shotguns will be held on certificate subject to conditions as to   **8–01**
them being held and used securely. "Firearms or shotguns to which a certificate
relates must be stored securely at all times so as to prevent, so far as is reasonably
practicable, access to the guns by unauthorised persons".[1]

On a Firearm or Shotgun Certificate the relevant statutory conditions are
expressed as follows:—

(4)   That the firearms and ammunition to which the certificate relates must at all
      times (except in the circumstances described in (5) below) be stored
      securely so as to prevent, so far as is reasonably practicable, access to them
      by unauthorised persons.
(5)   That, where a firearm or ammunition to which the certificate relates—
      (a)   is in use[2]; *or*
      (b)   the certificate holder has the firearm with him for the purpose of
            cleaning, repairing or testing, or for some other purpose connected
            with its use, transfer[3] or sale; *or*
      (c)   is in transit to or from a place in connection with its use for any of the
            purposes at (b) above,
      reasonable precautions must be taken for the safe custody of the firearm or
      ammunition.[4]

Similar conditions are imposed on Registered Firearms Dealers, Auctioneers,   **8–02**
Shooting Clubs, Museums and those who hold the Secretary of State's Authority

---

[1] Firearms Rules 1998.
[2] In a case decided under the earlier Firearms Rules of 1969, which referred to "actual use", it was
held that live ammunition concealed in the back of an unattended car for about half an hour was not in
actual use nor kept in a secure place with a view to preventing access to it by unauthorised persons
(*Marsh v Chief Constable of Avon & Somerset, The Independent*, May 8, 1987, DC).
[3] "Transfer" is defined to include let on hire, give, lend and part with possession (FA 1968 s.57(4)).
[4] Firearms Rules 1998 r.3(4). Further conditions can be imposed in the case of specialised weapons
and ammunition, such as humane killers, shot pistols and starting pistols, restricting their use to their
special purposes (Firearms Rules 1998 r.3(5)).

to possess prohibited weapons. In some of these cases the conditions relating to security may also require the firearms in question to be stored at particular premises (such as the RFD's place of business, or the clubhouse, as appropriate), unless in use. There are a large number of technical specifications, such as the thickness of the steel from which a gun cabinet should be made and the type of alarm that might be appropriate in particular circumstances, but these details are outside the scope of this book.[5] It should be said that whilst the law requires 'safekeeping', how that is to be achieved is not set out in the law. It is a matter of interpretation in each individual case and there is a wide discretion left to individual police forces. Set out below is some general guidance as to what is likely to be expected.

When considering the question of security it is important to bear in mind two matters. Firstly, it is a criminal offence to fail to comply with a condition of your certificate, and so if you were found to be in breach of the security requirements you are liable to be prosecuted. Secondly, failure to take security seriously is likely to lead the police to believe you are not a 'fit and proper person' to possess firearms and will lead to the loss of your certificate.

Following the two conditions set out above, there are two different sets of circumstances that need to be considered, with two different levels of security required.

STORAGE

8–03   As indicated in Chs 3 and 4, when you apply for a firearm or shotgun certificate you will be visited by an enquiry officer who will inspect your security arrangements for the storage of your firearms and ammunition. This will not only include checking that your cabinet is properly fixed to the wall, but good practice suggests that the officer should carry out a review of your general home security as well. This is the most important examination of your security and although you will receive a visit at every renewal, your security arrangements may not be examined again in detail, unless, for example, you apply to increase the number of guns you hold. The enquiry officer will look for window locks, secure doors and no other easy means of access for intruders. All firearms and shotguns must be stored in a lockable steel cabinet which is securely fixed to the fabric of your building. This also applies to s.1 ammunition, but not s.2 (shotgun) ammunition. There is no safe keeping requirement for ordinary shotgun ammunition, although most certificate holders choose to keep it under lock & key if they have the room. Although it is very difficult to generalise the following will usually be considered necessary:—

(a)   If possible the cabinets should be within an occupied building, not for example in an outhouse or garage.

(b)   Cabinets should be securely fixed to a wall, brick being preferable to breezeblock. If this is not possible, consideration should be given to a floor fixing.

---

[5] For those who require greater detail as to the specific requirements see *Firearm Security Handbook* (2000) (Home Office); *Consolidated Guidance on Firearm Security* 1999 (Home Office & ACPO, this is the one the police are most likely to look at) and Ch.19 and App.7 of the *Guidance*.

(c)   Security always involves an element of being discrete and cabinets should be located so as not to be seen by casual visitors to the property.

It is also acceptable to have a 'gunroom' if you are lucky enough to have sufficient space to spare. This will be expected to have a solid construction and a reinforced metal door.

The actual level of security the police require will depend on a large number of factors. Circumstances such as the building often being unoccupied; a high crime area; a large number of firearms, particularly ones which might be used in crime, and so on, are all factors which will increase the amount of security sought. Applicants sometimes feel that the police are being unreasonable in their approach. Disputes of this type can be difficult to resolve. If for example the police insist on an alarm being installed this can cause major additional expense to the applicant. Such a request is usually made where an applicant wishes to hold a large number of firearms. In some cases the police will ask for a 'central station alarm', where a call centre is automatically notified in the event of the alarm being triggered. If the police refuse a certificate because of the applicant's insistence that the security required is too great, then it is possible to appeal that decision. However, it is advisable to try to reach a compromise. The costs of installing an alarm system required by the police may well be less than the legal costs for an appeal to the Crown Court to resolve the dispute.

8–04

Bear in mind that it is also good practice, if possible, to keep ammunition apart from suitable firearms and to store rifle bolts separate from the rifle.

Unless your weapons are actually 'in use' as defined in Condition 5 they are expected to be locked up. Leaving them out overnight with a view to cleaning them in the morning is not considered acceptable, and most enquiry officers would revoke your certificate if they found you had that loaded shotgun propped up in the corner of the room in case you spotted a rabbit out of the window. In the second example you might argue that the gun was 'in use', but we have seen plenty of certificate holders lose their certificates in similar circumstances. Most breaches of security only come to light as a result of the theft or loss of a firearm or ammunition. As the certificate holder is under a duty to notify such a loss within seven days (14 if abroad)[6] it will quickly become apparent as to what has occurred and the police will conduct exhaustive enquiries as to the circumstances of the loss.

Note that Condition 4 does not require the certificate holder to always keep his firearms and ammunition in the approved cabinet at home, they simply have to be "stored securely". This could be (for example) in a similar cabinet at the owner's country house or with a gun dealer. The requirement is simply that they should be stored securely "so far as is reasonably practicable" to prevent access by unauthorised persons. Bear in mind however that placing guns in a friend's cabinet, to which they retain a key, would in law be giving possession to an unauthorised person, although in the case of shotguns this is acceptable if your friend is also a shotgun certificate holder, and it is for less than 72 hours.

8–05

Because of the fact that the vast majority of certificate holders follow these requirements the number of firearms subject to theft and loss in Great Britain is

---

[6] F(A)A 1997 ss.34 & 35. It is a criminal offence to fail to notify a loss, whether in Great Britain or abroad.

very small indeed. It is said that less than one per cent of firearms used in armed crime were taken unlawfully from their rightful owners.

8–06   "Unauthorised Persons". Bear in mind that the stated purpose of Condition 4 is "to prevent, so far as is reasonably practicable, access to them by unauthorised persons". In the case of a s.1 firearm the only person authorised to have possession is the certificate holder, and not for example their spouse or family, however much the holder might trust them! It is not unknown for the police to express concerns where it becomes apparent to them that the certificate holder's spouse has access to the keys to the gun cabinet. This applies equally to shotguns, with the single exception that another shotgun certificate holder can take possession (for up to 72 hours without entering it onto their certificate) of a shotgun without committing an offence.[7]

IN USE

8–07   'In Use' covers all the situations set out in Condition 5 where your firearms are not being stored in the approved cabinet at home. Such circumstances obviously vary widely and we cannot comment on every situation. Condition 5 (b) is widely drafted and covers most normal situations where a certificate holder might take a firearm or ammunition with them. We would suggest it covers any situation where you have taken your guns with you, so long as it is for a purpose reasonably connected with your ownership of them.[8] At its 'nearest' it covers the owner cleaning their guns on the kitchen table, at its furthest it is perhaps a two week trip to the Highlands to go stalking. What is required is for the owner to take 'reasonable precautions' for the safe custody of the firearm or ammunition. This is obviously going to be a matter of individual judgement in each set of circumstances. Examples of 'reasonable' precautions may include taking rifle bolts with you if the rifles are to be left unattended; securing guns in a hotel safe or strong room, or alternatively using a steel security cable to attach them to some immovable object (radiator perhaps?) in the hotel room. If firearms have to be left in a vehicle for any length of time they must be out of sight. The *Guidance* recommends that if firearms are to be regularly carried in a vehicle it might be appropriate to have a steel cable or cage attached to the chassis.[9]

In a recent case[10] a shooter travelled from his home address in Northumberland to Kirkham Abbey near York with his rifle and ammunition for the purpose of pest control. He then attended a county court hearing in York before intending to travel on further to Banbury in Oxfordshire, again for the purpose of pest control. At the court he placed his rifle in his locked Subaru Forester in the rear of his vehicle under clothing and bags. The safety catch was on; there was a round in the breech and 8 rounds in the magazine. He placed his ammunition in the compartment between the front seats; he deliberately parked his car outside the county court rather than in a public car park. There was a dog in the vehicle, so he

---

[7] The question of 'possession' is considered in detail at para.3–07.
[8] In any event it is an offence to have a firearm and suitable ammunition together in a public place without a reasonable excuse, FA 1968 s.19. See Ch.15 for more details.
[9] *Guidance,* Ch.19.
[10] *DPP v Frank Houghton-Brown* [2010] EWHC 3527, Silber J. We are grateful to barrister Jerome Silva for details of this case.

left a window partly open. The vehicle was unattended for three hours and the presence of the gun was discovered by a police officer who was concerned about the dog, it being a hot day. Mr Houghton-Brown was prosecuted for breach of the security conditions on his license, the terms being identical to those in Condition 5 b) and c). He was found not guilty by the magistrates. The police then appealed and the decision of the magistrates to find him not guilty was upheld. Two questions were posed for the High Court, firstly was he 'in transit'? The Appellants (the police) conceded that he was, given that he intended to travel on to Oxfordshire for more shooting. This is a sensible decision on their part and demonstrates the point that 'in transit' means what it says, a given journey does not have to be limited only to the purposes of shooting. The second question was that if he were in transit, had he taken reasonable precautions to ensure the safe custody of his firearm and ammunition? The High Court stated that this was 'a fact sensitive matter' and there was nothing to suggest that the magistrates had come to a conclusion which was not reasonable on the evidence. It has to be remembered that the burden is on the prosecution in a criminal trial to show beyond a reasonable doubt that the defendant did *not* take reasonable precautions. It was made clear in the judgement that all cases such as this must be decided on their own individual facts and the judge observed that "many people will regard him as having been fortunate". We would respectfully agree with that observation and in all cases certificate holders are advised to err on the side of caution. If there is a loss the police are likely to suggest that the precautions clearly weren't reasonable.

It is an offence for a person in possession of an air weapon to fail to take 'reasonable precautions' to prevent someone under the age of 18 from gaining unauthorised access to it.[11] Further details of this offence, and the defences to it, are set out at para.14–12.

8–08

---

[11] FA 1968 s.24(ZA), as amended by the Crime and Security Act 2010 s.46, in force February 10, 2011. Maximum penalty £1,000 fine.

CHAPTER 9

Imitation Firearms

IMITATION FIREARMS

It is an offence under the 1968 Act to commit a number of criminal offences with an imitation firearm, such as committing indictable offences (robbery for example), or resisting arrest, and is punishable in the same way as if the offender had used a real firearm. Details of such offences can be found in Ch.15. Further, some imitation firearms can be 'readily converted' to fire with lethal effect and possession of these is controlled in the same way as if they were real firearms of the same classification under the Acts.

9–01

IMITATION FIREARMS WHICH ARE 'READILY CONVERTIBLE'

Increasing concern about the use of imitation firearms for criminal purposes, and uncertainty about the extent to which the 1968 Firearms Act applied to them,[1] led to the passing in 1982 of a Firearms Amendment Act, which was brought into force on November 1, 1983. The expressed purpose of the Act is to apply (with some exceptions and qualifications) the provisions of the 1968 Act to imitation firearms if they fulfil certain conditions.[2]

9–02

An imitation firearm is defined in the 1982 Act, by reference to the 1968 Act, to mean anything which has the appearance of being a firearm (whether or not it is capable of discharging any shot, bullet or other missile) other than a weapon designed or adapted for the discharge of any noxious liquid, gas or other thing.[3]

---

[1] See, for example, the cases discussed in Ch.1.
[2] FA 1982 s.1(2).
[3] FA 1968 ss.5(1)(b), 57(4); FA 1982 s.1(3). See para.2–04 for weapons so designed or adapted.

There are two conditions, both of which must be fulfilled. First, that the imitation firearm shall have the appearance of being a s.1 firearm.[4] This is obviously a question of fact. In this context, component parts and accessories have been excluded.[5]

9–03 The second condition is that the imitation firearm shall be so constructed or adapted as to be 'readily convertible' into a s.1 firearm.[6] The 1982 Act goes on to say that the firearm shall be regarded as readily convertible if—

(a) it can be converted without any special skill on the part of the person converting it in the construction or adaptation of firearms of any description; *and*

(b) the work in converting it does not require equipment or tools other than such as are in common use by persons carrying out works of construction and maintenance in their own homes.[7]

The Home Office explains that the equipment and tools referred to are taken to mean tools and equipment that are normally on sale in retail tools shops, do-it-yourself shops and from mail order suppliers or discount catalogues. They include, the Home Office adds, electrically or hand-powered drills, with or without speed control and with or without vibratory or hammer device, hacksaws, rotating abrasive discs and wheels, high speed twist drills, tungsten carbide masonry drills, hacksaw blades, hammers, drifts, punches, files, etc.[8] It would not include, for example, a lathe.

9–04 If these two conditions are fulfilled, an imitation firearm will be subject to all the provisions of the 1968 Act which apply to firearms (other than those applying specifically to shot guns and air weapons), but excluding the provisions mentioned below.[9] The main effect is to require a firearm certificate to be obtained for the handling, etc. of imitation firearms in those circumstances where it would be needed for a real firearm, and the provisions described in Ch.3 will apply, as will the later provisions in that chapter referring to s.1 firearms.[10] An imitation firearm will also be a firearm for the purposes of the offences considered in Ch.15.

The provisions of the 1968 Act which do not apply to imitation firearms (so far as those provisions are discussed in this book) are those dealing with:

(a) Conversion into a firearm of anything incapable of discharging a missile.[11]

(b) Carrying a firearm in a public place.[12]

---

[4] FA 1968 s.1; FA 1982 s.1(1)(a), (4)(a); F(A)A 1988 s.25(7). For the definition of "Section 1 firearm" see paras 3–01 onwards. Note; For these purposes this will include having the appearance of any prohibited weapon such as a handgun or a machinegun, which are s.1 firearms as well as being s.5 prohibited weapons.

[5] FA 1968 s.57(1); FA 1982 s.1(3), (4)(b).

[6] FA 1968 s.1(3); FA 1982 s.1(1)(b).

[7] FA 1982 s.1(6).

[8] Home Office leaflet "Guidelines on the Design, Construction or Adaptation of Imitation Firearms".

[9] FA 1982 ss.1(2), (4), 2(1).

[10] For a leaflet defining measures which can be taken to prevent an imitation firearm becoming subject to the 1982 Act, see fn.8 above.

[11] FA 1968 s.4(3); FA 1982 s.2(2)(a).

[12] FA 1968 s.19; FA 1982 s.2(3). For such a carrying, see Ch.15.

(c)   Police powers in connection with item (b) above.[13]

It follows, then, from what has been said above that, with the exclusions just 9–05
mentioned, the provisions contained in Chs 2, 3, 6, 7, 8, 14, 15 and 16 apply to
imitation firearms meeting the required conditions in the same way as they apply
to real firearms, unless the provisions refer specifically to shot guns or to air
weapons. The same offences may be committed, and the exceptions to those
offences, where relevant, will apply.[14]

The 1982 Act includes an important defence which is available in any
prosecution involving an imitation firearm. It applies when the accused can
show[15] that he did not know and had no reason to suspect that the imitation
firearm was so constructed or adapted as to be readily convertible (as described at
para.9–03) into a firearm to which the Act applies.[16]

In conclusion, it may assist to highlight in summary form the points to be 9–06
considered in deciding whether an imitation firearm is to be treated as a firearm
for the purpose of the 1968 Act's provisions:

(1)   It must have the appearance of being a s.1 firearm.
(2)   Component parts and accessories of imitation firearms are excluded.
(3)   It shall be readily convertible into a real firearm.
(4)   It is not to be treated as a firearm in cases (a) to (c) above.

The position regarding imitation firearms, court cases about guns which were
incapable of being fired, and the 1982 Act is also dealt with in Ch.1.

REALISTIC IMITATION FIREARMS

Not content with the provisions set out above regarding imitation firearms, 9–07
Parliament made further provision in 2006 to prohibit the manufacture, sale,
modification of an imitation firearm, or importation into Great Britain of a
'realistic imitation firearm'[17] ('RIF'). A realistic imitation firearm is an imitation
firearm that is 'so realistic as to be indistinguishable, for all practical purposes,
from a real firearm'.[18] This does not however cover deactivated firearms, or
things that are in themselves antiques. The difference between an imitation
firearm under the 1982 Act and a realistic imitation firearm under the 2006 Act is
that the first Act prohibits items which are readily convertible to be a real firearm,
the second prohibits those which have the appearance of a real firearm,
convertible or not. A RIF is not to be regarded as distinguishable from a real
firearm if it can only be distinguished by an expert, on close examination, or by
attempting to load or fire it.[19] The court is entitled to take into account the size,

---

[13] FA 1968 s.47(1), (3)–(5); FA 1982 s.2(3).
[14] FA 1982 ss.1(2), 2(1).
[15] i.e. can convince the court before whom he is prosecuted.
[16] FA 1982 s.1(5). Contrast this defence with the absence of a corresponding defence if the firearm is
a real one under the ruling in *R. v Hussain*; see 3–08, fn.27 and the related text in Ch.3.
[17] VCRA 2007 s.36.
[18] VCRA 2006 s.38(1).
[19] VCRA 2006 s.38(2).

shape and principal colour in deciding the issue, although regulations[20] provide approved sizes and colours. In limited circumstances there are defences available on a prosecution under s.36. These are that the manufacture, sale, importation etc. was for the purpose only of placing the item in a museum or gallery; for theatrical productions and rehearsals or film production (this would include TV). There is also a defence for the organisation and holding of historical re-enactments by persons approved under the regulations by the Secretary of State.[21] Further, it is a defence to do such things by way of trade or business, if you intend to modify the RIF in such a way as it ceases to be a RIF. This would provide you with a defence if you imported RIFs with the intention of painting them bright purple, or some other 'approved' colour and then selling them as toys. Readers will have seen toy guns which have an orange cap on the 'muzzle'. This does not provide a defence in Great Britain, although it does in the State of California, and was widely copied here before the introduction of the 2006 Act. The purpose of the Act is to eventually reduce the number of imitation firearms (toys or otherwise) that are in circulation. Possession however is not an offence, unless you are committing some ulterior criminal offence with the realistic imitation firearm. The use of any type of imitation firearm in furtherance of another offence is punishable in the same was as if you had a real one, see Ch.15 for more details.

IMPORTATION OF REALISTIC IMITATION FIREARMS

9–08   Items intercepted by the UK Border Agency[22] on arrival into Great Britain which they consider are RIFs and do not meet the approved criteria in the regulations are liable to seizure and forfeiture.[23] If your goods are intercepted you will be served with a notice of seizure. This will initially invite you to make representations (if you wish) as to why the goods should not have been seized. If you wish to appeal against the legality of the seizure you must submit a notice of claim giving your reasons within one calendar month of the date of seizure. Be warned this time limit is very strictly applied by the Border Agency and any claim received later will be rejected.

Provided you submit a notice of claim challenging the legality of the seizure within the time limit, the Border Agency will then be obliged to issue 'Condemnation Proceedings' in a Magistrates Court, usually the one closest to where your items were seized. This will give you the opportunity to put your case before a court of law as to why your goods should not have been seized and should be returned to you. If the court does not find in your favour, or you do not lodge an appeal against seizure within the time limit, then your RIF will be 'condemned', i.e. forfeited to the Crown.

9–09   The Border Agency will tell you that you are not entitled to rely on the defences in s.36, set out above, when arguing that the seizure was not lawful. This

---

[20] The Violent Crime Reduction Act 2006 (Realistic Imitation Firearms) Regulations 2007 (SI 2007/2606). The size has to be less than 38mm high and 70mm long. Colours such as bright pink are permitted, or transparent, but black and silver don't appear in the list!

[21] VCRA 2006 s.37(2).

[22] Formerly border controls were administered by HM Customs.

[23] VCRA 2006 s.39(6).

seems to us to be wrong in principle. Surely if you are importing a RIF for use in a theatrical play (which is a permitted reason to import it) you should be allowed to say so?

In the notice of seizure you will also be offered the option of seeking 'Restoration'. This is an application to the Border Agency to have your goods returned, even if you accept the seizure was, or may have been, lawful. Any request for restoration must be put in writing no later than 45 days from the date of seizure. Restoration is considered by an officer of the Border Agency who will be independent of the officers who initially made the seizure. If you are dissatisfied with the decision notified to you there is an option within 45 days to request a review. If following the review you are still dissatisfied, you can appeal within 30 days to an independent Tribunal.

You can either apply for restoration alone or in conjunction with condemna- **9–10** tion proceedings, i.e. an appeal against the legality of the seizure. We would generally recommend doing both. Owners of goods often ignore 'Condemnation' and ask only for 'Restoration' at their peril. This can be a big mistake as your best prospect of getting your property back will usually be by having the matter heard in court. Perhaps not surprisingly, our experience is that where goods are considered by the Border Agency to have been lawfully seized, they are unlikely to agree to restore them.

You will receive with the notice of seizure an information Notice 12A outlining your rights of appeal. This claims to be written in plain English but those who have no previous experience of such matters may not appreciate from reading this leaflet the distinctions between condemnation and restoration proceedings, and the consequences of pursuing one route rather than the other. If the items are valuable and you want them back this is an area where you really need to consult a specialist solicitor quickly.

We should add that whilst we have dealt with the process for appealing against seizure of goods by the Border Agency in the context of importation of realistic imitation firearms, the above paragraphs apply equally to challenging the seizure of any other type of goods on entry into the UK.

CHAPTER 10

Shooting Game

WHAT IS MEANT BY "GAME"?

There are several Acts of Parliament dealing with the shooting of game. In some of those Acts the term 'game' is defined; however, the definitions are not always consistent. In some Acts there is no definition of the term. The definition, or the lack of it, will be mentioned in this chapter when each of the statutory provisions is dealt with.   **10–01**

It is also important to note that under the legislation the word 'game' is not always given its everyday meaning; for example, rabbits, (which are also referred to as conies), are included in the definition in some Acts.[1] Further, the expression will include, where appropriate, dead game[2] as well as live, and tame game as well as wild.[3]

Strictly speaking, deer cannot be regarded as game but, since most of the law in this chapter applies to game and deer, both are dealt with in the one chapter. The law relating specifically to the shooting of deer can be found at paras 12–10 to 12–20.   **10–02**

Finally, the reader will find references made to various different types of game such as black game, red game, moor game and ground game. These terms are taken from the legislation, which on the whole does not seek to define them, and so we are left to apply a common sense approach as to what might be included in these various types of game.[4]

---

[1] For example in the Prevention of Poaching Act (PPA) 1862 s.1.
[2] *Loome v Bailey* (1860) 3 E & F 444; Though the Game Act 1831 (GA 1831) does not apply to game killed abroad (*Guyer v R.* (1889) 23 QBD 100).
[3] *Cook v Trevener* [1911] K.B. 9; 74 JP 469. But tame pheasants are not "game" within the meaning of the Night Poaching Act 1828 (*R. v Garnham* (1861) 2 F & F 34).
[4] The exception is ground game which is defined; Ground Game Act 1880 s.8. See further Ch.13.

WHEN CAN I SHOOT GAME?

10–03 There are periods of the year, known as "close seasons", during which game and deer[5] must not be shot.[6] These periods vary according to the bird or animal protected.[7] For this purpose, 'game' means: pheasants, partridges, black game, grouse/red game or bustards.[8] A table of close seasons is set out in Appendix C at the end of the book.

Furthermore, there are certain days and times, outside the close seasons, during which game must not be killed. Game must not be killed on a Sunday or on Christmas Day.[9] For this purpose, the term 'game' includes: hares, pheasants, partridges, grouse, heath or moor game and black game.[10] Since the word "includes" is used, it is possible that other birds and animals may fall within the provision if they can be described as game.[11]

10–04 In addition to the different definitions of game, there is a further distinction between shooting out of season and shooting on a Sunday or on Christmas Day. In both instances, in the 1831 Game Act, the words "kill or take" are used, but in respect of Sundays and Christmas Day there are the added words: "or use any dog, gun, net, or other engine or instrument[12] for the purpose of killing or taking any game". This distinction has significance, as to shoot at and miss a pheasant on Christmas Day is an offence, but to do so on a week-day during the close season is not.

There are also restrictions on shooting game at night. You must not unlawfully[13] take or destroy any game[14] or rabbits at night[15] on any open or

---

[5] For this purpose deer are the species listed in s.3 of Appendix C at the end of the book (DA 1991 s.2(2) and Sch.1).

[6] Game Act (GA) 1831 s.3; Deer Act (DA) 1991 s.2(1); Game (Scotland) Act (G(S)A) 1772 s.1. A general exception arises under Agriculture Act 1947 (AA 1947) s.98. In this instance Government Ministers may require a person having the right to do so to take steps to kill particular birds and animals which are causing damage, even though they may be out of season. The only animals which may presently be the subject of this requirement are deer, though other animals and birds may be nominated by Government order. For special exceptions relating to deer, see para.12–12 and, in the case of deer, the maximum punishment on summary conviction is a fine at level 4 on the standard scale (currently £2,500), or three months' imprisonment, or both (DA 1991 s.9(1)). If an offence involves more than one deer, the maximum fine shall be regarded as if there was a separate offence against each deer (DA 1991 s.9(2)). In the case of game, the maximum penalty on summary conviction is a fine at level 1 on the standard scale (currently £200), for every head of game illegally taken (GA 1831 s3; G(S)A 1772 s.1).

[7] GA 1831 s.3; DA 1991 s.2(2) and Sch.1.

[8] GA 1831 s.3. In Scotland, the Game (Scotland) Act 1772 s.1 (G(S)A 1772) creates close seasons applicable to muir fowl, tarmagan (old spelling of ptarmigan), heath fowl, partridge or pheasant.

[9] GA 1831 s.3. The maximum punishment on summary conviction is a fine at level 1 on the standard scale (currently £200).

[10] GA 1831 s.2..

[11] However, the word "includes" has been interpreted in some statutory contexts to mean exclusively the items mentioned after it.

[12] e.g. a snare.

[13] i.e. without having the game rights. Thus, a tenant not having these rights could be convicted under this provision for these activities on land within his tenancy (*Liversedge v Whiteoak* (1893) 57 JPN 692 although this case does not specifically refer to night poaching the principle is of general application).

[14] "Game" includes hares, pheasants, partridges, grouse, heath or moor game and black game (Night Poaching Act (NPA) 1828 s.13). As to "includes", see fn.11 above.

[15] This is from one hour after sunset to one hour before sunrise (NPA 1828 s.12).

enclosed land.[16] By a later Act[17] this restriction was extended to include any public road, highway or path or the sides thereof and the openings, outlets or gates from any open or enclosed land leading onto any public road, highway or path.[18]

GAME LICENSES

Game licenses have now been abolished throughout the United Kingdom. In parts of the UK this change in the law was very recent at the time of going to press with this work. We have therefore included briefly here, for the benefit of anyone involved in legal proceedings relating to events that occurred prior to the abolition in their area, what the law was in relation to the requirement to have a game license, the key exemptions when a game license would not be needed, and when the legislation came into force in the various parts of the United Kingdom abolishing game licenses.

    Since August 1, 2007, there has no longer been any requirement to hold a game licence to shoot game in England and Wales.[19] The change was brought about as the cost of game licences had not kept up with inflation, and the requirements were not strictly adhered to, meaning that game licences did not generate significant revenue for the Crown. The fee payable for a game license varied, depending on whether it was to be valid for a full year or part thereof, but the maximum fee in 2007 was as little as £6, having not been increased in many years, and even thereafter remained unaltered for Scotland and Northern Ireland, where game licenses continued to be required for several more years. It is perhaps unsurprising therefore that game licenses were also finally abolished in both Scotland and Northern Ireland by legislation passed in 2011. In Northern Ireland the requirement to hold a game license in order to shoot game ceased with effect from June 13, 2011.[20] Scotland closely followed suit, with the change coming into force there from June 29, 2011.[21]

    Prior to those amendments the law provided that to "take, kill or pursue, or aid or assist in any manner in the taking, killing or pursuing by any means whatever, or use any dog, gun, net, or other engine for the purpose of taking, killing or

10–05

10–06

---

[16] NPA 1828 s.1. To do so is an offence with a maximum punishment on summary conviction of a fine at level 3 on the standard scale (currently £1,000). For an interpretation of "enclosed lands", though in another context, see para.10–07.

[17] NPA 1844 s.1.

[18] For restrictions on night shooting by tenants having the right to kill ground game, see paras 13–04 to 13–06. As to shooting deer at night, see para.12–14.

[19] The Regulatory Reform (Game) Order (RR(G)O) 2007. This repealed in its entirety the Game Licenses Act 1861 in respect of England and Wales and likewise the Hares Act 1848. Certain provisions of the Game Act 1831 were repealed, and various other consequential amendments made to legislation, to remove references to the requirement for a game license in England and Wales. See s.2 and Sch.1 RR(G)O 2007.

[20] Wildlife and Natural Environment (Northern Ireland) Act 2011 s.35 provides that Pt 4 of the Miscellaneous Transferred Excise Duties Act (Northern Ireland) 1972 (c.11) (game licences and game dealers' licences) shall cease to have effect. The Wildlife and Natural Environment (2011 Act) (Commencement No.1) Order (Northern Ireland) 2011 brought s.35 into force on the June 13, 2011.

[21] The Wildlife and Natural Environment (Scotland) Act 2011 received Royal assent on the April 7, 2011. Part 2 of Sch.1 to that Act repeals various Acts and provisions relating to the requirement for game licenses in Scotland. The Wildlife and Natural Environment (Scotland) Act 2011 (Commencement No. 1) Order 2011 brought those repeals into force on the June 29, 2011.

pursuing any game, or any woodcock, snipe, or any coney,[22] or any deer"[23] you would need a game licence.[24] The word 'game' was not defined in this context.

If you did any of the things described above for which a game licence was needed, without having taken out a licence which was still in force, you would have been liable on summary conviction to a maximum fine at level 2 on the standard scale (currently £500).[25]

Some examples taken from decided cases help to show how wide the scope of the requirement for a licence was. If you walked with a dog or a gun on land where there was game, or merely pointed a gun at game, there could be evidence of the commission of an offence.[26] From this it followed that if two or more persons, who held no licence, fired at the same bird and it was killed, but the person killing the bird could not be identified, each of those persons would have committed an offence.[27] Also if you killed game by accident and took it away, you would be guilty of an offence if you held no licence.[28] Thus, if you knocked over a pheasant with your car, stopped, picked it up, put it in the car and drove on, you would have committed an offence if you did not have a game licence. If you were caught with game in your possession, it was up to you to prove that you acquired it innocently, i.e. in circumstances in which a licence was not required.[29]

10–07   However, there were traditionally cases in which a game licence was not needed for shooting and they were as follows[30]:

(1)   The taking and killing of deer[31] in any enclosed lands by the owner or occupier of such lands, or by his direction or permission.[32] A decision in a court case usefully interpreted a point on this exception relating to the meaning of enclosed lands. The lower court had decided that the meaning of "enclosed lands" was restricted to a deer park or other enclosure where deer were kept, but the higher court considered this to be too narrow a meaning and widened it to include "lands used for farming and enclosed by normal agricultural hedges" in contrast with "moorland where there are no enclosures and where the deer can run free".[33]

(2)   The taking or destroying of rabbits by the proprietor of any warren or of any enclosed ground whatever, or by the tenant of lands,[34] either by himself or by his direction or permission.[35]

(3)   Shooting by the Royal Family and Her Majesty's gamekeepers.

---

[22]   i.e. rabbit, this is sometimes spelt cony in other contexts.

[23]   All ages and both sexes of deer are included (*R. v Strange* (1843) 1 LT (OS) 435).

[24]   GLA 1860 s.4.

[25]   GLA 1860 s.4.

[26]   *R. v Davis* (1795) 6 Term Rep 177.

[27]   *Hunter v Clark* (1902) 66 JP 247.

[28]   *Molton v Cheeseley* (1788) 1 Esp 123.

[29]   *Hemming v Halsey* (1823) 1 LJ (OS) KB 105.

[30]   GLA 1860 s.5.

[31]   For special restrictions on the shooting of deer, see Ch.12.

[32]   It seems that, to take advantage of this exception, the owner or occupier must have had the right to take or kill deer on the land. Similarly, the permission could only be given by whichever of the two had the right (*Halsbury's Laws of England*, 4th Edition Reissue, Vol.2(1), para.607, fn.7).

[33]   *Jemmison v Priddle* [1972] 1 All E.R. 539.

[34]   i.e. any lands, whether enclosed or not.

[35]   Some doubt existed as to whether both the proprietor and the tenant could permit another to take or destroy rabbits within this exception. Probably the latter only could do so (*Halsbury's Laws of England*, 4th Edition Reissue, Vol.2(1), para.607, fn.6).

(4)   A person aiding or assisting in the taking or killing of game[36] in the company or presence of, and for the use of, another person who has a game licence in his own right, who is taking some active part in the shoot with his own dog or gun and who is not acting "by virtue of any deputation or appointment". The effect of this was to exempt beaters, loaders and other assistants from the necessity of being licensed; but such unlicensed beaters, etc. could not assist a gamekeeper since he holds his position by "deputation or appointment". Moreover, they apparently could not use, or lend the use of any dog of their own, even to a licensed person who was, by virtue of his licence, taking and killing game there and then. Similarly, a loader could carry his employer's gun but he could not carry a gun of his own, and he could not fire either his own or his employer's gun.[37]

(5)   The actual occupier of any enclosed lands, or the owner thereof who has the right of killing hares on those lands, or a person authorised by either of them in writing, could kill hares on those lands without a game licence, but not at night.[38]

(6)   A person required by the Secretary of State to kill certain animals and birds as pests did not need to hold a game licence to kill them.[39]

(7)   An occupier of land, and certain persons who may be authorised by him in writing,[40] may kill hares and rabbits on that land.[41]

SALE OF GAME

Prior to the abolition of game licenses and the repeal of associated legislation, the **10–08** law restricted the sale of game at certain times. It was illegal to sell, or indeed buy, a game bird[42] after the expiration of ten days from the beginning of its close season.[43] Of those ten days, one was inclusive so that, for example, in the case of partridges, a sale after February 11, was illegal, the close season for partridges beginning on February 1. This rule did not apply to foreign game birds,[44] or to live birds bought or sold for rearing or exhibition purposes or for sale alive.[45]

In England and Wales, hares and leverets, unless imported, still must not be sold or exposed for sale during the months of March to July inclusive.[46] Although it is no longer an offence for dealers to buy, sell or possess game birds after ten

---

[36] As well as using the word 'game' (which is not defined), this exemption extended to woodcock, snipe, rabbits and deer.

[37] *Halsbury's Laws of England*, 4th Edition Reissue, Vol.2(1), para.607, fn.3; *Ex p. Sylvester* (1829) 9 B & C 61.

[38] Hares (Scotland) Act 1848 (H(S)A 1848) ss.1, 5; GLA 1860 ss.5, 6; "night" lasts from one hour after sunset to one hour before sunrise (H(S)A 1848 s.5).

[39] Agriculture (Scotland) Act 1948 ss.39, 53.

[40] As to who these persons may be, see para.13–03.

[41] GGA 1880 ss.4, 8. See further Ch.13 on the tenant's right to shoot.

[42] 'Game' is defined in the GA 1831 s.2 as including pheasants, partridges, grouse, heath or moor game, black game.

[43] GA 1831 s.4; For close seasons, see App.C at the end of the book.

[44] *Guyer v R.* (1889) 23 QBD 100.

[45] GA 1831 s.4. The maximum penalty on conviction is at level 1 on the standard scale (currently £200) for each head of game.

[46] HPA 1892 ss.2, 3. The maximum penalty on conviction is at level 1 on the standard scale (currently £200); this probably applies to each head of game. This Act has now been repealed in Scotland under the Wildlife and Natural Environment (Scotland) Act 2011.

days from the beginning of the close season[47] the sale of game birds in England and Wales is not without limitation. It is now an offence for any person to sell or offer or to expose for sale, or to have in his possession or transport for the purposes of sale, any bird of game, which has been taken or killed in circumstances which constitute an offence under the Night Poaching Act 1828, the Game Act 1831, the Poaching Prevention Act 1862, or Part 1 of the Wildlife and Countryside Act 1981, where the person concerned knows or has reason to believe that it has been so taken or killed.[48]

OWNERSHIP OF GAME AND NEIGHBOURS' RIGHTS

10–09   Whilst birds and animals are in a wild state they cannot be completely owned by anyone,[49] but in the following three cases there can be qualified ownership:

(1)   A person who lawfully takes, tames or reclaims a wild animal or bird may claim it as his property until it regains its natural liberty.[50]

(2)   An owner of land has a right to the young of wild animals or birds born on his land until they can run or fly away.[51]

(3)   A landowner also has the right[52] to shoot or otherwise take wild animals or birds whilst on his land.[53]

Tame or domesticated birds and animals may be owned as can wild birds kept in captivity or tamed.[54] The Theft Act 1968 creates an offence of theft of wild creatures. The offence is committed if—

(1)   they are domesticated, tamed or ordinarily[55] kept in captivity; or

(2)   their carcass has been reduced into possession[56] by or on behalf of another person and possession of them has not since been lost or abandoned; or

---

[47] RR(G)O 2007, which repealed s.4 of the Game Act 1831.

[48] GA 1831 s.3A. As of August 17, 2011, a similar offence exists in Northern Ireland under section 36 of the Wildlife and Natural Environment (Northern Ireland) Act 2011.

[49] Whilst there can only be qualified property in wild animals whilst they are alive, there can be absolute property in such animals when they are dead. This right is vested in the owner of the land, or the grantee of shooting rights over the land, and this is so even if the animals are not killed by them but by a trespasser.

[50] Known as qualified property obtained *per industriam Halsbury's Laws of England*, 5th Edition Reissue, Vol.2, para.712.

[51] Known as qualified property *ratione impotentiae et loci Halsbury's Laws of England*, 5th Edition Reissue, Vol.2, para 713; A claim of trespass will lie for young so born *Case of Swans* (1592) 7 Co Rep 15b at 17b; *Blades v Higgs* (1865) 11 HL Cas 621.

[52] For the cases when this right will be shared with or let to a tenant, see Ch.13.

[53] Known as qualified property *ratione soli* in respect of land owners and *ratione privilegii* in respect of grantees of those rights *Halsbury's Laws of England*, 5th Edition Reissue, Vol.2, para.714; *Blades v Higgs* (1865) 11 HL Cas.621.

[54] *Oke's Game Laws* (5th Edition, 1912) p.17. Note:— there are a number of references to *Oke's Game Laws* in the book. The current authors have been unable to obtain a copy of this great work in order to verify these references. We assume they are correct, given that they appeared in the previous six editions of *Gun Law*, presumably with corrections as appropriate.

[55] i.e. the offence can be committed whilst they are temporarily out of captivity.

[56] No statutory definition is given for the phrase "reduce into possession". It is suggested that this is akin to appropriation and means the doing of some act by the other person to assert his ownership, e.g. putting the carcass in his game bag or car or hiding it in some place.

(3)   another person is in the course of reducing them into possession.[57]

Rather difficult questions may arise when game (or other wild birds or animals) are put up on one person's land and are killed there or elsewhere. A person who puts up and kills game on another's land does not thereby own the carcass; it belongs to the person having the shooting rights over that land. But if you put up game on your land and kill it on or over another's land, the ownership is yours. Similarly, though for different reasons, if you, being a trespasser, start game on A's land, follow it on to B's land and there kill it, you are the owner of the game.[58] Mere ownership of the carcass will not necessarily entitle the owner to retrieve it, and he must take care that he does not commit the offence of trespassing in pursuit of game.[59] Simply to discharge your gun at game over your neighbour's land does not make you liable for this offence,[60] but personal entry to retrieve the game may do so. Unfortunately, the law on this point is confused, as is illustrated by the following four Court decisions: **10–10**

(1)   M, on land where he had a right to shoot, shot at and killed a pheasant on the ground on adjoining land occupied by U and over which M had no shooting rights. M then went on to U's land and picked up the pheasant. The Court decided that M should be convicted of trespassing in pursuit of game, since the shooting and picking up of the game was one transaction constituting the pursuit.[61]

(2)   A pheasant rose from H's land and, when it was over T's land, H, being on his own land, shot at it. The pheasant fell on T's land. H went on to T's land to pick up the pheasant, which was then dead. The Court decided there was no offence of trespass in pursuit of game. The offence refers to the pursuit of live game only.[62]

(3)   T, one of a party shooting pheasants, saw pheasants that had been shot fall into the adjoining wood of S. Two days afterwards, T went into S's wood to pick up the pheasants believing them to be dead. The Court decided that if the pheasants were dead, or if T believed them to be dead, there was no offence, but it would be otherwise if the pheasants were alive or believed to be alive.[63]

(4)   R stood on his own land and fired at and killed a grouse sitting on the adjoining land of G. Some hours later, R went on to G's land to pick up the bird, which had in the meantime been picked up by somebody else, namely the gamekeeper. The Court decided that the shooting and searching were sufficiently connected to form a continuous act and together constituted the pursuit of game. R was therefore guilty of the offence, and it mattered not whether the grouse was dead or alive when searched for.[64]

---

[57] Theft Act 1968 s.4(4) (TA 1968). Upon conviction on indictment for the offence the maximum term of imprisonment is.seven years (TA 1968 s.7).
[58] *Blades v Higgs* (1865) 34 LJCP 286, and cases there cited.
[59] As to this offence, see para.11–02.
[60] Although, technically, you will be committing the civil wrong of trespass.
[61] *Osbond v Meadows* (1862) 26 JP 439; 31 LJMC 238.
[62] *Kenyon v Hart* (1865) 29 JP 260; 34 LJMC 87.
[63] *Tanton v Jervis* (1879) 43 JP 784.
[64] *Horn v Raine* (1898) 62 JP 420; 67 LJQB 533.

In all cases the entry on the adjoining land without permission will constitute the civil wrong of trespass, as opposed to the criminal offence of trespass in pursuit of game. Permission to enter and retrieve game may not, however, easily be obtained.

SHOOTING GAME ON THE FORESHORE AND OVER WATER

10–11   The majority of the foreshore,[65] the bed of the sea for some distance below low-water mark, and the beds of estuaries, arms of the sea and tidal rivers are owned by the Crown Estate. The Crown has granted some of these lands to private individuals and other bodies, such as local authorities. Whether or not such a grant has been made, the only general rights of the public which may be exercised in these areas are rights of fishing and of navigation and their attendant rights, e.g. anchoring and mooring. The public has no general right of shooting or otherwise taking game and other birds and animals.[66] However, it has been suggested that the Crown, where it is the owner of the foreshore, would effectively acquiesce in the exercise of a right to shoot by the public when no mischief or injury is likely to arise from the exercise of that right.[67]

For a private individual to have the right of shooting in the areas mentioned he must be able to show—

(1)   that he owns or has acquired a title to the land or to the right of shooting by long uninterrupted usage[68]; or
(2)   that he is entitled to the benefit of a grant from the Crown of the land in question.[69]

Non-tidal waters are treated as if they were land not covered with water; for example, the right to shoot over a lake depends upon whether the area of the lake forms part of the land within the shooting. Where the land is bounded by a river or stream, the general rule is that the boundary of the land is the middle of the water.

---

[65] 'Foreshore' in England, Wales and Northern Ireland is generally defined as the land between the high water mark of medium high tides and the low water mark: *Halsbury's Laws of England*, 5th Edition Reissue, Vol.100, para.34. In Scotland the 'foreshore' is defined as the land between the mean high water of spring tides and the mean low water of spring tides.

[66] *Halsbury's Laws of England*, 5th Edition Reissue, Vol.100, para.52.

[67] *Halsbury's Laws of England*, 5th Edition Reissue, Vol.100, para.53.

[68] The acquisition of the right in this way is governed by strict legal rules and it is not, for example, sufficient for a claimant to say merely that he has shot over a particular stretch of foreshore for many years.

[69] The right to shoot and take birds on the foreshore is a profit à pendre: *Halsbury's Laws of England*, 4th Edition Reissue, Vol 14, paras 240 and following, and *Halsbury's Laws of England*, 5th Edition Reissue, Vol.100, para.52.

CHAPTER 11

Poaching

INTRODUCTION

In addition to being prosecuted,[1] the owner or occupier may take civil action against a poacher under the ordinary rules relating to trespass of the land.[2] If a person is trespassing on land, that is to say, is on land where they have no right to be, the owner or occupier of that land may order that person to leave at once. If they do not, the owner, the occupier or others under the direction of the occupier or owner, may use force to expel them provided that they only use such force as is necessary to remove them.[3] The occupier may also sue the trespasser in the civil courts for any damage caused whilst trespassing and, if that person is a persistent trespasser, may be able to obtain an injunction[4] against them.

11–01

Acts of Parliament have created a number of poaching offences whose ingredients and penalties vary according to whether the offences are committed in the daytime or by night, whether the poacher is alone or with others, whether or not he is armed, and whether he resists or co-operates when detected.

---

[1] A prosecution may be instituted by anyone, whether he is interested in the land trespassed on or not (*Halsbury's Laws of England*, 5th Edition Reissue, Vol.2, para.798).

[2] Though, where a prosecution for daytime poaching has been started, civil proceedings for trespass cannot be brought against the offender for the same act by a person at whose instance or with whose concurrence or assent the prosecution was instituted (GA 1831 s.46).

[3] *Halsbury's Laws of England*, 5th Edition Reissue, Vol.2, para.779.

[4] i.e. an order of the Court forbidding you to commit further trespass, the penalty for non-compliance usually being a fine or imprisonment.

POACHING IN THE DAYTIME

11–02   If you "commit any trespass"[5] by entering or being[6] in the daytime[7] upon any land in search or pursuit of game[8] or woodcocks, snipes … or conies",[9] you will commit an offence.[10] If five or more of you together do the same thing, each of you will upon conviction be liable to a greater penalty.[11]

If you are caught in the circumstances just mentioned by any one of a number of specified persons, you must, if asked to do so, leave the land at once and supply your full names and address. The persons who are entitled to make these requests are[12]:

(1)   The person having the right of killing game on the land.
(2)   The occupier of the land, whether or not he has the right of killing game on it.
(3)   The gamekeeper or other servant of, or any person authorised by, either of the persons described in (1) and (2) above.
(4)   A police constable.

11–03   If you refuse to give your real name and address, or give such a general description of your place of abode "as shall be illusory for the purpose of discovery", or wilfully continue or return upon the land, you may be apprehended by the person making the request, or by anybody acting by his order and in his aid, and later charged before a magistrate.[13] Any person so apprehended must be released if they are not brought before a magistrate within 12 hours.[14] Any of the persons listed above may also demand from you any game[15] in your possession which appears to have been recently killed and, if this is not delivered to them, they may seize it from you for the use of the person entitled to it.[16]

---

[5] i.e. entry without the prior permission of the occupier of the land or, where the shooting rights are held by some other person, of that other person (GA 1831 s.30).

[6] An entry or presence by a person is necessary to constitute the offence. The sending of a dog on to the land is not enough (*Pratt v Martin* [1911] 2 K.B. 90).

[7] This lasts from the beginning of the last hour before sunrise to the end of the first hour after sunset (GA 1831 s.34).

[8] The word "game" includes hares, pheasants, partridges, grouse, heath or moor game and black game (GA 1831 s.2).

[9] i.e. rabbits.

[10] GA 1831 s.30. The maximum penalty on summary conviction is a fine at level 3 on the standard scale (currently £1,000).

[11] GA 1831 s.30. The maximum penalty on summary conviction is a fine at level 4 on the standard scale (currently £2,500). Any vehicle used by you in committing the offence may be forfeited by order of the convicting court (Game Laws Amendment Act 1960 s.4A).

[12] GA 1831 ss.31, 31A.

[13] GA 1831 ss.31, 31A. You will be liable on summary conviction to a maximum fine at level 1 on the standard scale (currently £200).

[14] GA 1831 ss.31, 31A.

[15] This will be "game" as defined in fn.8. Thus the power of seizure will not extend to woodcock, snipe and rabbits which are the other birds and animals which may be the subject of daytime poaching. But see also the police powers of seizure mentioned at para.11–07.

[16] GA 1831 s.36. Although this section does not expressly refer to a police constable having the power to demand game.

If five or more of you together are found on land in pursuit of game, woodcock, snipe or rabbits in the daytime,[17] one or more of you having a gun, and you prevent or try to prevent "by violence, intimidation or menace" any of the persons described in items (1) to (4) above from approaching for the purpose of requiring you to leave the land or to give them your particulars, you will commit a further offence.[18]

POACHING BY NIGHT

As discussed in Ch.10, there are certain restrictions against shooting game at night. Additionally, Parliament has created a more serious offence to deal with armed trespass at night in pursuit of game by three or more persons. An offence is committed if persons in such numbers are or enter on any land[19] unlawfully[20] by night[21] for the purposes of taking or destroying game[22] or rabbits and any of them is armed[23] with a gun, crossbow, firearm, bludgeon or any other offensive weapon[24]; each of the party in these circumstances will be guilty.[25] It is not necessary that all of the party should enter the land; if all are associated for a common purpose and some enter while others remain near enough to assist, all of them may be convicted.[26] Nor is it necessary that all of them should be on the same piece of land or on land in the same occupation or ownership,[27] but they must have a plan in common[28]; and they may be convicted even though they may have abandoned their arms before being arrested.[29]

11–04

---

[17] This lasts from the beginning of the last hour before sunrise to the end of the first hour after sunset (GA 1831 s.34).

[18] GA 1831 s.32. The maximum fine on summary conviction is at level 5 on the standard scale (currently £5,000). If you aid or abet the commission of the offence you are likewise liable. This is so even though you may be on a road, and not on the land being trespassed upon (*Stacey v Whitehurst* (1865) 18 CB NS 344).

[19] This includes any public road, highway or path and the sides thereof, and the openings, outlets and gates from any land into them (NPA 1844 s.1).

[20] i.e. without having any necessary permissions or the right to take game.

[21] This means from one hour after sunset to one hour before sunrise (NPA 1828 s.12).

[22] This includes hares, pheasants, partridges, grouse, heath or moor game, black game and bustards (NPA 1828 s.13). As to "includes", see para.10–03, fn.11.

[23] If one of the party is armed, all are deemed to be so (*R. v Goodfellow* (1845) 1 Car & Kir 724 CCR).

[24] This can include a large stone, provided it is capable of inflicting serious injury if used offensively and brought and used for that purpose, (*R. v Grice* (1837) 7 C & P 803) and, if taken with the intention of it being used offensively, a stick (*R. v Fry & Webb* (1837) 2 Mood & R 42). A definition of "offensive weapon" is given in another Act of Parliament as "any article made or adapted for use for causing injury to the person, or intended by the person having it with him for such use by him or by some other person" (Prevention of Crime Act 1953 s.1(4)). See Ch.15 for a full discussion of offensive weapons.

[25] NPA 1828 s.9. The Criminal Law Act 1977 s.15(4) provides that this offence is triable summarily only and the maximum punishment on summary conviction is six months' imprisonment, or a fine at level 4 on the standard scale (currently £2,500), or both. Originally the offender could have been transported overseas for 7–14 years or sentenced to hard labour!

[26] *R. v Whittaker* (1848) 2 Car & Kir 636 CCR.

[27] *R. v Uezzell* (1851) 2 Den 274 CCR.

[28] There must be a joint act for each to be guilty of the offence: *R. v Nickless* (1839) 8 C & P 757. In modern criminal law a 'joint enterprise'.

[29] *R. v Nash & Weller* (1819) Russ & Ry 386.

There are also the offences of unlawfully by night: taking[30] or destroying game or rabbits on any land; or entering[31] or being on any land with any gun, net, engine[32] or instrument for the purpose of taking or destroying game.[33] Any person found upon land committing either of these offences may be seized and apprehended by any of the following people who may also apprehend him in any other place to which he may have escaped to and been pursued:

(1)   The owner or occupier of the land.
(2)   The lord of the manor or reputed manor in which the land lies.
(3)   Any gamekeeper or servant of any of the persons listed at (1) and (2).
(4)   Any person assisting such gamekeeper or servant.

The person so apprehended must be delivered as soon as possible into the custody of a police officer to be brought before the magistrates.

11–05   If the offender assaults, or offers any violence to, a person so authorised to arrest him with any gun, crossbow, firearm, bludgeon, stick, club or any other offensive weapon whatsoever, he commits an offence.[34]

The powers to demand and seize game, which have been discussed above in relation to daytime poaching, apply equally to offences of nocturnal poaching.[35]

POACHING BY DAY OR NIGHT

11–06   If you obtain game[36] by unlawfully going on any land, in search or pursuit of game, you will commit an offence.[37] "Unlawfully in search or pursuit of game" means a trespass by the offender on land of which he is neither the owner, nor occupier, nor the gamekeeper, nor the servant of either, nor having any *bona fide* right to kill the game thereon; the trespass being also without the consent of the owner, or of any person having the right to kill game there, or of any person having any right to authorise the offender to enter or be upon the land for the purpose of searching for or pursuing game.[38]

---

[30] Taking does not necessarily involve the offence of theft. It means, not to take away, but to catch, e.g. catching game in a snare with a view to keeping or killing it (*R. v Glover* (1814) Russ & Ry 269, CCR).

[31] Personal entry is necessary (*R. v Pratt* (1855) 4 E & B 860); thus, the sending of a dog on to land to drive out game does not constitute entry (*Pratt v Martin* [1911] 2 KB 90).

[32] The words "engine" and "instrument" include a snare (*Allen v Thompson* (1870) LR 5 QB 336 at 339). This case was concerned with the use of a snare on a Sunday but is of general application. Further, it was held that leaving a trap or snare is sufficient; there is no need for the person to be present when it is operated.

[33] NPA 1828 s.1. The maximum punishment on summary conviction for this offence is a fine at level 3 on the standard scale (currently £1,000).

[34] NPA 1828 s.2. The Criminal Law Act 1977 s.15(4) provides that this offence is triable summarily only and the maximum punishment on summary conviction is six months' imprisonment or a fine at level 4 on the standard scale (currently £2,500), or both.

[35] GA 1831 s.36.

[36] "Game" includes hares, pheasants, partridges, woodcocks, rabbits, snipe, grouse and black or moor game (PPA 1862 s.1). As to "includes", see para.10–03, fn.11.

[37] The maximum penalty on summary conviction is a fine at level 3 on the standard scale (currently £1,000). Game, guns and ammunition in the offender's possession may also be forfeited by order of the Court (PPA 1862 s.2; Game Laws (Amendment) Act (GLA) 1960 s.3(2)).

[38] GA 1831 s.30.

If you use[39] any gun, part of a gun, cartridges or other ammunition, or nets, traps, snares or other devices of a kind used for the killing or taking of game, for unlawfully killing or taking game, that will be an offence.[40]

A person who is an accessory[41] to either of the last two offences is liable to the same penalties as the offender himself.[42]

POWERS OF POLICE

The powers of the police to arrest suspected persons are governed by the Police and Criminal Evidence Act 1984 which is of general application. However, statutes dealing with poaching contain a number of provisions enabling the police to stop and search suspected persons and their vehicles, to arrest suspected persons and to seize and detain things found on those arrested. If a police officer has reasonable grounds for suspecting that a person is committing an offence of poaching in the day or at night he may enter on that land to arrest him.[43] A police officer may, in any highway or public place, search any person whom he has good cause to suspect of coming from land where he has been unlawfully in search or pursuit of game,[44] or any person aiding or abetting him, and of having in his possession any game unlawfully obtained, or any gun, part of gun, cartridges or other ammunition, or any nets, traps, snares or other devices of a kind used for the taking of game.[45] The police officer has the power to seize any game or rabbits or any gun or article used for killing or taking game or rabbits, which are in his possession.[46] The police officer also has the power to stop and search any cart or conveyance in or on which the officer suspects any such game or article is being carried.[47]

11–07

---

[39] So far as this offence is concerned, a gun may be said to be used for these purposes, even though it has not been fired. If you go onto land with a gun for the purposes of shooting game with that gun then you are deemed to be using that gun for the purpose of taking game within the meaning of the Act (*Gray v Hawthorn* [1961] Crim L.R. 265).

[40] The maximum penalty on summary conviction is a fine at level 3 on the standard scale (currently £1,000). Game, guns and ammunition in the offender's possession may also be forfeited by order of the Court (PPA 1862 s.2; GLA 1960 s.3(2)).

[41] An accessory is one who assists an offender before, during or after the commission of the offence.

[42] See fn.40 above.

[43] GL(A)A 1960 s.2(1)(a), (b) (Amended by the Police and Criminal Evidence (PACE) Act 1984 Sch.6 para 10; and the Serious Organised Crime and Police Act 2005 s.111 Sch.7, para.52(2)).

[44] 'Game' for these purposes means: hares, pheasants, partridges, eggs of pheasants and partridges, woodcocks, snipes, rabbits, grouse, black or moor game, and eggs of grouse, black or moor game (PPA 1862 s.1).

[45] PPA 1862 s.2; GL(A)A 1960 s.3(2).

[46] GLA(A) 1960 s.4(1).

[47] PPA 1862 s.2.

CHAPTER 12

Protected Birds and Animals

INTRODUCTION

Wild birds and animals are protected by a number of Acts of Parliament. The **12–01** principal measure is the Wildlife and Countryside Act 1981[1] which contains wide ranging provisions protecting most kinds of wild birds and animals. Deer, seals and badgers are each singled out for individual protection in their own Acts.

Less important are: the Criminal Damage Act 1971, which affects wild creatures no longer in a wild state; and the Wild Mammals (Protection) Act 1996, which is concerned with the unnecessary infliction of suffering on wild animals.

The following sections of this chapter consider each of the foregoing measures in turn. Except for the last section, discussion is confined to those measures which relate to shooting and to those wild creatures which may be the subject of shooting.

---

[1] In Northern Ireland the relevant legislation is The Wildlife (Northern Ireland) Order 1985.

WILDLIFE AND COUNTRYSIDE ACT 1981

12–02   It is first necessary to look at a number of definitions which the 1981 Act uses. A "wild bird" is defined as any bird of a species which is ordinarily resident in, or is a visitor to, the European territory of any Member State in a wild state, but does not include poultry or (except in the three instances later mentioned) any game bird.[2] Within this definition, further terms are defined: "poultry" means domestic fowls, geese, ducks, guinea-fowls, pigeons and quails, and turkeys; a "domestic duck" and a "domestic goose" mean, respectively, any domestic form of duck or goose; "game bird" means any pheasant, partridge, grouse (or moor game), black (or heath) game or ptarmigan.[3] A wild animal is defined as any animal (other than a bird) which is or was (before it was killed or taken) living wild.[4] The Act's provisions extend to the Scilly Isles and the territorial waters adjacent to Great Britain.[5]

With the exceptions set out below, it is an offence[6] to intentionally kill, injure or take any wild bird[7] or to intentionally or recklessly kill, injure or take any of the animals listed in Sch.5 to the Act.[8] These animals collectively are referred to below as listed animals.

12–03   The exceptions to these offences are:

(1)   A person shall not be guilty of an offence under s.1 by reason of the killing or taking of a bird included in Part I of Sch.2 outside the close season for that bird, or the injuring of such a bird outside that season in the course of an attempt to kill it,[9] except—

(a)   in Scotland on Sundays and Christmas Day,[10] and

---

[2] WCA 1981 s.27(1). This exception relating to game birds has been repealed in Scotland pursuant to s.2(b) of the Wildlife and Natural Environment (Scotland) Act 2011.

[3] WCA 1981 s.27(1). This definition has been repealed in Scotland pursuant to s.2(a) of the Wildlife and Natural Environment (Scotland) Act 2011.

[4] WCA 1981 s.27(1).

[5] The breadth of territorial waters adjacent to Great Britain is 12 nautical miles (1 nautical mile = 1852 metres). The baselines from which this measurement is taken are to be laid down by Orders in Council from time to time (Territorial Seas Act 1987 s.1).

[6] The offence in respect of wild birds is set out in WCA 1981 s.1(1) and s.9(1) in respect of wild animals. WCA 1981 s.18(1) provides that anyone who attempts to commit such offences will be punishable in a like manner for the offence. The maximum punishment on summary conviction for either of these offences is a term of imprisonment not exceeding six months and/or a fine at level 5 on the standard scale (currently £5,000). Where more than one animal or bird is involved in an offence, the maximum fine is as if the offender were convicted of a separate offence for each bird or animal (WCA 1981 s.21(1) and (5)).

[7] In this instance "wild bird" does not include any bird which is shown to have been bred in captivity unless it has been lawfully released into the wild as part of a re-population or re-introduction programme. A bird shall not be treated as bred in captivity unless its parents were lawfully in captivity when the egg was laid (WCA 1981 ss.1(6), 27(2)).

[8] WCA 1981 s.9(1) and Sch.5. The listing may be varied by Government order (WCA 1981 s.22(3), (4)). In proceedings for an offence these animals will be presumed to have been wild unless the contrary is shown (WCA 1981 s.9(6)).

[9] WCA 1981 s.2(1).

[10] The Wildlife and Natural Environment (Scotland) Act 2011 s.3(8) introduces Part 1A to Sch.2 in respect of Scotland. This Part lists a number of species of birds which cannot be shot in Scotland on Sundays or Christmas Day. See Appendix E.

(b)   in England and Wales in any area prescribed for the purpose by Government order.[11]

The names of the birds so listed and the close seasons for them are given in Appendix E at the end of the book. Both may be varied by Government order, and orders may be made giving special protection to any listed bird, which have the same effect as a close season for it. Prior to making an order giving any special protection the Secretary of State shall consult a representative of persons interested in the shooting of birds of the kind proposed to be protected by the order.[12]

(2)   To prevent damage to crops, pasture, animal or human foodstuffs, livestock,[13] trees, hedges, banks or any works on land, Government Ministers may require the person having the right to do so to kill wild birds and animals causing such damage. Such a killing or an injuring of a wild bird or a listed animal is excused in these circumstances.[14]

(3)   Any act done in pursuance of the provisions of the Animal Health Act 1981, or of any order made under it, is excused.[15]

(4)   A person shall not be guilty of the killing of a wild bird or listed animal if it is shown that it had been so seriously disabled, otherwise than by his unlawful act, that there was no reasonable chance of its recovering.[16] Similarly, he shall not be guilty of taking a wild bird or listed animal if it is shown that the animal had been disabled otherwise than by his unlawful act and was taken solely for the purpose of tending it and releasing it when no longer disabled.[17]   **12–04**

(5)   Any act done if it is shown that the act was the incidental result of a lawful operation[18] and could not reasonably have been avoided.[19]

(6)   The killing, injuring or taking of a wild bird (except one included in Sch.1 of the Act)[20] by an authorised person[21] shall not be an offence if it is shown   **12–05**

---

[11] WCA 1981 s.2(3).

[12] WCA 1981 ss.2(5)–(7), 22(1). Notice of the making of all orders must be published in the London Gazette, or the Edinburgh Gazette for orders affecting Scotland (WCA 1981 s.26(5)).

[13] "Livestock" includes any animal which is kept: for the provision of food, wool, skins or fur; for the purpose of its use in the carrying on of any agricultural activity; or for the provision or improvement of shooting or fishing (WCA 1981 s.27(1)).

[14] AA 1947 s.98 and in respect of Scotland, A(S)A 1947 s.39; WCA 1981 ss.4(1)(a), 10(1)(a).

[15] WCA 1981 ss.4(1)(b) and (c), 10(1)(b); Animal Health Act 1981 ss.21 and 22. This does not apply in all instances to wild birds listed in Schs ZA1 and 1 to the WCA 1981, for which see Appendix D at the end of the book.

[16] WCA 1981 ss.4(2)(b), 10(3)(b). However, a person shall not be permitted to rely on the defence under s.10(3)(c) as respects anything done in relation to a bat otherwise than in the living area of a dwelling house unless he had notified the conservation body for the area in which the house is situated or, as the case may be, for the area where the act is to take place, or of the proposed action or operation, and has allowed them a reasonable time to advise him as to whether it should be carried out and, if so, the method to be used. (WCA 1981 s.10(5)).

[17] WCA 1981 ss.4(2)(b), 10(3)(a).

[18] e.g. an accidental killing or injury of a wild bird or listed animal by a moving vehicle or by a shot lawfully fired at something else.

[19] WCA 1981 ss.4(2)(c), 10(3)(c). However, a person shall not be permitted to rely on the defence under s.10(3)(c) as respects anything done in relation to a bat otherwise than in the living area of a dwelling house unless he had notified the conservation body for the area in which the house is situated or, as the case may be, for the area where the act is to take place, of the proposed action or operation, and has allowed them a reasonable time to advise him as to whether it should be carried out and, if so, the method to be used. (WCA 1981 s.10(5)).

[20] For the birds listed in Sch.1, see Appendix D.

that it was necessary for the purpose of preventing serious damage to livestock,[22] foodstuffs for livestock, crops, vegetables, fruit, growing timber, fisheries or inland waters.[23]

But this exception cannot be relied on if any of the following apply—

(a)   the authorised person was unable to show that, as regards the purpose of preventing the serious damage his action was necessary, as there was no other satisfactory solution;

(b)   it had become apparent, before the time of killing or injuring, that that action would prove necessary for the purpose of preventing the serious damage *and either*—

     (i)   a licence[24] authorising the action had not been applied for as soon as reasonably practicable after the fact had become apparent; *or*

     (ii)   an application for a licence had been determined[25];

(c)   the authorised person, as respects any action taken at any time, does not notify the Ministry of Agriculture as soon as reasonably practicable after that time that he had taken the action.[26]

(7)   The killing or injuring by an authorised person[27] of a wild animal listed in Sch.5 to the Act if it is shown that that was necessary for the purpose of preventing serious damage to livestock,[28] foodstuffs for livestock, crops, vegetables, fruit, growing timber or any other form of property or to fisheries.[29]

But this exception cannot be relied on if it had become apparent before the time of killing or injuring that that would prove necessary for the purpose of preventing serious damage of any of the kinds described, *and either*—

(a)   a licence authorising the action had not been applied for as soon as reasonably practicable after that fact had become apparent; *or*

---

[21] An "authorised person" means: the owner or occupier, or any person authorised by the owner or occupier, of the land on which the action authorised is taken; any person authorised in writing by the local authority for the area within which the action authorised is taken; a person authorised in writing by certain authorities and other statutory bodies who may also authorise persons for this purpose. (WCA 1981 s.27(1)).

[22] "Livestock" includes any animal which is kept: for the provision of food, wool, skins or fur; for the purpose of its use in the carrying on of any agricultural activity; or for the provision or improvement of shooting or fishing (WCA 1981 s.27(1)).

[23] WCA 1981 s.4(3)(c). The expression "inland waters" "inland waters" means: (a) inland waters within the meaning of the Water Resources Act 1991; (b) any waters not falling within paragraph (a) which are within the seaward limits of the territorial sea; (c) controlled waters within the meaning of Part II of the Control of Pollution Act 1974 other than ground waters as defined in s.30A(1)(d) of that Act (WCA 1981 s.27(1)).

[24] For licences, see item (9).

[25] To meet the requirements of sub-paras (b)(i) and (ii) of item (6) above, it appears that it is only necessary to apply for a licence promptly.

[26] WCA 1981 s.4(3)–(6).

[27] An "authorised person" means: the owner or occupier, or any person authorised by the owner or occupier, of the land on which the action authorised is taken; any person authorised in writing by the local authority for the area within which the action authorised is taken; a person authorised in writing by certain authorities and other statutory bodies who may also authorise persons for this purpose. (WCA 1981 s.27(1)).

[28] "Livestock" includes any animal which is kept: for the provision of food, wool, skins or fur; for the purpose of its use in the carrying on of any agricultural activity; or for the provision or improvement of shooting or fishing (WCA 1981 s.27(1)).

[29] WCA 1981 s.10(4).

(b)   an application for a licence had been determined.[30]

(8)   The killing or injuring by an authorised person[31] of a wild bird (except one included in Sch.1 to the Act)[32] if it is shown that that was necessary for the purpose of preserving public health, or public or air safety, or preventing the spread of disease.[33]

(9)   Any killing or injuring of a wild bird or listed animal, or an attempt to kill or injure either, which is done under and in accordance with the terms of a licence granted by the appropriate authority.[34] Licences are obtainable only for particularised purposes, and those which may be relevant to shooting are listed in Appendix F at the end of the book with details of the authorities from whom they can be obtained.[35]

It is an essential ingredient of the offence of killing or injuring a wild bird, or   **12–06**
attempting to do so, that there was intent to kill or injure. Therefore, if there is no such intent, no offence is committed. However, the offence of killing or injuring a listed animal has been drafted to include a reckless basis also. Therefore, it is not necessary to prove intent, it is sufficient to show that the killing or injuring of the animal was a foreseeable consequence of the action taken.

The Wildlife and Countryside Act 1981 creates a number of other offences which are connected directly or indirectly with shooting, and these, together with the available defences, will now be considered.

It is an offence to intentionally or recklessly disturb any wild bird included in Sch.1 to the 1981 Act[36] while it is building a nest or is in, on or near a nest containing eggs or young, or to intentionally or recklessly disturb the dependent young of such a bird.[37] Similarly, it is an offence to intentionally or recklessly damage or destroy any structure or place which any listed animal uses for shelter or protection, or to intentionally or recklessly disturb any listed animal while it is occupying a structure or place, which it uses for shelter or protection or to obstruct access to any such place.[38]

---

[30] WCA 1981 s.10(6).

[31] An "authorised person" means: the owner or occupier, or any person authorised by the owner or occupier, of the land on which the action authorised is taken; any person authorised in writing by the local authority for the area within which the action authorised is taken; a person authorised in writing by certain authorities and other statutory bodies who may also authorise persons for this purpose. (WCA 1981 s.27(1)).

[32] For the birds listed in Sch.1, see Appendix D.

[33] WCA 1981 s.4(3)(a), (b).

[34] WCA 1981 s.16(1)–(3).

[35] Game birds, for which see para.12–02, may be the subject of a licence (WCA 1981 ss.16, 27(1)). Although, pursuant to the Wildlife and Natural Environment (Scotland) Act 2011 s.2 game birds may not be the subject of a licence in Scotland.

[36] The birds included in Sch.1 are listed in App.D at the end of the book. The Sch.1 listing may be varied by Government order (WCA 1981 s.22(1)).

[37] WCA 1981 s.1(5). WCA 1981 s.18(1) provides that anyone who attempts to commit such an offence will be punishable in a like manner for the offence. The maximum punishment on summary conviction for this offence is a term of imprisonment not exceeding six months and/or a fine at level 5 on the standard scale (currently £5,000). Where more than one bird, nest or egg is involved in an offence, the maximum fine is as if the offender were convicted of a separate offence for each bird, nest or egg (WCA 1981 s.21(1) and (5)).

[38] WCA 1981 s.9(4)(a),(b),(c). WCA 1981 s.18(1) provides that anyone who attempts to commit such an offence will be punishable in a like manner for the offence. The maximum punishment on summary conviction for this offence is a term of imprisonment not exceeding six months and/or a fine

12–07　　　The exceptions listed at items (3) and (5) above apply to all the above offences, and the disturbance of a bird or animal as the result of such a requirement by the Ministry of Agriculture as described in item (2) above will also be an exception.[39] Any disturbance of a listed animal shall not be unlawful if it takes place in a dwelling house[40] except where the listed animal is a bat, which has been disturbed in a place other than the living area of a dwelling house. In that instance, the conservation body for the area in which the house is situated should be notified.[41]

The 1981 Act prohibits certain methods of killing wild birds and wild animals. Some methods are prohibited only in respect of the kinds of wild animal set out in Sch.6 to the Act reproduced in Appendix G at the end of the book,[42] whereas other prohibited methods apply to all wild birds and to all wild animals respectively. There is some duplication of the methods prohibited in respect of wild birds and wild animals, therefore, for convenience the prohibited methods have been organised into the four groupings, which appear below.

12–08　　　The list of prohibited methods may be varied by Government order.[43] However, in respect of any method of killing or taking wild birds, which involves the use of a firearm, or any method of killing or taking wild animals, that power shall not be exercised, except for the purpose of complying with an international obligation.[44] To use a prohibited method, or knowingly to cause or permit the use of such a method, is an offence[45] unless approved by a licence issued by the appropriate authority.[46] The prohibited methods, so far as they relate or may relate to shooting, are as follows:

(1)　Methods applying to all wild birds[47] and to wild animals[48] listed in Sch.6 WCA 1981:

　　(a)　Using for the purpose of killing—

---

at level 5 on the standard scale (currently £5,000). Where more than one animal is involved in an offence, the maximum fine is as if the offender were convicted of a separate offence for each animal (WCA 1981 s.21(1) and (5)).

[39] WCA 1981 ss.4(1), (2)(c), 10(1), (3)(c). Although the exception under s.10(3)(c) shall not apply where the listed animal concerned is a bat unless the relevant conservation body have been notified WCA 1981 s.10(2), (5) (see para.12–04 above).

[40] WCA 1981 s.10(2).

[41] WCA 1981 s.10(2), (5) (see para.12–04 above).

[42] The listing may be varied by Government order (WCA 1981 s.22(4)(a)).

[43] WCA 1981 ss.5(2), 11(4).

[44] WCA 1981 ss.5(3), 11(4).

[45] WCA 1981 ss.5(1), 11(1). WCA 1981 s.18(1) provides that anyone who attempts to commit such an offence will be punishable in a like manner for the offence. The maximum punishment on summary conviction for this offence is a term of imprisonment not exceeding six months and/or a fine at level 5 on the standard scale (currently £5000). Where more than one bird or animal is involved in an offence, the maximum fine is as if the offender were convicted of a separate offence for each bird or animal (WCA 1981 s.21(1) and (5)).

[46] WCA 1981 ss.5(1)(f), 11(2)(f), 16(1), (3). See App.F at the end of the book for the purposes for which licences may be obtained.

[47] In England and Wales, game birds are included in this instance and, for these purposes, "game bird" means any pheasant, partridge, grouse (or moor game), black (or heath) game or ptarmigan (WCA 1981 ss.5, 27(1)). However, game birds will not be included in respect of Scotland pursuant to the Wildlife and Natural Environment (Scotland) Act 2011 s.2.

[48] In any proceedings for an offence the animal in question shall be presumed to have been wild unless the contrary is shown (WCA 1981 s.11(5)).

(i) any automatic or semi-automatic weapon,[49]

(ii) any device for illuminating a target or any sighting device for night shooting,

(iii) any form of artificial light or any mirror or other dazzling device.

(b) For the purpose of killing, using as a decoy any sound recording.

(c) Using any mechanically propelled vehicle[50] in immediate pursuit of a bird or animal for the purpose of killing or taking it.[51]

(2) Methods applying to all wild birds[52] :

(a) Using, for the purpose of killing, any shot gun of which the barrel has an internal diameter at the muzzle of more than 1.75 inches.

(b) For the purpose of killing, using as a decoy any live bird or other animal whatever which is tethered, or which is secured by means of braces or other similar appliances, or which is blind, maimed or injured.[53]

(3) Method applying to all wild animals[54]:

Using as a decoy, for the purpose of killing any wild animal, any live mammal or bird whatever.[55]

(4) Method applying to wild animals listed in Sch.6 to the WCA 1981[56]:

Using any mechanically propelled vehicle[57] in immediate pursuit of an animal for the purpose of driving, killing or taking that animal.[58]

The 1981 Act makes it an offence for a person to have in his possession,[59] for the purpose of committing any of the offences which have been described, anything capable of being used for committing one of those offences.[60] Many things so capable may be innocently possessed. However, it is an element of the offence, and hence must be proven beyond reasonable doubt, that the object in question was possessed for the purpose described; to that end, the prosecution would have to adduce evidence to demonstrate a link between possession and the commission, or intended commission, of one of the offences.

12–09

---

[49] "Automatic weapon" and "semi-automatic weapon" do not include any weapon the magazine of which is incapable of holding more than two rounds (WCA 1981 s.27(1)).

[50] The word "vehicle" includes aircraft, hovercraft and boat (WCA 1981 s.27(1)).

[51] WCA 1981 ss.5(1)(c)–(e), 11(2)(c)–(e).

[52] In England and Wales, game birds are included in this instance and, for these purposes, "game bird" means any pheasant, partridge, grouse (or moor game), black (or heath) game or ptarmigan (WCA 1981 ss.5, 27(1)). However, game birds will not be so included in respect of Scotland pursuant to the Wildlife and Natural Environment (Scotland) Act 2011 s2.

[53] WCA 1981 s.5(1)(c)(iv), (d).

[54] In any proceedings for an offence the animal in question shall be presumed to have been wild unless the contrary is shown (WCA 1981 s.11(5)).

[55] WCA 1981 s.11(1)(c).

[56] The names of the animals in Sch.6 are listed in App.G at the end of the book.

[57] "vehicle" includes aircraft, hovercraft and boat WCA 1981 s27(1).

[58] WCA 1981 s.11(2)(e).

[59] For commentary on the meaning of "possession", see para.3–07.

[60] Anyone convicted of this offence shall be punished in like manner as for the offence for which it is alleged that the person had the thing in his possession to commit (WCA 1981 s.18(2)).

Constables,[61] with reasonable cause to suspect that a person is committing or has committed an offence under the 1981 Act, may without warrant stop and search the person, search and examine things the person has or is using and seize and detain things, which may be evidence of an offence, or which may be forfeited by a convicting court.[62] They may also arrest the person suspected if they fail to give their name and address to the constable's satisfaction.[63] Constables may also enter any premises other than a dwelling to exercise these powers, and to make arrests if they reasonably suspect that an offence is being committed.[64] A constable will need to obtain a warrant from a justice of the peace to enter upon and search any premises where there are reasonable grounds to suspect that an offence has been committed and that evidence of that offence may be found on those premises.[65]

As well as imposing fines, a convicting court is compelled to order the forfeiture of any bird or animal in respect of which the offence was committed.[66] The court *may* also order forfeiture of any vehicle,[67] animal, weapon, or other thing which was used to commit the offence.[68]

DEER ACT 1991

Introduction

12–10   The earliest modern legislation specifically protecting deer was the Deer Act of 1963. Further protection was added by the Deer Acts of 1980 and 1987 and the Roe Deer (Close Seasons) Act of 1977, the 1980 and 1987 Acts legislating for the newer trends in deer farming, deer poaching and the selling of venison. These Acts have now been repealed and their provisions, with amendments, consolidated in the Deer Act of 1991.[69] The 1991 Act has recently been reformed in England and Wales by the Regulatory Reform (Deer)(England and Wales) Order 2007.

The shooting of deer is considered in the following pages under five headings: close seasons; killing deer at night; use of unlawful methods and illegal possession of objects; powers of police and powers of courts on conviction of offences; and deer poaching. The 1991 Act also legislates for licences for taking live deer and for trading in venison.[70] These, not being matters connected with shooting, are not further dealt with.

12–11   The provisions of the 1991 Act apply throughout to "deer"[71] which term is defined as "deer of any species and includes the carcass of any deer or any part

---

[61] As well as police constables, including special police constables, "constables" includes others holding that office, e.g. harbour constables. The hallmark of a constable is his attestation as such before, usually, a Magistrate.

[62] WCA 1981 s.19(1)(a), (b), (d). For police powers of general application, see para.11–07.

[63] WCA 1981 s.19(1)(c).

[64] WCA 1981 s.19(2).

[65] WCA 1981 s.19(3).

[66] WCA 1981 s.21(6)(a).

[67] The word "vehicle" includes aircraft, hovercraft and boat (WCA 1981 s.27(1)).

[68] WCA 1981 s.21(6)(b).

[69] In respect of Scotland the relevant legislation is the Deer (Scotland) Act 1996.

[70] DA 1991 ss.8, 10, 11.

[71] Except in relation to close seasons for particular species of deer.

thereof", unless the context otherwise requires; and "species" includes any hybrid of different species of deer".[72] Thus, deer of either sex, of all ages and tame deer are included.

Close seasons

There are close seasons for six species of deer, and these are shown in s.3 of App.C at the end of the book.   **12–12**

It is an offence to take or intentionally to kill deer[73] of these species, or to attempt to do so, during their respective close seasons,[74] except where one of the following defences (listed as A–E below) is available.

The defences are as follows:

(A) That the deer was killed or taken, or was injured in an attempt to kill or take   **12–13**
    it, by one of the persons described at (a) to (e) below by means of shooting,
    and the act was done on any cultivated land, pasture or enclosed
    woodland.[75] But this defence cannot be relied upon unless that person
    shows that—

    (i) he had reasonable grounds for believing that deer of the same species
    were causing, or had caused, damage to crops, vegetables, fruit,
    growing timber or any other form of property on the land[76]; *and*

    (ii) it was likely that further damage would be so caused *and* such
    damage was likely to be serious; *and*

    (iii) his action was necessary for the purpose of preventing any such
    damage.[77]

The above defence is available only to the following named classes of persons—

    (a) the occupier of the land on which the action is taken;

    (b) any member of the occupier's household[78] normally resident on the
    occupier's land, and acting with the occupier's written authority;

    (c) any person in the ordinary service[79] of the occupier on the occupier's
    land, acting as above;

---

[72] DA 1991 s.16.

[73] The word "deer" will include deer of either sex and all ages (*R. v Strange* (1843) 1 Cox CC 58), and tame deer as well as wild deer.

[74] DA 1991 ss.2(1), 5(1). The maximum punishment on summary conviction is a fine at level 4 on the standard scale (currently £2,500), or 3 months' imprisonment, or both (DA 1991 s.9(1)). If an offence involves more than one deer, the maximum fine shall be regarded as if there was a separate offence against each deer involved (DA 1991 s.9(2)).

[75] DA 1991 s.7(1).

[76] i.e. the land upon which the act was done, being land of one of the three descriptions given earlier in the text.

[77] DA 1991 s.7(3)(a)–(c). Government Ministers may by order add further conditions to those listed in sub-paragraphs (i)–(iii) of item (A) above and may vary and delete such further conditions (DA 1991 s.7(5)(b)). For restrictions on the types of guns and ammunition which the authorised person may use, see item (3) at para.12–15 below and item (D) at para.12–16 below.

[78] As to household membership and "ordinary service" see the definition at para.13–03, fn.18. Though derived from the law relating to ground game, those notes may serve as a guide pending any court decision on the words' meanings in this text.

[79] As above.

(d)   any person having the right to take or kill deer on the land on which the action is taken; and

(e)   any person acting with the written authority of a person at (d) above.[80]

(B)   That the killing or attempting to kill was done for the purpose of preventing suffering by an injured or diseased deer.[81]

(C)   That the taking or killing of the deer was because he reasonably believed that the deer had been deprived in any way (other than by an unlawful taking or killing by that person) of a female deer on which it was dependent; or; was about to be deprived, by death from disease or a lawful taking or killing, of a female deer on which it is dependent.[82]

(D)   That the killing or attempting to kill was done in pursuance of a Government Minister's requirement under s.98 of the Agriculture Act 1947.[83]

(E)   That the deer was killed by a person, or his authorised servant or agent, and that person, by way of business, kept the deer on land enclosed by a deer–proof barrier for the production of meat or other foodstuffs or skins or other by–products, or as breeding stock; and the deer so kept was conspicuously marked so as to identify it as kept by that person in the way described above.[84]

Killing deer at night

12–14   It is an offence intentionally to kill a deer at night,[85] or attempt to do so,[86] except where one of the defences described at (B), (C) or (D) above is available.[87]

Use of unlawful methods and illegal possession of objects

12–15   Subject to the defences later described, the following acts done in relation to deer, and attempts to commit those acts, are offences[88]:

---

[80] DA 1991 s.7(4).

[81] DA 1991 s.6(2).

[82] DA 1991 s.2A.

[83] DA 1991 s.6(1). This is a reference to Ministers' powers to require the person having the right to do so to kill deer (and other animals and birds) which are causing damage, even though they may be out of season.

[84] DA 1991 s.2(3).

[85] "Night" extends from the expiry of one hour after sunset to the beginning of one hour before sunrise (DA 1991 s.3).

[86] DA 1991 ss.3, 5(1). The maximum punishment on summary conviction is a fine at level 4 on the standard scale (currently £2500), or 3 months' imprisonment, or both (DA 1991 s.9(1)). If an offence involves more than one deer, the maximum fine shall be regarded as if there was a separate offence against each deer involved (DA 1991 s.9(2)).

[87] DA 1991 s.6(1) and (2)

[88] The maximum punishment on summary conviction is a fine at level 4 on the standard scale (currently £2500), or 3 months' imprisonment, or both (DA 1991 s.9(1)). If an offence involves more than one deer, the maximum fine shall be regarded as if there was a separate offence against each deer involved (DA 1991 s.9(2)).

(1)   Setting in position any trap, snare or poisoned or stupefying bait which is of such a nature or so placed as to be calculated to cause bodily injury to any deer coming into contact with it.[89]

(2)   Using, for the purpose of taking or killing any deer, any trap, snare or poisoned or stupefying bait, or any net.[90]

(3)   Using, or attempting to use, for the purpose of taking, injuring or killing any deer—

(a)   any smooth bore gun or any cartridge for use in it, *or*

(b)   any rifle of a calibre less than 0.240 inches or a muzzle energy of less than 1,700 foot pounds (2,305 joules), *or*

(c)   any bullet for use in a rifle, other than a soft-nosed or hollow-nosed bullet,[91] *or*

(d)   any arrow, spear or similar missile, *or*

(e)   any missile, whether discharged from a firearm[92] or otherwise, carrying or containing any poison, stupefying drug or muscle relaxing agent.[93]

(4)   Discharging any firearm[94] or projecting any missile from any mechanically propelled vehicle[95] at any deer when the vehicle is moving or when its engine is running.[96]

(5)   Using, or attempting to use, any mechanically propelled vehicle or aircraft for the purpose of driving deer.[97]

(6)   Possessing[98] any object described at items (2), (3)(d) or (e) above, or possessing any firearm or ammunition, for the purposes of committing any of the following offences: those described at items (1) to (5) above; or for the taking or killing certain deer during the close season; or for the killing or taking of deer at night.[99]

The defences to the offences listed above are: **12–16**

(A)   In the case of the offences at (1) and (2) above, that any trap or net set in position or used was for the purpose of preventing the suffering of an injured or diseased deer.[100]

(B)   A person shall not be guilty of the offences set out at (1), (2) and (3)(a)–(e) above, by reason of the use of any reasonable means for the purpose of

---

[89] DA 1991 ss.4(1)(a), 5(1).

[90] DA 1991 ss.4(1)(b), 5(1).

[91] The descriptions of guns and ammunition in item (3)(a)–(c) above may be varied by order of the Home Office (DA 1991 s.4(3)).

[92] The definition of "firearm" examined in Ch.1 applies (DA 1991 s.16; FA 1968 s.57(1)).

[93] DA 1991 ss.4(2), 5(1) and Sch.2. Sch.2 contains a prospective provision prohibiting the using, or the attempting to use, for the purpose of taking, injuring or killing any deer any air gun, air rifle or air pistol. This provision is not in force and as yet there is no date for it to be brought into force. Therefore, at the time of writing it is not an offence to use the items aforementioned.

[94] The definition of "firearm" examined in Ch.1 applies (DA 1991 s.16; FA 1968 s.57(1)).

[95] "vehicle" includes an aircraft, hovercraft or boat (DA 1991 s.16).

[96] DA 1991 ss.4(4)(a), 5(1).

[97] DA 1991 ss.4(4)(b), 5(1).

[98] For some notes on the meaning of "possession", though in another context, see para.3–07.

[99] DA 1991 ss.4(1)(b), 4(2)(b), 4(2)(c), 5(2). To secure a conviction for this offence, it would be necessary for the prosecution to prove to the court's satisfaction a link between possession and the commission, or intended commission, of one of the offences.

[100] DA 1991 s.6(3).

killing any deer if he reasonably believes that the deer has been so seriously injured, otherwise than by his unlawful act[101], or is in such condition, that to kill it is an act of mercy.[102] For these purposes any "reasonable means" means any method of killing a deer that can reasonably be expected to result in rapid loss of consciousness and death and which is appropriate in all the circumstances (including in particular what the deer is doing, its size, its distance from the closest position safely attainable by the person attempting to kill the deer and its position in relation to vegetative cover).[103]

(C) In the case of the offence at (3)(a) above, that the gun was used as a slaughtering instrument[104] to kill deer, provided the gun—
   (i)   was of not less gauge than 12 bore, *and*
   (ii) had a barrel less than 24 inches (609.6mm) in length, *and*
   (iii) was loaded with a cartridge purporting to contain shot none of which was less than 0.203 inches (5.16mm) in diameter (size AAA or larger).[105]

(D) In the case of the offence at (3)(a) above, if the gun is used for the purpose of taking or killing or injuring any Chinese water deer (*Hydropotesinermis*) or muntjac deer (*Muntiacusreevesi*), provided the gun—
   (a) was a rifle having a calibre of not less than .220 inches and a muzzle energy of not less than 1,356 joules (1000 foot pounds), and
   (b) was loaded with a soft-nosed or hollow-nosed bullet weighing not less than 3.24 grammes (50 grains).[106]

(E) In the case of the offence at (3)(a) above, that a smooth-bore gun of not less gauge than 12 bore was used by one of the persons described at items A (a) to (e) to take or kill deer on any land, and the gun was loaded with—
   (i)   a cartridge containing a single non-spherical projectile weighing not less than 350 grains (22.68 grammes); *or*
   (ii) a cartridge purporting to contain shot each of which was 0.203 inches (5.16mm) in diameter (size AAA).[107]

But this defence cannot be relied upon unless the person using the gun can show he had reasonable grounds for believing that deer of the same species were causing, or had caused, damage to crops, vegetables, fruit, growing timber or any other form of property on the land; it was likely that further

---

[101] The words "unlawful act" are not restricted to acts made unlawful by the Deer Act 1991, and will thus, it seems, embrace acts which are otherwise unlawful, e.g. the improper use of a gun without a firearm or shot gun certificate.

[102] DA 1991 s.6(4).

[103] DA 1991 s.6(4A).

[104] Though the matter is not entirely clear, it appears that this defence is intended to apply when deer are killed preparatory to the use of their carcasses as venison, as on a deer farm.

[105] DA 1991 s.6(5).

[106] DA 1991 s.6(6).

[107] DA 1991 s.7(2). The Secretary of State and agriculture minister acting jointly may by order either generally or in respect of a species of deer repeal this section or amend it by adding any firearm or ammunition or by altering the description of, or deleting, any firearm or ammunition for the time being mentioned in it (DA 1991 s.7(5)(a)).

damage would be so caused and any such damage was likely to be serious; and his action was necessary for the purpose of preventing any such damage.[108]

(F)　In the case of the offences at (4) and (5) above, that the prohibited act was done by, or with the written authority of, the occupier of any enclosed land[109] where deer are usually kept and was done in relation to deer on that land.[110]

Powers of police and powers of court on conviction of offences

Constables[111] are given wide powers by the 1991 Act. They may, if they suspect with reasonable cause that a person is committing or has committed an offence under the Act, without a warrant stop and search suspected persons, search or examine vehicles,[112] weapons, animals and other things for evidence, and seize and detain things which are such evidence and deer, venison,[113] vehicles, animals, weapons and other things which a court may order to be forfeited on conviction.[114]
 12–17

A constable may enter any land,[115] other than a dwelling house, to exercise the foregoing powers or to arrest a person under the general powers of arrest available to him.[116] He may also sell any deer or venison[117] seized, and the net proceeds are to be forfeited in the same manner as the deer or venison sold.[118]

In addition to any sentence passed, a convicting court may order the forfeiture of—
 12–18

"(a)　any deer or venison in respect of which the offence was committed or which was found[119] in the defendant's possession; and

(b)　any vehicle,[120] animal, weapon or other thing which—

(i)　was used to commit the offence, or

---

[108] DA 1991 s.7(2),(3),(4). The Secretary of State and agriculture minister acting jointly may by order, either generally or in respect of one species of deer, may amend this proviso by adding any conditions which must be satisfied or by varying or deleting any conditions attached (DA 1991 s7(5)(b)).

[109] No definition is given of "enclosed land" but see para.10–07 for a judicial interpretation in another context.

[110] DA 1991 s.4(4), (5).

[111] As well as police constables, including special police constables, "constables" includes others holding that office, e.g. harbour constables. The hallmark of a constable is his attestation as such before, usually, a Magistrate.

[112] "Vehicle" includes an aircraft, hovercraft or boat (DA 1991 s.16).

[113] "Venison" includes imported venison and means (a) any carcass of a deer or (b) any edible part of the carcass of a deer which in either case has not been cooked or canned (DA 1991 s.16).

[114] DA 1991 s.12(1). For police powers of general application, see para.11–07.

[115] "Land" includes building and other structures, land covered with water, and any estate, interest, easement, servitude or right in or over land (Interpretation Act (IA) 1978 s.5 and Sch.1).

[116] DA 1991 s.12(2). For the powers of arrest, see the Police and Criminal Evidence Act 1984 s.24.

[117] "Venison" includes imported venison and means (a) any carcass of a deer or (b) any edible part of the carcass of a deer which in either case has not been cooked or canned (DA 1991 s.16).

[118] DA 1991 s.12(3).

[119] "Found" presumably refers to things found by a constable and seized or detained by him under the powers described at para.11–07.

[120] "Vehicle" includes an aircraft, hovercraft or boat (DA 1991 s.16).

(ii)   was capable of being used to take, kill or injure deer and was found in the defendant's possession.[121]"

Deer poaching

12–19   The following acts are, subject to the exemptions mentioned below, made offences by the Deer Act 1991:

(1)   To enter land[122] in search or pursuit of any deer[123] with the intention of taking, killing or injuring it.[124]

(2)   While on any land—

     (a)   intentionally to take, kill or injure, or attempt to take, kill or injure, any deer; *or*

     (b)   to search for or pursue any deer with the intention of taking, killing or injuring it; *or*

     (c)   to remove the carcass of any deer.[125]

     But these offences are not perpetrated if the person committing the act—

     (a)   has the consent of the owner or occupier of the land; *or*

     (b)   has lawful authority[126] to do it[127]; *or*

     (c)   believes that he would have the consent of the owner or occupier of the land if the owner or occupier knew of his doing the act and the circumstances of it; *or*

     (d)   believes that he has other lawful authority[128] to do the act.[129]

12–20   If an authorised person[130] suspects with reasonable cause that another person is committing or has committed any of these offences on any land, he may require that person to give his full name and address and to leave the land at once; the failure to comply with those requests is an offence.[131]

The powers of convicting courts and of the police in relation to deer poaching are as given at paras 12–17 to 12–18, but, in addition, a court may cancel any firearm or shot gun certificate held by the convicted person.[132] Where a court

---

[121] DA 1991 s.13(1).

[122] "Land" includes building and other structures, land covered with water, and any estate, interest, easement, servitude or right in or over land (IA 1978 s.5 and Sch.1).

[123] "Deer" means deer of any species and includes the carcass of any deer or any part of the carcass (DA 1991 s.16).

[124] DA 1991 s.1(1).

[125] DA 1991 s.1(2).

[126] No definition or explanation of "lawful authority" is given, but these words would cover acts by a tenant holding rights to kill or take deer on the land, or by Ministry of Agriculture officers acting under powers given to them to deal with animal diseases.

[127] DA 1991 s.1(1), (2).

[128] For the belief to be effective as a defence, it is suggested that, though the belief may be mistaken, it must be honestly and reasonably held.

[129] DA 1991 s.1(3).

[130] "Authorised person" is defined as the owner or occupier of the land or a person authorised by either of them, and includes any person having the right to take or kill deer on the land (DA 1991 s.1(5)).

[131] DA 1991 s.1(4). This provision does not enable an authorised person to eject the suspected person, but an owner or occupier of the land, or an employee acting under their orders, may eject a trespasser at common law, using only such force as is necessary.

[132] DA 1991 s.13(2).

cancels a firearm or shot gun certificate the court shall give notice in writing to the chief officer of police by whom the certificate was granted. That officer shall require, by notice in writing, the holder to surrender that certificate. If the holder fails to surrender the certificate within twenty-one days from the date of that requirement, he shall be guilty of an offence.[133]

CONSERVATION OF SEALS ACT 1970

As of January 31, 2011, this Act has been repealed in respect of Scotland only. **12–21** The regime for the protection of seals in Scotland is now dealt with by the Marine (Scotland) Act 2010. This regime will be considered later. The Conservation of Seals Act 1970 does not extend to Northern Ireland.

It is an offence to use, or attempt to use, for the purpose of killing, injuring or taking any seal,[134] any firearm[135] other than a rifle using ammunition[136] having a muzzle energy of not less than 600 foot pounds and a bullet weighing not less than 45 grains.[137] The following defences are available in respect of this offence:

(1) In the case of killing a seal, that it had been so seriously disabled otherwise than by an act of the killer that there was no reasonable chance of its recovering.[138]
(2) That the act done was authorised by a licence granted by the Home Office.[139]
(3) That the act was done outside the seaward limits of the territorial waters adjacent to Great Britain.[140]

The annual close seasons for seals are as follows: **12–22**

Grey seals (*Halichoerusgrypus*): September 1 to December 31
Common seals (*Phocavitulina*): June 1 to August 31.[141]

---

[133] DA 1991 s.13(3). The maximum punishment on summary conviction is a fine not exceeding level 2 on the standard scale (currently £500).

[134] Although this means all seals, the grey and common seals are the only species known to inhabit the coasts of Britain.

[135] This word has the same meaning as in the Firearms Act 1968 (CSA 1970 s.15), as to which see Ch.1.

[136] This word has the same meaning as in the Firearms Act 1968 (CSA 1970 s.15), as to which see Ch.1.

[137] CSA 1970 ss.1(1), 8(1). The descriptions given of firearms and ammunition may be altered by order of the Home Office (CSA 1970 s.1(2)). The maximum punishment on summary conviction is a fine at level 4 on the standard scale (currently £2500) (CSA 1970 s.5(2)).

[138] CSA 1970 ss.1(1), 9(2).

[139] CSA 1970 ss.1(1), 10. For further details of such a licence, see para.12–23 below.

[140] CSA 1970 s.17(2). For the extent of territorial waters, see para.12–03 above.

[141] CSA 1970 s.2(1). All dates are inclusive.

It is an offence wilfully[142] to kill or injure, or attempt to kill or injure, these seals during their close seasons.[143] The killing, injuring or taking of seals is also an offence if done at any time of the year in an area designated for the conservation of seals by way of a Home Office order.[144] One such order, which affects grey seals and common seals, is currently in force. In general terms, it extends to counties and metropolitan districts in England which border the North Sea and to their territorial waters.[145]

The following defences are available to an accused for either a close season offence or an offence under the terms of the Home Office 1996 order:

(i)   That the killing or injuring of the seal was unavoidable and the incidental result of a lawful action.[146]

(ii) That the killing or attempted killing of any seal was to prevent it from causing damage to a fishing net or fishing tackle in the accused's possession or in the possession of a person at whose request he killed or attempted to kill the seal, or to any fish for the time being in such fishing net, provided that at the time of the killing or attempted killing the seal was in the vicinity of such net or tackle.[147]

(iii) The defences described in items (1), (2) and (3) at para.12–21 above.[148]

12–23   The Home Office may grant a licence to any person to kill or take seals and, provided this is done within the terms and conditions of the licence, no offence will be committed. The purposes for which a licence may be given are:

(a)   For scientific or educational purposes;
(b)   for preventing damage to fisheries;
(c)   for preventing a population surplus of seals for management purposes;
(d)   for using a population surplus of seals as a resource; or
(e)   for the protection of flora and fauna in certain areas.

In all cases, the licence will authorise a killing or taking in the area described in the licence which will also specify the means to be used and the number of seals to be killed or taken.[149] The licence may be revoked at any time by the

---

[142] This means deliberately and intentionally, and not by accident or inadvertence (*R. v Senior* [1899] 1 Q.B. 283 at pp.290–91). Although this case involved offences concerning the welfare of children it is submitted that the interpretation of the term 'wilfully' shall apply equally to animal welfare cases.
[143] CSA 1970 ss.2(2), 8(1). The maximum punishment on summary conviction is a fine at level 4 on the standard scale (currently £2,500) (CSA 1970 s.5(2)).
[144] CSA 1970 ss.3, 8(1). The maximum punishment on summary conviction is a fine at level 4 on the standard scale (currently £2,500) (CSA 1970 s.5(2)).
[145] Conservation of Seals (England) Order 1999. The order defines precisely the area in which it has effect. For the extent of territorial waters, see para.12–02 above.
[146] CSA 1970 ss.2(2), 3(2), 9(1)(b).
[147] CSA 1970 ss.2(2), 3(2), 9(1)(c).
[148] CSA 1970 ss.2(2), 3(2), 9(2), 10, 17(2). A further defence is available to a person who takes or attempts to take a seal which has been disabled otherwise than by his act, if it was taken or to be taken solely for the purpose of tending it and releasing it when no longer disabled (CSA 1970 ss.2(2), 3(2), 9(1)(a)).
[149] CSA 1970 s.10(1). The use of strychnine cannot be authorised by a licence. The taking of seals for a zoological garden or a collection may also be covered by a licence.

Home Office.[150] A person who: contravenes, attempts to contravene, or fails to comply with, any condition of the licence commits an offence.[151]

Any person, who, for the purpose of committing any of the offences described,[152] has in his possession,[153] or attempts to have in his possession, any poisonous substance or any prohibited firearm or ammunition[154] commits an offence.[155]

12–24

A court convicting a person of any of the offences described[156] may order the forfeiture of any seal or seal skin in respect of which the offence was committed, or any seal, seal skin, firearm, ammunition or poisonous substance in his possession[157] at the time of the offence.[158]

Constables[159] are given wide powers to enforce the Act. They may stop any person suspected by them with reasonable cause of committing any of the offences described and may—

(1)   without warrant arrest that person if he fails to give his name and address to the constable's satisfaction;

(2)   without warrant search any vehicle or boat which that person may be using at the time he is stopped by the constable; and

(3)   seize any seal, seal skin, firearm, ammunition or poisonous substance which is liable to be forfeited by order of a court as described above.[160]

A constable may also sell or otherwise dispose of any seal seized in this way, and the net proceeds of sale are liable to forfeiture in the same manner as the seal sold.[161]

---

[150] No reasons for revocation are laid down, thus giving the Home Office a free hand in this respect. Before granting a licence, the Home Office must consult English Nature or the Countryside Council for Wales. The consent of these bodies is required prior to granting a licence in National Parks, sites of scientific interest or marine nature reserves except where the licence is granted to prevent damage to fisheries (CSA 1970 s.10(3)).

[151] CSA 1970 ss.8(1), 10(2). The maximum punishment on summary conviction is a fine at level 4 on the standard scale (currently £2,500) (CSA 1970 s.5(2)). Prosecution for this offence will not affect liability for another penalty under this or any other Act.

[152] And also the offences of wilfully obstructing or attempting to obstruct the entry on land or water of a person authorised in writing to enter by the Minister of Agriculture (CSA 1970 ss.8(1), 11(7)).

[153] For commentary on the meaning of "possession", though in another context, see para.3–07.

[154] i.e. any firearm or ammunition other than the types described at para.12–21.

[155] CSA 1970 ss.1(1)(b), 8. The maximum punishment on summary conviction is a fine at level 4 on the standard scale (currently £2,500) (CSA 1970 s.5(2)).

[156] And also the offences of wilfully obstructing or attempting to obstruct the entry on land or water of a person authorised in writing to enter by the Minister of Agriculture (CSA 1970 ss.8(1), 11(7)).

[157] For commentary on the meaning of "possession", though in another context, see para.3–07.

[158] CSA 1970 s.6.

[159] As well as police constables, including special police constables, "constables" includes others holding that office, e.g. harbour constables. The hallmark of a constable is his attestation as such before, usually, a Magistrate.

[160] CSA 1970 s.4(1).

[161] CSA 1970 s.4(2). For police powers of general application, see para.11–07.

MARINE (SCOTLAND) ACT 2010

12–25   Part 6 of the Marine (Scotland) Act 2010 now governs the conservation of seals in Scotland. Killing, injuring or taking a live seal, either intentionally or recklessly, is an offence.[162] However, it shall not be an offence for a person to end a seal's life humanely (or to injure a seal when attempting to do so) provided that it has been seriously disabled (otherwise than by the person's unlawful conduct), it has no reasonable chance of recovering, and ending its life is the only satisfactory way to end its suffering and is not detrimental to the maintenance of the population of any species of seal at a favourable conservation status in their natural range (within the meaning of art.1(e) of the Habitats Directive).[163]

    Similarly, it shall not be an offence to take a seal (or to kill or injure a seal when attempting to take it) if it has been seriously disabled (otherwise than by the person's unlawful conduct), it is to be taken only in order to tend it with a view to releasing it when it is recovered or release it after it has been tended, it is taken in a manner and in circumstances unlikely to cause the seal to suffer unnecessarily and taking it is the only satisfactory way to help it recover, and is not detrimental to the maintenance of the population of any species of seal at a favourable conservation status in their natural range (within the meaning of art.1(e) of the Habitats Directive).[164] It is the duty of anyone killing or taking a seal lawfully in the manner described above to report the matter to the Scottish Ministers as soon as reasonably practical after doing so.[165] The failure to do so shall be an offence.[166]

12–26   It shall not be an offence to kill or take a seal in accordance with a seal licence.[167] Scottish Ministers have the power to grant seal licenses authorising the killing or taking of seals for a variety of reasons described in the Act.[168] A seal licence must specify the method which the licensee must use to kill or take seals and Scottish Ministers must not grant a seal licence authorising a person to kill seals by shooting unless they are satisfied that the person has adequate skills and experience in using firearms.[169]

    A seal licence which authorises the killing of seals by shooting must impose conditions—

(a)   specifying the type of firearm which must be used,

(b)   specifying the weather conditions in which a person may attempt to shoot a seal,

(c)   specifying how close a person must be to a seal before attempting to shoot it,

---

[162] M(S)A 2010 s107. A person guilty of this offence is liable on summary conviction to imprisonment for a term not exceeding six months or to a fine not exceeding level 5 on the standard scale (currently £5,000), or to both (M(S)A 2010 s.128(1)).

[163] M(S)A 2010 s.108(1).

[164] M(S)A 2010 s.108(2).

[165] M(S)A 2010 s.108(3).

[166] M(S)A 2010 s.108(4). A person guilty of this offence is liable, on summary conviction, to a fine not exceeding level 4 on the standard scale (currently £2,500) (M(S)A 2010 s.128(2)).

[167] M(S)A 2010 s.109.

[168] M(S)A 2010 s.110.

[169] M(S)A 2010 s.111(1) and (2).

(d)   prohibiting a person from attempting to shoot a seal from an unstable platform, and

(e)   about the recovery of carcasses.[170]

There are reporting requirements for those who hold seal licences and the failure, without reasonable excuse, to send a seal licence report is an offence.[171] A seal licence may be varied or revoked at any time.[172]   **12–27**

Harassing a seal (intentionally or recklessly) at a haul-out site is an offence. The term "haul-out site" is defined as any place which the Scottish Ministers, after consulting the Natural Environment Research Council, by order designate as such.[173]

A court convicting a person of any of the offences detailed above may order the forfeiture of any seal or seal skin in respect of which the offence was committed, or anything, which the person possessed or controlled at the time of the offence which was capable of being used in connection with the offence.[174] A constable may stop any person who he suspects with reasonable cause of committing any of the offences described above and may—

(a)   without warrant, search any vehicle or vessel which the constable reasonably believes to have been used in connection with the commission of the offence,

(b)   seize any seal, seal skin or other thing liable to be forfeited as described above.[175]

PROTECTION OF BADGERS ACT 1992

This Act states that it is an offence[176] wilfully[177] to kill or injure, or to attempt to kill or injure, any badger.[178] If, in a prosecution for attempt, there is evidence from which it could be reasonably concluded that at the material time the accused   **12–28**

---

[170] M(S)A 2010 s.112(2).

[171] M(S)A 2010 s.113. A person guilty of this offence is liable, on summary conviction, to imprisonment for a term not exceeding 3 months or to a fine not exceeding level 5 on the standard scale (currently £5,000), or to both (M(S)A 2010 s.128(3)).

[172] M(S)A 2010 s.114.

[173] M(S)A 2010 s.117. A person guilty of this offence is liable, on summary conviction, to imprisonment for a term not exceeding six months or to a fine not exceeding level 5 (currently £5,000) on the standard scale, or to both (M(S)A 2010 s.128(1)).

[174] M(S)A 2010 s.127.

[175] M(S)A 2010 s.126.

[176] The maximum punishment on summary conviction is a term of imprisonment not exceeding six months' and/or a fine at level 5 on the standard scale (currently £5,000), for each badger against which the offence is committed (PBA 1992 s.12(1), (2)).

[177] This means deliberately and intentionally, and not by accident or inadvertence (*R. v Senior* [1899] 1 QB 283 at pp.290-91). In addition in Scotland pursuant to the Wildlife and Natural Environment (Scotland) Act 2011 s.33 a person will be guilty of an offence if they knowingly cause or permit any act rendered unlawful by s.1(1)–(3) of the Act to be done.

[178] PBA 1992 s.1(1). Except that in Scotland the words to 'attempt to kill or injure' have been repealed by Nature Conservation (Scotland) Act 2004 s.26(2)(a) and attempts are now classified as offences pursuant to s.11 of the 2004 Act. "Badger" means any animal of the species *melesmeles* (PBA 1992 s.14).

was attempting to kill or injure, he shall be presumed to have been so attempting unless the contrary is shown.[179] A number of defences are available and, so far as shooting is concerned, these are:

(1) In the case of a killing or attempted killing, or in the case of injuring a badger in the course of attempting to kill it, that the defendant can show that his action was necessary for the purpose of preventing serious damage to land,[180] crops, poultry or any other form of property; *but* this defence is *not* available in relation to any action taken at any time if it had become apparent, before that time, that that action would prove necessary for the purpose mentioned, *and either*

    (a) a licence authorising that action had not been applied for as soon as reasonably practicable after the fact of the action proving necessary had become apparent; *or*

    (b) an application for such a licence had been determined.[181]

(2) That it was a killing or attempted killing of a badger which appeared to be so seriously injured or in such a condition that to kill it would be an act of mercy.[182]

(3) That it was an unavoidable killing or injuring as an incidental result of a lawful action.[183]

(4) That the act was done under the authority of, and within the conditions of, a licence, the provisions for which are next considered.[184]

12–29   Licences related to shooting of badgers may be granted for the following purposes:

(i) For scientific or educational purposes, to kill within the area and by the means described in the licence, or to sell or have in the licensed person's possession the number of badgers stipulated by the licence.

(ii) For the purpose of preventing the spread of disease, to kill badgers within the area and by the means described in the licence.

(iii) For the purpose of preventing serious damage to land,[185] crops, poultry or any other form of property, to kill badgers within the area and by the means described in the licence.[186]

In the first case, licences are granted by Natural England or, in Wales, by the Countryside Council for Wales. In the last two cases, licences are issued by the

---

[179] PBA 1992 s.1(2). Except that this provision has been repealed with respect to Scotland by s.26(2)(b) NC(S)A 2004.

[180] "Land" includes buildings and other structures and land covered with water (IA 1978 s.5 and Sch.1).

[181] PBA 1992 s.7. For comment on the same defence in another context, see para.12–23 above.

[182] PBA 1992 s.6(b). Except that in Scotland the provision has been amended to read: "killing or attempting to kill a badger which has been so seriously disabled otherwise than by his unlawful act that there was no reasonable chance of it recovering" (s.26(4)(b) NC(S)A 2004).

[183] PBA 1992 s.6(c). An example of this defence would be an accident between a vehicle and a badger on a road.

[184] PBA 1992 ss.1(1), 10.

[185] "Land" includes buildings and other structures and land covered with water (IA 1978 s.5 and Sch.1).

[186] PBA 1992 s.10(1)(a), (2)(a), (b).

Regional Offices of the Ministry of Agriculture. A licence may be revoked at any time,[187] and breach of its conditions is an offence.[188]

The Protection of Badgers Act 1992 creates a number of other offences related to badgers, some with special defences, which will now be considered.

12–30

Unless permitted by or under the 1992 Act,[189] it is an offence[190] for any person to have in his possession,[191] or under his control, any dead badger or any part of, or anything derived from, a dead badger,[192] but it is a defence if the person shows that—

(a) the badger had not been killed[193]; *or*

(b) it had been killed otherwise than in contravention of the 1992 Act or the Badgers Act 1973[194]; *or*

(c) the object in the person's possession or control had been sold (whether to him or any other person) *and*, at the time of purchase, the purchaser had no reason to believe that the badger had been killed in contravention of the 1973 or 1992 Acts.[195]

Described as offences of cruelty,[196] the following acts are forbidden—[197]

12–31

(a) to cruelly ill-treat any badger;

(b) to use any badger tongs in the course of killing, or attempting to kill, any badger;

(c) to use, for the purpose of killing or taking any badger, any firearm[198] other than a smooth-bore weapon of not less than 20 bore or a rifle using ammunition[199] having a muzzle energy of not less than 160 foot pounds and a bullet weighing not less than 38 grains.[200]

---

[187] Licences may not be unreasonably withheld or revoked (PBA 1992 s.10(9)) but otherwise the issuing authorities have a free hand in these respects.

[188] PBA 1992 s.10(8). The maximum punishment on summary conviction is imprisonment of a term not exceeding six months and/or a fine at level 5 on the standard scale (currently £5,000) for each badger against which the offence is committed (PBA 1992 s.12(1), (2)).

[189] e.g. under the terms of a licence.

[190] The maximum punishment on summary conviction is imprisonment of a term not exceeding six months and/or a fine at level 5 on the standard scale (currently £5,000) for each badger against which the offence is committed (PBA 1992 s.12(1), (2)).

[191] For commentary on the meaning of "possession", though in another context, see para.3–07.

[192] PBA 1992 s.1(3).

[193] i.e. had died naturally.

[194] The Badgers Act 1973, which was repealed by the 1992 Act s.15(2), contained substantially the same provisions as the 1992 Act.

[195] PBA 1992 s.1(4).

[196] PBA 1992 s.2.

[197] The maximum punishment on summary conviction is a term of imprisonment not exceeding six months and/or a fine at level 5 on the standard scale (currently £5,000) for each badger against which the offence is committed (PBA 1992 s.12(1), (2)).

[198] The definitions of these words in the Firearms Act 1968 are applied (PBA 1992 s.4). For a discussion of them, see Ch.1.

[199] The definitions of these words in the Firearms Act 1968 are applied (PBA 1992 s.4). For a discussion of them, see Ch.1.

[200] PBA 1992 s.2(1). Digging for badgers is also forbidden unless permitted by or under the Act, e.g. by a licence (PBA 1992 s.2(1)(c)).

12–32   Constables[201] are given wide powers to enforce the legislation. If a constable has reasonable grounds for suspecting that any person is committing or had committed an offence under the 1973 or 1992 Acts *and* that evidence of the commission of the offence is to be found on that person or any vehicle or article he may have with him,[202] he may—

(1)   without a warrant stop and search that person and search any vehicle or article he may have with him; *and*
(2)   seize and detain for the purposes of a prosecution under the 1973 or 1992 Acts anything which may be evidence of the commission of the offence or which may be liable to be forfeited by a convicting court.[203]

12–33   On conviction of any offence under the Act the court *must* order forfeiture of any badger or badger's skin in respect of which the offence was committed, and *may* order forfeiture of weapons and articles connected with the offence.[204]

          If any person is found on land committing any of the offences described on this and the preceding page, the owner or occupier of the land, or an employee of either, or a constable, may require that person to leave the land at once and give his name and address. If the person then deliberately remains on the land or refuses to give his particulars, he commits an offence.[205]

OTHER LEGISLATION

12–34   It is an offence[206] to destroy or damage[207] wild creatures no longer in a wild state[208] "without lawful excuse".[209] A person shall be deemed to have a lawful excuse if at the time of the act he believed that the person or persons whom he believed to be entitled to consent to the destruction of or damage to the property in question had so consented, or would have so consented to it if he or they had known of the destruction or damage and its circumstances; or if he destroyed or damaged the property in order to protect property belonging to himself or another or a right or interest in property which was or which he believed to be vested in

---

[201] As well as police constables, including special police constables, "constables" includes others holding that office, e.g. harbour constables. The hallmark of a constable is his attestation as such before, usually, a Magistrate.

[202] For an interpretation of the words "have with him", though in another context, see para.14–11, fn.29.

[203] PBA 1992 s.11. For the powers of the police generally to make searches, etc. See para.11–07.

[204] PBA 1992 s.12(4).

[205] PBA 1992 s.1(5). The maximum punishment on summary conviction for this offence is a fine at level 3 on the standard scale (currently £1,000) (PBA 1992 s.12(3)).Note that this provision gives no right to the persons named forcibly to eject the offender from the land. If he is a trespasser, the common law powers of ejectment summarised at para.11–01 will apply.

[206] The maximum punishment on conviction is 10 years' imprisonment (Criminal Damage Act 1971 s.4).

[207] The word "damage" is used because the Act of Parliament creating the offence is primarily concerned with damage to lifeless property.

[208] i.e. tamed, ordinarily kept in captivity or otherwise reduced or being reduced into possession.

[209] CDA 1971 ss.1(1), (2), 5, 10(1)(a).

himself or another and that property was in need of immediate protection and the means of protection was reasonable in the circumstances.[210]

The Wild Mammals (Protection) Act 1996 lists several acts of cruelty against wild mammals which, if done with intent to inflict unnecessary suffering, constitute an offence.[211] Shooting is not one of those acts.

---

[210] CDA 1971 s.(10)(2).

[211] WMA 1996 s.1. The maximum punishments on summary conviction are a fine at level 5 on the standard scale (currently £5,000), or six months' imprisonment, or both (WMA 1996 s.5(1)).

CHAPTER 13

The Tenant's Right to Shoot

COMMON LAW RIGHTS

Under the **Common Law**, the right to possession of land carries with it the right   **13–01**
to take all birds and animals naturally on the land, whether they be game or not.[1]
Thus a land owner has such rights and he may reserve those rights to himself or
grant them to another. When he grants such game rights, the grantee may exercise
those rights in the same manner and to the same extent as the owner of the land.
Where the owner, whether in occupation or not, has let the shooting rights he has
no right at Common Law to shoot over the land. However, an owner in
occupation has a statutory right to shoot ground game.[2]

If the owner does not occupy his land but lets it to another under a tenancy
then, unless the shooting is "reserved" to the landlord, the tenant will have an
absolute right to shoot as against any other person. Conversely, if the right to take
game is "reserved", the tenant will have no right to shoot at Common Law.[3] This
rule is expressly preserved by the Game Act 1831.[4] Further, it is an offence under
that Act for an occupier to pursue, kill or take game, or to permit another to do so,
where the owner has reserved the game rights or granted them to another.[5]
However, any reservation of rights will be void in so far as it purports to exclude
the owner's rights to destroy ground game.[6] An occupier, such as a tenant, with
full shooting rights may authorise any person to kill and take game and other
birds and animals and may also let or assign his shooting rights.

---

[1] Rare exceptions to this rule apply where sporting rights are given to lords of manors under Inclosure
Acts and Awards.
[2] GGA 1880 s.1. 'Ground game' means hares and rabbits (GGA 1880 s.8).
[3] Unless he is expressly permitted to do so by the landlord.
[4] GA 1831 s.8, which also forbids the occupier to permit another person to shoot.
[5] GA 1831 s.1. The punishment for such an offence is a fine at level 1 on the standard scale, and a
person can be fined such an amount for each head of game so killed or taken.
[6] GGA 1880 s.3.

RIGHTS UNDER LEGISLATION

13–02   As can be seen above, the position at Common Law was much altered by the **Ground Game Act** passed in 1880. The objective of the Act was to allow tenants without shooting rights to protect their crops against hares and rabbits. It did so by permitting occupiers of land to kill and take ground game[7] on their land concurrently with any other person who may have the right to do the same thing.[8] Within certain limitations, tenants may also claim compensation from their landlords for damage to crops caused by any wild animals or birds.[9] There are some extensions to, and several limitations on, this right of the occupier to take ground game, and these will now be considered.

Firstly, who shall be deemed an occupier for the purposes of the Act? Clearly, an occupying owner, tenant or sub-tenant of land will be. The Act says that a person having a right of common or "an occupation for the purpose of grazing or pasturage of sheep, cattle, or horses for not more than nine months" will not be an occupier.[10] It would seem to follow from this that if the occupation for the purposes quoted exceeds nine months, the occupier will be qualified under the Act. However, this proposition has been questioned and the contrary view put that the occupier must have the right to full possession of the land and not a limited right to its use, as in the case of a licensee.[11] Doubts also arise in cases where land is used for grazing other animals such as goats and pigs. Where there are joint occupiers, all are entitled to the rights conferred by the Act.[12]

13–03   In addition to the occupier, the occupier can authorise one other person in writing[13] to shoot[14] ground game.[15] This person can only be—

(1)   a member of the occupier's household[16] resident[17] on the land in his occupation, the shooting authority extending only to that land; or

(2)   a person in the occupier's ordinary service[18] on the land occupied, the shooting authority extending only to that land; or

---

[7] "Ground game" means hares and rabbits (GGA 1880 s.8).

[8] GGA 1880 s.1.

[9] AHA 1986 s.20.

[10] GGA 1880 s.1(2).

[11] See *Oke's Game Laws*, 5th edition, p.103.

[12] See *Oke's Game Laws*, 5th edition, pp.101–2.

[13] The authority needs not be in any prescribed form, and no provision expressly requires it to be signed or dated, but it would be desirable for it to describe the person to whom it is given and precisely state the situation and extent of the land over which it is to operate.

[14] More than one person may, however, be authorised to take ground game otherwise than by using firearms.

[15] GGA 1880 s.1(1)(a). Where there are joint occupiers, it seems that all must give their authority to one other person to shoot and that each cannot authorise a different person (*Oke's Game Laws*, 5th edition, p.102).

[16] This will include servants who live and board at the house, but not those living in other houses on the farm (*Re Drax, Savile v Yeatman* (1887) 57 LT 475; *Ogle v Morgan* (1852) 1 De GM & G 359).

[17] This is a question of fact and could include a visitor staying at the house but presumably not one who comes for a day. A person invited to stay for a week and shoot rabbits for one week was held to satisfy the condition of residence (*Stuart v Murray* (1884) 12 R 9, Ct of Sess.).

[18] "Ordinary service" is not further defined in the Act but presumably means those in regular service so as to exclude casual labour but may include labour regularly employed for a certain season only.

(3)   any one other person *bona fide* employed by the occupier for reward[19] in the taking and destruction of ground game.[20]

More than one person from classes (1) and (2) above, but only one from class (3), may, at the same time, kill and take ground game otherwise than by shooting if, again, they are authorised in writing by the occupier.[21] Only one person, aside from the occupier himself, may be authorised by him to kill ground game with firearms.[22]

An authorised person must produce his written authority, if asked to do so, to any person having a concurrent right to take or kill ground game on the land or to any person authorised by the latter in writing to make the demand. In default, the authorised person's rights cease.[23]   **13–04**

In the case of moorlands and unenclosed non-arable land, except detached portions of either which are less than 25 acres in extent and adjoin arable lands, the time at which the right of the occupier to kill ground game may be exercised is limited. Between December 11 of one year and March 31 (both inclusive) of the following year the right may be exercised and ground game may be killed in any legal way by the occupier and persons authorised by him in accordance with the Act.[24] Between April 1 and August 31 (both inclusive) the right is suspended altogether. Between September 1 and December 10 (both inclusive) the right may be exercised otherwise than by the use of firearms.[25] The occupier may make an agreement with the owner of, or any other person having the right to take game on, lands of this description, for the joint exercise, or the exercise for their joint benefit, of the right to kill and take ground game within this period of the year.[26]

The occupier of land, *or one other person*[27] authorised by him, may now[28] use firearms[29] to kill hares and rabbits at night[30] on that land if—

(a)   the occupier has the exclusive right to kill and take hares and rabbits on the land; *or*

---

[19] The fact of, for example, a rabbit-catcher being allowed to keep all or some of the rabbits taken would probably be sufficient evidence of such employment for reward (*Bruce v Prosser* (1898) 35 Sc LR 433), but a similar gift to a friend asked to come and shoot would hardly be so. Further, the person must be definitely employed for this purpose, verbal instructions to kill ground game is insufficient and shall be a trespass (*Richardson v Maitland* (1897) 34 S.L.R. 426).

[20] GGA 1880 s.1(1)(b).

[21] GGA 1880 s.1(1)(b).

[22] GGA 1880 s1(1)(a).

[23] GGA 1880 s.1(1)(c).

[24] GGA 1880 s.1(3).

[25] GGA 1906 s.2. This Act refers to the occupier only whereas GGA 1880 s.1(3) also mentions persons authorised by him. Thus, it seems, only the occupier himself may take ground game, otherwise than by shooting, between September 1 and December 10.

[26] GGA 1906 s.3.

[27] Who must be a person within one of the descriptions given in items (1)–(3) at para.13–03 above. As to the form of authority, see the suggestions at para.13–03, fn.13 above.

[28] Since February 16, 1982 after the WCA 1981 came into effect. Previously, what is now permitted was, for occupying tenants, an offence.

[29] The definition of "firearm" discussed in Ch.1 applies (FA 1968 s.57(1); WCA 1981 ss.12, 27(1) and Sch.7, para.1(1)).

[30] From one hour after sunset to one hour before sunrise (WCA 1981 s.12 and Sch.7, para.1(1)).

(b)   the occupier has the written authority[31] of the other person, or one of the other persons,[32] who has that right.[33]

13–05   However, where the above does not apply, any occupier of land (other than the owner) who is entitled to kill ground game, either by virtue of the Ground Game Act or because the rights have not been reserved, uses firearms in the exercise of this right between the expiration of the first hour after sunset and the commencement of the last hour of sunrise, will be guilty of an offence.[34]

The Ground Game Act 1880 is at pains to ensure that an occupier retains the shooting rights which it gives to him. Thus, if an occupier has the right to shoot hares and rabbits, otherwise than by the powers given to him by the Act, and he transfers that right to another person, he nevertheless retains his statutory shooting rights.[35] Again, any agreement, condition or arrangement which tries to divest the occupier of his rights under the Act, or which gives him an advantage in return for his forbearing to exercise those rights, is declared to be void.[36] As the Act twice declares,[37] the rights which it gives to the occupier are "incident (*sic*) to and inseparable from" his occupation of the land.

13–06   On the other hand, nothing in the Ground Game Act 1880 operates so as to restrict the occupier's shooting rights to those rights which it gives to him. An occupier may still acquire, and exercise, the right to shoot ground game and other game and shall not be limited by the restrictions contained in the Act.[38] This means, for example, that an occupying tenant, whose lease does not reserve shooting rights to his landlord, may shoot ground game with freedom from the restrictions which the Act would impose if his right to shoot was acquired solely from the provisions of the Act.

Where the occupier has no shooting rights (except those given to him by the Ground Game Act) and he shoots game,[39] other than hares and rabbits, or gives permission to any other person to do so, and does so without, in either case, the authority of the person who has the right of killing that game, then he shall commit an offence.[40]

---

[31] Impliedly, this will be an authority to the occupier to use firearms at night for the purpose described; which need not, it is suggested, embrace others whom the occupier himself might authorise under this provision.

[32] As to who these persons may be, see para.13–03 above. As to the form of authority see para.13–03, fn.13.

[33] WCA 1981 s.12 and Sch.7, para.1.

[34] GGA 1880 s.6. The punishment for an offence of this nature is a fine not exceeding level 1 on the standard scale (currently £200).

[35] GGA 1880 s.2. This means that both persons have concurrent rights to shoot hares and rabbits.

[36] GGA 1880 s.3.

[37] GGA 1880 ss.1 and 2.

[38] GGA 1880 s.2.

[39] Game in this context includes hares, pheasants, partridges, grouse, heath or moor game and black game (GA 1831 s.2). Note that "includes" has been interpreted in some statutory contexts to mean exclusively the things mentioned after it.

[40] GA 1831 s.12. The maximum punishment on summary conviction is a fine at level 1 on the standard scale (currently £200) plus a similar fine for each head of game so taken.

CHAPTER 14

Young People and Guns

INTRODUCTION

To all the other regulations and restrictions affecting the use of guns and their ammunition Parliament has added special provisions for young people under 18 years of age.[1] These provisions vary according to age, depending upon whether the person is under 14, under 15, under 17 or under 18, vary again according to the kind of act done in relation to firearms and ammunition, and vary yet again according to the type of firearm or ammunition which is involved. A number of offences are created, many of them with exceptions. This produces a complex situation which may perhaps best be examined by considering each of the offences in turn and seeing how each applies to the different age groups and what exceptions each may have. For further clarity, a table is given at para.14–14 of this chapter dealing with all these elements in summary form.

    The general exceptions to firearms' law in the cases of the Proof Houses and antique firearms, which are considered at the end of Ch.1, apply to young people as to others. It must be borne in mind that the possession of and other dealings

14–01

---

[1] FA 1968 ss.22-24A, as amended by the Anti-Social Behaviour Act 2003 and the Violent Crime Reduction Act 2006. A person attains a particular age expressed in years at the beginning of the relevant anniversary of the date of his birth (Family Law Reform Act 1969 s.9(1)). Thus, a person becomes 18 at the midnight immediately preceding his 18th birthday.

with firearms by young people which are permitted under the headings now to be discussed will nevertheless in many cases be illegal unless covered by the necessary firearm or shot gun certificate, the need for which is discussed in Chs 3 and 4. To be granted a firearm certificate a young person will need to be aged 14 or over, but a shotgun certificate may be granted at an earlier age (see *Guidance* Ch.7). In our experience, it would be highly exceptional for a shotgun certificate to be granted to a child aged less than 12.

FIREARMS AND AMMUNITION

14–02   Both these words are given lengthy definitions in the Firearms Act of 1968 and are fully discussed in Ch.1. These definitions catch all ordinary kinds of firearms and ammunition (including, as we shall see, restrictions on air weapons) and, in the case of firearms, component parts and accessories for reducing noise or flash are included. Imitation Firearms and Realistic Imitation Firearms fulfilling the conditions described in Ch.9 will also be subject to the following rules.

Buying or hiring

14–03   It is an offence:—

(a)   for a person under the age of 18 to purchase or hire an air weapon or ammunition for an air weapon.
(b)   for a person under the age of 17 to purchase or hire a firearm or ammunition of any other description.[2]
(c)   for a person under 18 to purchase an imitation firearm.[3]

There are also corresponding offences for any person to sell[4] or let on hire any firearm or ammunition to a youngster under 17, or an air weapon or ammunition for it to a youngster under 18, or an imitation firearm to a youngster under 18,[5] unless the supplier can prove that he believed the youngster to be of or over that age, and had reasonable ground for the belief.[6]

---

[2] FA 1968 s.22(1), as amended by the VCRA 2006, s.33. The maximum punishment on summary conviction is six months' imprisonment, or a fine at level 5 on the standard scale (currently £5,000), or both (FA 1968 s.51(1), (2) and Sch.6 Pt I).

[3] FA 1968 s.24A(1), as amended by the VCRA 2006, s.40.The maximum punishment on summary conviction is six months' imprisonment, or a fine at level 5 on the standard scale, or both (FA 1968 s.51(1), (2) and Sch.6 Pt I as amended by VCRA 2006, s.40(2)).

[4] A sale, a condition of which is that the seller retains possession of the firearm and where the seller in fact retains subsequent physical possession, allowing the buyer only to have it to use at a rifle club, is nevertheless a sale for the purpose of this offence (*Watts v Seymour* [1967] 1 All E.R. 1044).

[5] FA 1968 s.24(1) & 24A(2), as amended by the VCRA 2006, s.33 & 40.

[6] FA 1968 s.24(1), (5) and, in relation to imitation firearms, s.24A(3 & 4). The maximum punishment for the supplier is the same as for the young person purchasing or hiring the relevant item.

Possession

Youngsters aged 14 or over may have s.1 firearms or s.1 ammunition[7] in their **14–04** possession.[8] Those under 14 are allowed to possess those firearms and that ammunition (including muzzle-loading pistols and their ammunition) only in the following situations[9]:

(1) They may carry any firearm or ammunition belonging to a person holding a firearm certificate or shot gun certificate, the carrying being under instructions from, and for the use of, that person for sporting purposes only.[10]

(2) As a member of an approved rifle club,[11] he may possess a rifle and ammunition for it, and use them, whilst engaged as such a member in connection with target shooting.[12]

(3) For conducting or carrying on a miniature rifle range (whether for a rifle club or otherwise) or shooting gallery at which, in either case, no firearms are used other than air weapons[13] or miniature rifles not exceeding .23 inch calibre, a person under 14 may have in his possession such miniature rifles and ammunition suitable for them; and he and other persons may use there those rifles and that ammunition.[14]

It is an offence for a person to part with the possession of s.1 firearms and s.1 **14–05** ammunition to any child under the age of 14, except in those cases where the under-14 is allowed to have possession as described above.[15] It will be a defence for the accused person to prove that he believed the child to be aged at least 14 and had reasonable ground for the belief.[16]

It is an offence for a youngster under the age of 18 in possession of a firearm as the holder of a firearm or shot gun certificate to use it for a purpose not authorised by the European Weapons Directive.[17] The authorised purposes are: sporting purposes; shooting of vermin, or other activities in the connection with the management of any estate, or other wildlife; target shooting and competitions.[18]

---

[7] For the meanings of "s.1 firearm" and "s.1 ammunition", see Ch.3.

[8] For commentary on the meaning of "possession" see para.3–07.

[9] Otherwise an offence is committed; FA 1968 s.22(2), as amended by the F(A)A 1988, s.23(4). The maximum punishment on summary conviction is six months' imprisonment, or a fine at level 5 on the standard scale (currently £5,000), or both.

[10] FA 1968 s.11(1), 22(2). This is intended to cover 'gun bearers' and only allows carrying but not use of the firearm and ammunition by the youngster. The shooting of rats in a barn is not shooting for a 'sporting purpose' (*Morton v Chaney* [1960] 3 All E.R. 632), although as Dr. Barry Peachey, the wildlife expert, once observed of the judge who made this decision, "His Lordship had obviously never tried it"!

[11] As to the approval of rifle clubs, see para.3–11.

[12] FA 1968 ss.22(2)& 11(3), as amended by F(A)A 1988 s.15.

[13] This means any air gun, air rifle or air pistol, not being of a type declared by rules made by the Home Office to be specially dangerous (FA 1968 ss.1(3)(b), 57(4)).

[14] FA 1968 ss.11(4), 22(2). At a fairground for example.

[15] FA 1968 ss.11(1), (4), 22(2), 24(2)(b). For the maximum punishment, see fn.9 above.

[16] FA 1968 s.24(5).

[17] FA 1968 s.22(1A); Firearms Acts (Amendment) Regulations.1992, reg.4(1). "European Weapons Directive" means European Council's Directive 91/477/EEC.

[18] FA 1968 s.57 (4A), SI 1992/2823.

Gifts and loans

14–06   A person may not make a gift of or lend s.1 firearms or s.1 ammunition[19] to a youngster aged under 14. To do so is an offence[20] unless the person accused can prove that he believed the youngster to be 14 or over and had reasonable ground for that belief.

It is no longer expressly made an offence for a child under 14 to accept a gift or loan in a case where the donor or lender commits an offence though, technically, if the child assists the offender, the child is guilty as an accessory to the offence.

SHOT GUNS AND SHOT GUN AMMUNITION

14–07   The definition of "shot gun" is given in Ch.4; "shot gun ammunition" must be given the meaning set out in (a) at para.3–05.

Gifts

14–08   A person may make a gift of a shot gun or shot gun ammunition to a youngster aged 15 or over, but not to one aged under 15.[21] Again, it is a defence if the accused person can prove that he believed the youngster to be 15 or over and had reasonable ground for that belief.[22]

Having an assembled shot gun

14–09   A child aged less than 15 must not have an assembled shot gun with him[23] except while under the supervision of a person at least 21 years old or while the gun is so covered with a securely fastened gun cover that it cannot be fired.[24] Youngsters of 15 and over may have assembled shot guns with them without either of these restrictions. The person 'supervising' does not need to be a certificate holder (although the youngster has to be), but we suggest the supervisor cannot be someone who is 'prohibited' under s.21 of the Act, see Ch.5.

---

[19] For the meanings of "s.1 firearm" and "s.1 ammunition", see Ch.3.

[20] FA 1968 s.24(2)(a). The maximum punishment on summary conviction is six months' imprisonment, or a fine at level 5 on the standard scale (currently £5,000), or both.

[21] FA 1968 s.24(3). The maximum punishment on summary conviction is a fine at level 3 on the standard scale (currently £1,000) (FA 1968 s.51(1), (2) and Sch.6 Pt I).

[22] FA 1968 s.24(5).

[23] It seems that the words "with him" will cover the case of a gun being on or in a vehicle carrying a youngster. He will only be liable for conviction if he knew that the gun was with him (*R. v Cugullere* [1961] 2 All E.R. 343). See also para.14–11.

[24] FA 1968 s.22(3). The maximum punishment is as per in fn.21 above.

AIR WEAPONS AND AIR WEAPON AMMUNITION

The following rules about young persons having air weapons and ammunition with them and about gifts of these to them relate only to air weapons not declared to be specially dangerous[25] and to air weapon ammunition generally.[26] If they are specially dangerous, they fall into the same category, for the purposes of this chapter, as s.1 firearms and must be considered under the heading "Firearms and ammunition" at para.14–02.   **14–10**

In the following paragraphs "air weapon" means an air rifle, air gun or air pistol,[27] and will include an air weapon powered by compressed carbon dioxide.[28]

Having possession of an air weapon and its ammunition in a public place and elsewhere

No person under the age of 18 shall have with him[29] an air weapon or ammunition for it, unless either;   **14–11**

(1)   The youngster is engaged in connection with target shooting as a member of a rifle club or miniature rifle club, and that club is approved by the Home Office.

(2)   The youngster is using the air weapon at a shooting gallery where the only firearms used are either air weapons which are not specially dangerous or miniature rifles not exceeding .23 inches in calibre.[30]

(3)   The youngster may have with him on any premises an air weapon and ammunition for it, provided he is under the supervision of a person aged at least 21.[31] However, if the air weapon is used to fire a missile beyond those premises,[32] both the young person and the supervisor should be aware they will each be liable for an offence.[33] That said, it shall be a defence if it can be shown that the only premises into or across which the missile was fired were premises the occupier of which had given their consent to the firing of the missile (whether specifically or by way of general consent).[34]

Note in these circumstances there is no lower age limit. In relation to item (3) above, a child aged 14 or over does not require the supervision of an

---

[25]   For details, see para.3–01.

[26]   FA 1968 ss.22(4), (5), 23, 24(4), 57(4).

[27]   FA 1968 ss.1(3)(b), 57(4).

[28]   F(A)A 1997 s.48.

[29]   It seems that the words "with him" will cover the case of a gun being on or in a vehicle carrying a youngster. He will only be liable for conviction if he knew that the gun was with him (*R. v Cugullere* [1961] 2 All E.R. 343).

[30]   FA 1968 ss.22(4), 23(2), as amended by s.33 VCRA 2006. It would appear that these two provisions permit the young person under 18 to have the air weapon and ammunition with them in a public place if they are in transit for either of these purposes.

[31]   FA 1968 s.23(1).

[32]   The word "premises" is defined as including any land (FA 1968 s.57(4)).

[33]   FA 1968 ss.21A & 23(1) as amended by s.34 VCRA 2006. The maximum punishment on summary conviction is a fine at level 3 on the standard scale (currently £1,000) (FA 1968 s.51(1), (2) and Sch.6, Pt I).

[34]   FA 1968 s.21A(2) as amended by VCRA 2006 s.34(2).

adult, provided he has the air weapon and ammunition with him on private premises and with the consent of the occupier.[35]

Parting with possession of an air weapon and its ammunition to a youngster

14–12   It is an offence to part with the possession of an air weapon or air weapon ammunition to a person under the age of 18, except where they are not prohibited from having it as set out at items (1) to (3) above.[36] In addition, it will always be an offence to sell or let on hire an air weapon or ammunition for it to a person under the age of 18.[37] In any of these circumstances, the supplier of the air weapon or ammunition will have a defence if he can prove that he believed the youngster to be at least 18 and had reasonable ground for that belief.[38]

Yet another offence has recently been created, and that is where a person in possession of an air weapon fails to take reasonable precautions to prevent someone under the age of 18 from gaining unauthorised access to it.[39] A defence is provided where a person can show he had reasonable grounds for believing the other person to be aged 18 or over. It is not an offence under this section to permit someone under 18 to have possession of an air weapon in any of the permitted circumstances already set out here in this Chapter; supervised by someone over 21, shooting galleries etc. This places an onus on those who keep air weapons to prevent access to them by those under 18. There is no requirement to prevent access by adults. The guidance issued by the Home Office is very similar to the security advice they issue in relation to firearms. It is a matter of looking at each situation on the individual merits of the case. They suggest using steel cables, gun cabinets and the like. Further information on this topic is set out in Ch.8. Given that the only risk that is required to be assessed is that from those under 18, the necessary steps that will need to be taken are obviously less stringent.

Gifts

14–13   A person may make a gift of an air weapon or air weapon ammunition to a youngster aged 18 or more, but not if under 18.[40] Again, the person making the gift has a defence if he can prove that he believed the youngster to be at least 18 and had reasonable ground for that belief.[41]

By way of conclusion to this section, it is worth noting that the 1968 Act as originally enacted allowed youngsters aged 14 or over to purchase, be given or

---

[35] FA 1968 s.23(3) as amended by VCRA 2006 s.34(2).

[36] FA 1968 ss.23, 24(4)(b) as amended by VCRA 2006 s.33. The maximum punishment on summary conviction is a fine at level 3 on the standard scale (currently £1,000) (FA 1968 s.51(1), (2) and Sch.6 Pt I).

[37] FA 1968 s.24(1)(a). The maximum punishment on summary conviction is six months' imprisonment, or a fine at level 5 on the standard scale (currently £5,000), or both.

[38] FA 1968 s.24(5).

[39] FA 1968 s.24(ZA), as amended by s.46 Crime and Security Act 2010, in force February 10, 2011. The maximum punishment on summary conviction is a fine at level 3 on the standard scale (currently £1,000).

[40] Except in circumstances (clubs etc.) set out above. FA 1968 s.24(4)(a) as amended by VCRA 2006 s.33. The maximum punishment on summary conviction is a fine at level 3 on the standard scale (currently £1,000) (FA 1968 s.51(1), (2) and Sch.6 Pt I).

[41] FA 1968 s.24(5), as amended by VCRA 2006 s.33.

otherwise have in their possession air weapons and air weapon ammunition. However, the successive increases in that age limit firstly to 17 by virtue of the Anti-Social Behaviour Act 2003 and then more latterly to 18 by virtue of the Violent Crime Reduction Act 2006 have created a somewhat illogical situation. We are now left with the position where the possession by and transfer to under 18s of air weapons and their ammunition is on the face of it more tightly controlled than is the case in relation to s.1 firearms or shotguns. The counter view would be that any youngster aged under 18 will generally, although not always, have been assessed as to their suitability to hold a firearm or shotgun certificate before acquiring possession of the s.1 firearm or shotgun, whereas no corresponding vetting process will have taken place before a young person takes possession of an air weapon.

TABLE OF RESTRICTIONS IN RELATION TO YOUNG PERSONS

Upon conviction for an offence mentioned in this chapter (except an offence relating specifically to air weapons and the offence of having an assembled shot gun) the Court may order the forfeiture or disposal of any firearm or ammunition found in the convicted person's possession,[42] and may cancel that person's firearm certificate or shot gun certificate.[43]   **14–14**

Many of the restrictions discussed above are complicated enough in themselves, but a greater difficulty is caused, when trying to find the answer in a particular case, by the considerable overlapping and duplication of the restrictions. In an attempt to overcome this, there are set out below in summary form the restricted acts which apply to the different age groups, and underneath the exceptions which operate in some cases. The word "Yes" under the "Age" heading indicates that the prohibited act may be done; the word "No" shows it may not be, except where it is followed by a capital letter referring to an exception, in which case the prohibition is eased to the extent of the exception. The exceptions appear underneath the table.

It is advisable that great care must be taken when using the table. Because of the similarities of some of the expressions and the different descriptions of guns which are used, it is advisable, when considering any particular case, to check the position under each of the prohibited acts. Most gun shops which sell firearms and air weapons should be able to advise you as to your particular circumstances and certainly it is advisable to ask.

Table of restrictions in relation to young persons

Restricted Acts	Up to and including 13	15	15 to 16 inclusive	17	18

---

[42] For commentary on the meaning of "possession" see para.3–07.
[43] FA 1968 s.52(1).

I. Acts by youngsters which are prohibited					
1. Buying or hiring any section 1 firearm or shotgun or ammunition for either.	No	No	No	Yes	Yes
2. Buying or hiring an air weapon or Imitation firearm	No	No	No	No	Yes
3. Having an assembled shot gun with him.	No A, D	No A, D	Yes	Yes	Yes
4. Possessing a Section 1 firearm or ammunition.	No B, C, E	Yes	Yes	Yes	Yes
5. Having with him an air weapon[44] or ammunition for one.	No B, C, D	No B, C, D	No B, C, D	No B, C, D	Yes

---

[44] The air weapon, and this applies to all references to air weapons in this table, must not be of a kind declared to be specially dangerous. If of such a kind, the rules relating to s.1 firearms apply.

6. Using a firearm for a purpose not authorised by the European Weapons Directive.	No	No	No	No	Yes
II. Acts by others[45] in relation to young-sters[46]					
7. Selling or letting on hire a Section 1 firearm or shotgun or ammunition for either.	No	No	No	Yes	Yes
8. Selling or letting on hire an air weapon or Imitation firearm	No	No	No	No	Yes
9. Giving a shot gun or ammunition	No	No	Yes	Yes	Yes
10. Giving or lending a Section 1 firearm or ammunition.	No	Yes	Yes	Yes	Yes

---

[45] These may include other youngsters as well as adults.

[46] In the case of each of the acts under this heading, it will be a defence for the accused person to prove that he believed the youngster to be of or over the age of 14, 15 or 17 (as the case may be) and that he had reasonable ground for that belief.

11. Parting with possession of a Section 1 firearm or ammuni-tion.	No B, C, E	Yes	Yes	Yes	Yes
12. Giving an air weapon or ammuni-tion for an air weapon.	No	No	No	No	Yes
13. Parting with possession of an air weapon or ammuni-tion for one.	No	No	No	No	Yes

Exceptions

A.   Gun so covered with a securely fastened gun cover so that it cannot be fired.
B.   Member of a rifle club or miniature rifle club approved by the Home Office whilst engaged, as a member, in, or in connection with, target shooting.
C.   Having the weapon or ammunition at a shooting gallery where the only firearms used are air weapons which are not specially dangerous or miniature rifles not exceeding .23 inches calibre.
D.   Supervision by a person at least 21 years old. Note there is no requirement for supervision in the case of a youngster aged 14 or over who has an air weapon with him if he is on private premises, and provided he is there with the consent of the occupier.
E.   As a gun bearer a youngster under the age of 14 can carry a s.1 firearm for another's use but may not use it himself.

CHAPTER 15

Criminal Offences Relating to Firearms—General Restrictions on Shooting and Carrying Guns

INTRODUCTION

In addition to the requirements of the law referred to in earlier chapters relating to the possession of firearms, shotguns and specially dangerous air weapons, a number of criminal offences have been created relating to the possession and use of them and their associated ammunition. For these offences it matters not that you may be the lawful owner of the item found in your possession. Further, with the exception of the 'possession only' offences dealt with directly below, it should be noted that where a firearm or shotgun certificate is required for the gun in question, even if you have been granted the relevant certificate, this will not provide you with a defence to these offences.

15–01

The usual range of penalties will be available to the criminal courts, which may include anything from a fine up to imprisonment. Depending on the length of the prison sentence, this may then result in a prohibition on possessing all types of firearms including air weapons, which could last for the rest of your life.[1] In addition, upon conviction for any of these offences the court may also order forfeiture and disposal or destruction of the firearm and any ammunition found in your possession at the time of the offence. If that were not enough, where you are a certificate holder, the court may cancel your certificate, and even if the court does not, a conviction for any of these offences will almost certainly result in your certificate being revoked by the police. Your firearms licensing department may not wait until you are convicted to revoke your certificate and seize your guns. Indeed, even if the offence is ultimately not proved in the criminal court, the mere fact that you have been arrested on suspicion of such an offence may well be relied on as sufficient justification for revocation. Therefore, if you value your certificate, you would be well advised to avoid any activity that might cast you under suspicion for these or indeed any criminal offences.

This is not a criminal law textbook and therefore does not seek to address every possible offence in detail. We shall confine ourselves to focusing on the more common offences where those who are ordinarily in legitimate possession of firearms may find themselves inadvertently falling foul of the law.

UNLAWFUL POSSESSION OF FIREARMS AND AMMUNITION

15–02 This section deals with what are referred to above as the 'possession only' offences. Chapters 1 to 4 explain in detail the classification of s.1 firearms, shotguns, prohibited firearms and the ammunition corresponding to each. Also set out in those chapters are the need for a firearm or shotgun certificate, as appropriate, and the exceptions where the person in possession will be exempt from the usual requirement to hold a certificate. Perhaps unsurprisingly, if you are found in possession of any such item without holding a valid certificate,[2] and you cannot demonstrate you fall within one of the exemptions, you will be liable for the offence of unlawful possession.[3] If you do hold a firearm or shotgun certificate, but possession of the particular firearm or ammunition in question is not authorised by it, and is not exempt from certification, you will similarly be guilty of unlawful possession of that item. In relation to ammunition for a s.1 firearm, bear in mind that the offence of unlawful possession can occur where you are in possession of a quantity that exceeds the amount authorised under your

---

[1] For further details on prohibition, see Ch.5.

[2] This would include where your certificate has been cancelled, revoked or has expired and you have failed to promptly surrender your firearms to the police on demand, or to a registered firearms dealer or other person authorised to possess them. In the case of renewals, provided you submitted your application for renewal in good time before the expiry of your certificate, it is unlikely the police would take action against you for this offence.

[3] In the case of possession of a s.1 firearm or its ammunition, or a shotgun (but not shotgun ammunition, the possession of which does not require a certificate), the maximum punishment on summary conviction is imprisonment for six months or a fine of the prescribed sum (currently £5,000), or both; or on indictment, five years' imprisonment (unless it is a shotgun with a shortened barrel, in which case seven years) or an unlimited fine, or both (FA 1968 ss.1, 2, 51(1), (2) and Sch 6 Pt I). Be aware that unless the court accepts that there are 'exceptional circumstances' committing this offence with most, although not all, categories of prohibited weapon or prohibited ammunition (see Ch.2) attracts a minimum custodial sentence of five years, FA 1968 s.51A(1A), as amended by VCRA 2006 s.30.

firearm certificate for that calibre. This would also apply to prohibited ammunition authorised under a certificate.

For these offences, essentially all that needs to be proved is that you were in possession of the firearm or ammunition in question, which is often not in dispute, and that it does fall in law to be classified as a s.1 firearm or ammunition, a shotgun, or as a prohibited firearm or prohibited ammunition, as charged. This will be enough for the offence to have been committed and there is no need to establish that you had it with you in a public place, fired it or did anything else with it, nor that you had any particular intent. Neither will it afford you a defence that you had the item in your possession in your own home or other private premises. Your mistaken belief or lack of knowledge as to the correct legal status of the item is equally irrelevant to the question of your guilt, although it may serve to reduce the penalty. These are therefore what lawyers refer to as offences of strict liability.

CARRYING FIREARMS IN A PUBLIC PLACE

"Any person who without lawful authority or reasonable excuse, the proof whereof shall lie on him, has with him in a public place any loaded shot gun; an air weapon (whether loaded or not); or any other firearm (whether loaded or not) together with ammunition suitable for use in that firearm, or an imitation firearm, commits an offence".[4] So having a shotgun (unloaded, even if you have ammunition with you) or a s.1 firearm (without suitable ammunition) in public is not an offence under this section, but having an imitation firearm in public does contravene this section.   **15–03**

The ingredients of this offence are:—

> "Lawful authority": these words are not defined in the Act, and there is no certain authority for their interpretation, but we suggest it would be taken to include the police and others in the service of the Crown and those other examples where persons have authority to possess firearms without a certificate, as set out in the Chs 1 to 4 of this book. In relation to this offence it is not a defence likely to apply to private individuals. The grant of a firearm or shotgun certificate does not confer 'lawful authority' to carry it in public outside of the terms of the certificate.[5]
>
> "Reasonable excuse": The carrying of a gun to a rifle range for shooting or the crossing of a public road with a gun during the course of a shoot are, it is suggested, examples of situations in which there is a reasonable excuse, as would be any other situation which is in accordance with the conditions of the relevant license, if there is one. If a license is not required, for example with an air weapon or an imitation firearm, then the facts of each

---

[4] FA 1968 s.19, as amended by the Anti-Social Behaviour Act 2003 s.37(1). The maximum punishment on summary conviction is imprisonment for six months or a fine of the prescribed sum (currently £5,000), or both; or (unless the firearm is an air weapon) on indictment, seven years' imprisonment or an unlimited fine, or both (FA 1968 s.51(1), (2) and Sch.6 Pt I). Be aware that unless the court accepts that there are 'exceptional circumstances' committing this offence with a prohibited weapon (see Ch.2) attracts a minimum custodial sentence of five years, FA 1968 s.51A(1A), as amended by VCRA 2006 s30.

[5] *R. v Jones (T)* [1995] 1 Cr. App. R. 262 CA.

case need to be examined. Although the meaning of the words is somewhat different, the question 'did you have a good reason for having the firearm in public?' is a good starting point. If the answer is 'yes' you may well have a reasonable excuse. It is obviously reasonable to take *both* the firearms and ammunition to go shooting, despite the wording of the Act implying that they should be kept separate. There is no requirement to make two trips each way! The certificate holder in the case detailed at para.8–07 (relating to leaving his rifle in his car while he went to the County Court) could have been prosecuted under s.19 if the police had argued that he no longer had the gun with him in connection with its use. This does not seem to have been the position taken in that case.

Apart from having a firearm and ammunition in a public place in connection with their use or ownership, other circumstances may arise where an owner might be tempted to take a gun into public. Self-defence, the defence of others and (perhaps) protection of property are all permitted in law, as long as the amount of force used (or threatened) is reasonable in the circumstances as you believe them to be. Certificate holders should be aware however that except in the most extreme cases the police will take a serious view of those who use lawfully held firearms 'to take the law into their own hands'. Not only would you risk revocation of your certificate you would almost certainly be prosecuted for serious criminal offences. For there to be a reasonable excuse in respect of this offence under s.19 it must be shown that there was an imminent particular threat affecting the circumstances in which the weapon was carried. The constant carriage of a weapon on account of some enduring threat or danger, supposed or actual, to the carrier cannot be excused,[6] and neither can threatening the use of a weapon to enforce a private argument.[7] In short, don't do it.

15–04 "The proof whereof shall lie on him": if charged, it will be enough for the defendant to satisfy the Court of the probability of existence of the lawful authority or reasonable excuse, in other words, on the balance of probabilities.[8]

"Has with him": this should be read as "knowingly has with him".[9] Thus, for example, the person is entitled to be acquitted if he can satisfy the Court that the gun was in the vehicle he was driving without his knowledge. The words have a more restricted meaning than is implied by possession,[10] and extend to any situation where there is a close physical link between the defendant and the gun.[11]

15–05 "A public place": this is defined in the Act as including any highway and any other premises or place to which at the material time the public have or are permitted to have access, whether on payment or otherwise.[12] This definition clearly covers places of public entertainment and hotels and public houses during licensing hours and also, it is suggested, buses, trains,

---

[6] *Evans v Hughes* [1972] 3 All E.R. 412.

[7] *Taylor v Mucklow* (1973) Crim L.R. 750. He hadn't paid his builder and threatened him with an air weapon when the builder started to demolish the extension he had built.

[8] *R. v Carr-Briant* [1943] 2 All E.R. 156.

[9] *R. v Cugullere* [1961] 2 All E.R. 343.

[10] For commentary on the meaning of "possession", see para.3–07.

[11] *R. v Kelt* [1977] 1 W.L.R. 1365; Crim L.R. 556.

[12] FA 1968 s.57(4).

aeroplanes and ships running on scheduled services, and taxis whilst available for hire. The space behind the counter in a shop is a public place[13] "Loaded": the Act declares that the weapon shall be deemed to be loaded if there is ammunition in the chamber or barrel or in any magazine or other device which is in such a position that the ammunition can be fed into the chamber or barrel by the manual or automatic operation of some part of the weapon.[14] An interesting anomaly is that in respect of firearms other than shotguns and air weapons the offence arises if you have suitable ammunition with you, whether the gun is loaded or not. This might lead to the logical conclusion that (assuming you have a reasonable excuse for having the gun and ammunition in a public place), you might as well have it loaded! This is perhaps not what Parliament intended, but this offence does not prevent the gun being loaded, indeed it specifically envisages that might be the case with a shotgun.

"Shot gun": is defined in Ch.4.　　　　　　　　　　　　　　　　　　　**15–06**

"Air weapon": the Act defines this as an air gun, air rifle or air pistol, not being of a type declared by rules made by the Home Office to be specially dangerous.[15]

"Firearm": the definition discussed at paras 1–03 onwards applies[16]; briefly, it includes virtually every type of gun, any component part of it and some accessories, and an imitation firearm.[17]

"Ammunition": the definition at para.1–20 applies;[18] but the point is that the ammunition is to be suitable for use in the firearm carried at the time.

In summary this offence arises where a shot gun is loaded, but other firearms need not be, provided suitable ammunition is carried, and there is no reasonable excuse.[19]

HAVING OFFENSIVE WEAPONS IN A PUBLIC PLACE

Any person who without lawful authority[20] or reasonable excuse, the proof　**15–07** whereof shall lie on him, has with him in any public place any offensive weapon commits an offence.[21] The term "offensive weapon" is defined as "any article made or adapted for use for causing injury to the person, or intended by the

---

[13] *Anderson v Miller and Spearman* [1976] Crim L.R. 743, DC.
[14] FA 1968 s.57(6)(b).
[15] FA 1968 ss.1(3)(b), 57(4).
[16] FA 1968 s.57(1).
[17] For imitation firearms, see Ch.9.
[18] FA 1968 s.57(1).
[19] The offence under s.19 is in identical terms to that under the Prevention of Crimes Act 1953 (PCA) s.1 which concerns the carrying of offensive weapons in public. Many of the authorities regarding that legislation are equally applicable to this, and vice versa, as is obvious from the following paragraph.
[20] The different meanings of these ingredients of the offence are discussed at paras 15–03 to 15–06.
[21] PCA 1953 s.1(1). The maximum punishments are: on indictment four years' imprisonment, or an unlimited fine, or both; on summary conviction, six months' imprisonment, or a fine of the prescribed sum (currently £5,000), or both (PCA 1953 s.1(1); CLA 1977 s.32(1)). Upon conviction the court may order the forfeiture or disposal of any weapon in respect of which the offence was committed (PCA 1953 s.1(2)).

person having it with him for such use by him or by some other person".[22] As the wording suggests, there are three categories of offensive weapon.[23] If an item was 'made (type 1) or adapted (type 2)' for causing injury it is said to be an offensive weapon 'per se'. In these cases the offence is committed unless the person concerned demonstrates a reasonable excuse for having the item with them in public. If the item is not offensive per se (an ordinary pocket knife, for example, type 3) then the prosecution have to prove that the person had it with them with the intention of using it as a weapon of offence. Carrying an item with the intention to defend yourself with it comes within the Act; the 'intention' covers lawful as well as unlawful injury, although the threat of imminent attack may be a reasonable excuse.[24] The fact that an item was used as a weapon of offence does not mean that it was being carried in contravention of the Act.[25] It is the intention before it is used as a weapon that is important, if the item is actually used this can be appropriately dealt with by prosecuting for one of the offences of violence under the Offences Against the Person Act. Clearly, any gun is made or adapted for causing injury and therefore is offensive per se[26] and so, although the Act was aimed at persons with criminal inclinations, the ordinary citizen must beware lest he commits this offence whilst carrying a gun in a public place; in other words, he should be sure that he has "lawful authority or reasonable excuse". Many hunters will carry a knife for dealing with their quarry and so this offence should be borne in mind by all those who do so.

BLADED ARTICLES

15–08   The reader should also be aware that it is an offence to have an article with a blade or sharp point in a public place without 'good reason or lawful authority'.[27] This offence does not apply to a folding pocket knife with a cutting edge under three inches in length (7.6 cm). However, it covers a lock knife of any size. Lawful authority will have the same meaning as in the offences above. 'Good reason' can be any purpose, but is said to include use at work, for religious reasons or as part of any national costume.[28] It would include a knife for gutting game taken on a shoot. As above, it is for the person charged to prove the good reason on the balance of probabilities.

---

[22] PCA 1953 s.1(4).

[23] *R. v Simpson* (1978) Cr. App. R. 115.

[24] *Evans v Hughes* (1956) Cr. App. R. 813.

[25] *R. v Jura* [1954] 1 Q.B. 503 This concerned a rifle at a rifle range.

[26] As are swords; bayonets; 'death stars' and many other items used in martial arts; truncheons and knuckle dusters. Except with flick knives (which are offensive per se as a matter of law) it is a matter for the jury in each case to decide whether the item is made or adapted as an offensive weapon.

[27] Criminal Justice Act 1988 s.139.

[28] CJA 1988 s.139 (5).

TRESPASSING WITH A FIREARM

It is an offence for any person who, while he has a firearm or imitation firearm[29] with him,[30] enters or is on any land[31] or in any building or part of a building as a trespasser and without reasonable excuse, the proof whereof shall lie on him.[32] This is a corresponding offence for private land and buildings to the offence of carrying a firearm in a public place. The same criteria largely applies, although the offence is committed with any firearm (including an air weapon), and whether loaded or not, or an imitation firearm.

    Points arising on the words "firearm", "without reasonable excuse", "the proof whereof shall lie on him" and what is meant by a person having a firearm with him have been discussed above at paras 15–03 to 15–06, but the following two small matters should be mentioned.

    "Land", as the Act says,[33] includes "land covered with water", so the mere fact that an offender is afloat will not enable him to escape the penalties of the law.

    The word "trespasser" is not defined. As well as having its ordinary meaning, e.g. a person who is on premises without the permission of the occupier of the premises, it includes a person on a public road who is not using it for a legitimate purpose.

    Lastly, it should be noted that the police have wide supporting powers in connection with the offences discussed under this head. These include[34] power to require a suspected person to hand over a firearm and ammunition to a constable[35] for examination[36]; power to search a suspected person and detain him for that purpose; power to stop and search suspected vehicles; and power to arrest a suspected person and to enter any place.[37]

15–09

15–10

---

[29] For imitation firearms, see Ch.9.

[30] But there will be no offence where there is no evidence that the firearm worked or could be made to work (*Grace v DPP* [1989] Crim L.R. 365, DC).

[31] "Land" is defined to include land covered with water (FA 1968 s.20(3)).

[32] FA 1968 s.20(1), (2). If the offence relates to a building, the maximum punishment on summary conviction is imprisonment for six months or a fine of the prescribed sum (currently £5,000), or both; or (unless the firearm is an air weapon or an imitation firearm), on indictment, seven years' imprisonment or an unlimited fine, or both. Be aware that unless the court accepts that there are 'exceptional circumstances' committing this offence with a prohibited weapon (see Ch.2) attracts a minimum custodial sentence of five years, FA 1968 s51A(1A), as amended by VCRA 2006 s.30. If the offence relates to land, the maximum punishment on summary conviction is imprisonment for three months or a fine at level 4 on the standard scale (currently £2,500), or both (FA 1968 s.51(1), (2) and Sch.6, Pt I).

[33] FA 1968 s.20(3).

[34] FA 1968 s.20 actually creates two separate offences, one relating to buildings or parts thereof and the other to land. The powers specified apply to one or other of the offences but not necessarily to both of them.

[35] As well as police constables, including special police constables, "constables" includes others holding that office, e.g. harbour constables. The hallmark of a constable is his attestation as such before, usually, a Magistrate.

[36] Failure to do so is itself an offence carrying a maximum punishment on summary conviction of 3 months' imprisonment, or a fine at level 4 on the standard scale (currently £2,500), or both (FA 1968 ss.47(2), 51(1), (2) and Sch.6 Pt I).

[37] FA 1968 ss.20, 47(1), (3)–(6), 50(2). For police powers of general application, see para.11–07.

TRESPASSING WITH A WEAPON OF OFFENCE

15–11   A person who is on premises as a trespasser, after having entered as such, is guilty of an offence if, without lawful authority or reasonable excuse, he has with him on the premises any weapon of offence.[38] Several ingredients of this offence require individual examination.

The word "premises" is defined to mean any building, any part of a building under separate occupation, any land ancillary to a building and the site comprising any building or buildings together with any land ancillary to the building or buildings.[39] The word "building" in this definition is itself defined to extend its meaning to any structure other than a movable one, and to any movable structure, vehicle or vessel designed or adapted for use for residential purposes. Part of a building is to be treated as under separate occupation if anyone is in occupation or entitled to occupation of that part as distinct from the whole. Land is to be treated as ancillary to a building if it is adjacent to it and used or intended for use in connection with the occupation of that building or any part of it.[40]

15–12   A trespasser is, briefly, a person who is on premises without the permission of the occupier. Additionally, for the purpose of the offence now being considered, a person is treated as a trespasser if he enters or is on or in occupation of any premises "by virtue of any title derived from a trespasser or any licence or consent given by a trespasser or by a person deriving title from a trespasser".[41] The effect of the legal phraseology quoted here is that a person who is on premises by some arrangement with a trespasser is himself a trespasser; the word "title" means entitlement to ownership or tenancy of premises, and "licence" is used in the sense of leave or permission.

Anyone who is on any premises as a trespasser does not cease to be a trespasser because he has been allowed time to leave the premises.[42]

The expressions "without lawful authority or reasonable excuse" and "has with him" are discussed earlier at paras 15–03 to 15–06.

15–13   "Weapon of offence" is defined to mean any article made or adapted for use for causing injury to or incapacitating a person, or intended by the person having it with him for such use.[43] Clearly, any gun capable of causing injury comes within this definition.

A constable[44] in uniform may arrest without warrant anyone who is, or whom he with reasonable cause suspects to be, in the act of committing the offence described.[45]

---

[38] CLA 1977 s.8(1). The maximum punishment on summary conviction is a fine at level 5 on the standard scale (currently £5,000), or 3 months' imprisonment, or both (CLA 1977 s.8(3)).

[39] CLA 1977 s.12(1)(a).

[40] CLA 1977 s.12(2).

[41] CLA 1977 s.12(6).

[42] CLA 1977 s.12(7).

[43] CLA 1977 s.8(2).

[44] As well as police constables, including special police constables, "constables" includes others holding that office, e.g. harbour constables. The hallmark of a constable is his attestation as such before, usually, a Magistrate.

[45] CLA 1977 s.8(4).

Though this offence was created primarily to deal with modern squatters who use offensive weapons to retain possession of property, those who, within the terms of the offence, trespass carrying guns in other circumstances may also be prosecuted.

SHOOTING ON OR NEAR THE HIGHWAY

The first point to bear in mind is that the only right which the public has on a public road is to pass to and fro on it and to use it for other purposes reasonably necessary to that right of passage (although case law has given the public rights of demonstration on public roads). Thus, roads are not places where anybody may shoot at will. The land on which roads are made belongs to the adjoining landowners, subject to the rights of road users and of the highway authority, or to the highway authority itself, or, in some cases, to the builder of the adjoining houses. **15–14**

To this general proposition, Parliament has added a number of offences dealing with shooting on or near roads. First, under the Highways Act 1980 it is an offence, without lawful authority[46] or excuse,[47] to discharge any firearm within 50 feet[48] of the centre of a highway which consists of or comprises a carriageway, as a consequence of which a user of the highway is injured, interrupted or endangered.[49]

A carriageway is defined in the Act as meaning a way constituting or comprised in a highway,[50] being a way (other than a cycle track) over which the public have a right of way for the passage of vehicles.[51] Thus, the offence will operate in the case of all public roads, and will not apply to independent footpaths and bridleways. **15–15**

A highway is generally taken to be the full width of the road between its boundary hedges or ditches and this will include wide verges in some cases. Additionally, for the purposes of this offence, a highway includes bridges and tunnels where it passes over or through them.[52]

---

[46] See the comments on this phrase at para.15–03.

[47] In order to have a lawful excuse (which is to be distinguished from "reasonable excuse" as explained at para.15–03) a person must show—

(a) that he honestly, but mistakenly, believed on reasonable grounds that the facts were of a certain order; *and*

(b) that if those facts had been of that order, his conduct would have been lawful (*Cambridgeshire and Isle of Ely CCl v Rust* [1972] 3 All E.R. 232). An innocent motive alone will not be enough to establish a lawful excuse (*Dickens v Gill* [1896] 2 Q.B. 310).

[48] This is to be measured in a straight line on a horizontal plane (IA 1978 s.8).

[49] HA 1980 s.161(2). The maximum punishment is a fine at level 3 on the standard scale (currently £1,000).

[50] i.e. a public road.

[51] HA 1980 s.329(1).

[52] HA 1980 s.328(2).

Except in the Greater London area, an offence is committed[53] by any person who in any street[54] to the obstruction, annoyance or danger of its residents or passengers wantonly discharges a firearm.[55]

In the Metropolitan Police District[56] an offence is committed[57] by any person who in any thoroughfare or public place[58] wantonly discharges any firearm to the damage or danger of any person.[59]

SHOOTING BEYOND PREMISES

15–16   A person commits an offence if they use an air weapon on any premises to shoot a missile beyond those premises,[60] although a defence is provided if you can show that the owner of the adjoining land consented. In those cases where the law requires a young person to be supervised whilst using an air weapon (see Ch.14) the person supervising will commit an offence if he permits shooting onto adjoining land without consent.[61]

SHOOTING IN CEMETERIES AND BURIAL GROUNDS

15–17   In certain cemeteries and burial grounds[62] it is an offence to discharge firearms except at a military funeral.[63] In the case of cemeteries provided and maintained by local authorities no such offence exists,[64] but it is made an offence wilfully[65] to create a disturbance, to commit any nuisance or to play any game or sport[66]; depending on the circumstances, shooting may constitute one of these offences.

---

[53] The maximum fine on summary conviction is a fine at level 3 on the standard scale (currently £1,000) (CJA 1967 s.92(1) and Sch.3 Pt I). A policeman may arrest an offender without warrant if the offence is committed in his sight (TCPA 1847 s.28).

[54] The word "street" includes any road, square, court, alley, thoroughfare or public passage (TCPA 1847 s.3). The word does not include a place from which the public may be excluded, such as a roadway to a station or other private property (*Curtis v Embery* (1872) LR 7 Exch 369).

[55] TCPA 1847 s.28; PHA 1875 s.171; LGA 1972 s.180 and Sch.14, paras 23, 26.

[56] The District comprises Greater London (except the City of London and the Inner and Middle Temples) and parts of Essex, Hertfordshire and Surrey (LGA 1963 s.76(1)).

[57] The maximum fine is at level 2 on the standard scale (currently £500) (MPA 1839 s.54). A constable belonging to the Metropolitan Police Force may arrest an offender without warrant if the offence is committed in his sight (MPA 1839 s.54).

[58] "Public place" is not defined in this context. See para.15–05 for a description of places which might be considered as being within the meaning of the term.

[59] MPA 1839 s.54, para.15.

[60] FA 1968 s.21A as amended by VCRA 2006 s.34 (2). The maximum punishment is fine is at level 3 on the standard scale (currently £1,000).

[61] FA 1968 s.22 (1) as amended by VCRA 2006 s.34. The maximum punishment is fine is at level 3 on the standard scale (currently £1,000).

[62] These are cemeteries and burial grounds made under the authority of an Act of Parliament which incorporates the Cemeteries Clauses Act 1847 (CCA 1847 s.1).

[63] CCA 1847 ss.3, 59. The maximum punishment is a fine at level 1 on the standard scale (currently £200).

[64] LGA 1972 s.214(7), (8) and Sch.26, para.14.

[65] This means deliberately and intentionally, and not by accident or inadvertence (*R. v Senior* [1899] 1 Q.B. 283 at pp.290–91).

[66] Local Authorities' Cemeteries Order 1977 art.18(1). The maximum fine is at level 2 on the standard scale (currently £500) (1977 Order, art.19).

POSSESSION OF FIREARMS WHEN DRUNK

A person who is drunk[67] when in possession[68] of any loaded firearm[69] commits an offence[70] and may be arrested.[71]

15–18

POSSESSION OF A FIREARM OR IMITATION FIREARM WITH INTENT TO CAUSE FEAR OF VIOLENCE

It is an offence to have in your possession a firearm (or an imitation[72]) with the intent to cause, or enable another person to cause, someone else to fear that unlawful violence will be used against them or another person.[73] 'Unlawful' is an important part of this offence. Doing acts such as defending yourself, or others, or your property, might be considered lawful in some circumstances.

15–19

SERIOUS CRIMINAL OFFENCES WITH FIREARMS

In addition to the offences set out above, there are also firearms offences under the Firearms Act 1968 as follows:—

15–20

(a)   "Possession of a firearm with intent to resist arrest, s.17.

(b)   Possession of a firearm with intent to endanger life, s.16.

(c)   Possession of a firearm with intent to commit any indictable offence, or to resist arrest, or to prevent the arrest of another, s.18.

All of these offences are punishable with life imprisonment (as a maximum), apply to imitation firearms as well as real ones, and if committed with a prohibited weapon carry a five year minimum sentence. These offences are not dealt with in detail here as they will not be of concern to the average reader. In the event that you, or someone you know, have been charged with such an offence, you need a good solicitor!

---

[67] There is no test of drunkenness in this instance, and it will be for the magistrates to decide on the evidence before them whether the accused was drunk.

[68] It is suggested that a narrower meaning for "possession" than that given at para.3–07 would be applicable, i.e. that the defendant was carrying the firearm or perhaps had it within easy reach.

[69] The case of *Seamark v Prouse*[1980] 3 All E.R. 26 decided that an air rifle is a firearm for this purpose.

[70] The maximum penalties are a fine at level 1 on the standard scale (currently £200) or one month's imprisonment.

[71] LA 1872 s.12. It appears that the offence is committed wherever the drunken person may be.

[72] See also Ch.9.

[73] FA 1968 s.16A, inserted by the Firearms Amendment Act 1994 s.1. Maximum penalty 10 years imprisonment, and if committed with some prohibited weapons, five year minimum.

CHAPTER 16

Firearms Dealers

WHO IS A FIREARMS DEALER?

For the purposes of the regulations relating to firearms dealers, a firearms dealer is defined as a person who, by way of trade or business, manufactures, sells, transfers,[1] repairs, tests or proves any s.1 firearm[2] or s.1 ammunition[3] or a shot gun.[4]

16–01

REGISTRATION OF FIREARMS DEALERS

The police are obliged to keep a register of firearms dealers and, with the exceptions mentioned later, to enter in it the name and places of business of any person who, having or proposing to have a place of business in the police area, applies to be registered.[5] Application should be made to the local police firearms licensing department on a form provided by them if you are or wish to become a firearms dealer within the definition discussed above.[6] Upon registration a certificate will be issued to you.[7] A £150 fee[8] is payable.[9] The certificate lasts for

16–02

---

[1] "Transfer" is defined as including letting on hire, giving, lending and parting with possession (FA 1968 s.57(4)).

[2] For the meanings of these words, see Ch.1. An imitation firearm may also fall to be treated as a s.1 firearm (FA 1982 s.2(1)). See further, Ch.9.

[3] For the meanings of these words, see Ch.4.

[4] FA 1968 s.57(4). The meaning of "shot gun" includes any component part of it and any accessory to it designed or adapted to diminish the noise or flash caused by firing it (FA 1968 s.57(4)).

[5] FA 1968 ss.33, 57(4). For the form of register, see Firearms Rules 1998 r.10(3) and Sch.5 Pt III.

[6] FA 1968 s.33(3); Firearms Rules 1998 r.10(1) and Sch.5, Pt I.

[7] FA 1968 s.33(4).

three years from the date on which it was granted[10] unless the registration is cancelled under the provisions later to be considered. But in the following cases the police may, and in one case must, refuse registration:

(a)   Registration of the applicant **must** be refused where a Court, following conviction of the applicant, has ordered that he shall not be registered.[11]

(b)   Registration of the applicant **may** be refused if the police are satisfied that the applicant cannot be permitted to carry on his business without danger to the public safety or to the peace.[12]

(c)   Registration of a place of business **may** be refused if the police are satisfied that it is a place at which the applicant cannot be permitted to carry on business as a firearms dealer without danger to the public safety or to the peace.[13]

(d)   Registration of the applicant **may** be refused unless the police are satisfied that the applicant will engage in business as a firearms dealer to a substantial extent or as an essential part of another trade, business or profession.[14]

16–03   There is an appeal to the Crown Court against a refusal of the police in any of these cases.[15] Notice of the appeal must be given within 21 days from the receipt of the decision of the police to refuse.[16]

A registered firearms dealer must, on or before the expiration of three years from the date of its grant, surrender his certificate of registration to the police and apply on the appropriate form for a new certificate. If granted, it will cost £150[17] and will last for a further three-year period unless the registration is cancelled under the provisions later to be considered.[18] It can only be refused if the police are satisfied that the applicant is no longer carrying on business as a firearms

---

[8] The amount of the fee may be varied, or abolished altogether, by order of the Home Office (FA 1968 s.43(1)).

[9] FA 1968 s.35(1), as amended by the Firearms (Variation of Fees) Order 1994. No fee is, however, payable when your only place of business was already registered in one police area and by boundary changes falls into a new police area, or when, being already registered in one police area, you propose transferring your only place of business to another police area (FA 1968 s.35(2)). If you apply to be registered for dealing at a game fair, trade fair or exhibition, agricultural show or similar event, and your principal place of business is registered for another area, the fee is £12 (FA 1968 s.35(1A); Firearms (Variation of Fees) Order 1994).

[10] FA 1968 s.33(5); F(A)A 1988 s.13(1).

[11] FA 1968 s.34(1). For the cases where a Court in Great Britain may make such an order, see para.16–13. Courts in Northern Ireland may also make these orders.

[12] FA 1968 s.34(2). There can, however, be no refusal on this ground where the applicant has been authorised by the Home Office to deal in prohibited weapons or prohibited ammunition, [for which see Ch.2] (FA 1968 ss.5, 34(3), 57(4); Transfer of Functions (Prohibited Weapons) Order 1968 arts 2(a) and 3(1)). For some decisions on "danger to the public safety or to the peace", although in another context, see paras 5–11 to 5–14 and also para. 4–06.

[13] FA 1968 s.34(4). See also second part of note directly above.

[14] FA 1968 s.34(1A); F(A)A 1988 s.13(2).

[15] FA 1968 ss.34(5), 44(1), (2).

[16] FA 1968 ss 34, 44 and Sch.5 Pt II. You should consult a solicitor at once if you are considering making an appeal.

[17] The amount of the fee may be varied, or abolished altogether, by order of the Home Office (FA 1968 s.43(1)).

[18] FA 1968 ss.33(5) and 35(3), as amended by the Firearms (Variation of Fees) Order 1994; F(A)A 1988 s.13(1).

dealer, or that he has ceased to have a place of business in the police area, or that he cannot be permitted to carry on such a business without danger to the public safety or to the peace.[19]

It is an offence if—

(1)   any person, by way of trade or business, manufactures, sells, transfers,[20] tests, proves, exposes for sale or transfer, or has in his possession for sale, transfer, repair, test or proof, any s.1 firearm,[21] s.1 ammunition[22] or shot gun[23] without being registered as a firearms dealer[24];

(2)   any person knowingly or recklessly makes a statement which is false in any material particular for the purpose of procuring the registration of himself or another person as a firearms dealer or of procuring, whether for himself or another person, the entry of any place of business in the register.[25]

Registration as a firearms dealer enables the dealer to do certain other things in relation to firearms and ammunition which others are not allowed to do. For example, the dealer may, within limitations, shorten the barrel of a shot gun and convert firearms and may possess, purchase and acquire,[26] firearms and ammunition without holding a firearm certificate or shot gun certificate.[27]   **16–04**

CONDITIONS OF REGISTRATION

The police may at any time impose conditions on the registration of a person as a firearms dealer, and may, either on their own initiative or on the application of the dealer, vary or revoke any condition.[28] Where conditions are imposed on the issue of the certificate, they are to be written into it. When imposed, or varied or revoked, during the currency of a certificate, the police must give notice[29] to the dealer of the conditions or variations (giving particulars) or revocation. The   **16–05**

---

[19] FA 1968 ss.33(5), 38(1). The last ground of refusal does not apply where the dealer has been authorised by the Home Office to manufacture or deal in prohibited weapons or prohibited ammunition (FA 1968 ss.5, 38(2); Transfer of Functions (Prohibited Weapons) Order 1968 arts 2(a) and 3(1)). For an interpretation of "danger to the public safety or to the peace", see paras 5–11 to 5–14 and also para. 4–06.

[20] "Transfer" is defined as including letting on hire, giving, lending and parting with possession (FA 1968 s.57(4)).

[21] For the definition of these terms, see Ch.3 para.3–01.

[22] For the definition of these terms, see Ch.3 para.3–05.

[23] For the definition of this term, see paras 3–02 and 4–01.

[24] FA 1968 s.3(1). The maximum punishment upon summary conviction is six months' imprisonment or a fine of the prescribed sum (currently £5,000), or both; and upon indictment, five years' imprisonment or an unlimited fine, or both (FA 1968 s.51(1), (2) and Sch.6, Pt I).

[25] FA 1968 s.39(1). The maximum punishment upon summary conviction is six months' imprisonment, or a fine at level 5 on the standard scale (currently £5,000), or both (FA 1968 s.51(1), (2) and Sch.6 Pt I).

[26] "Acquire" means hire, accept as a gift or borrow (FA 1968 s.57(4)).

[27] FA 1968 ss.4(2), (3), 8(1).

[28] FA 1968 s.36(1).

[29] This notice may be sent by registered post or by recorded delivery service in a letter addressed to the dealer at his last or usual place of abode or at any place of business in respect of which he is registered (FA 1968 s.56). It may also, of course, be delivered to him personally, or alternatively can now be sent by email, provided the dealer has given the police his consent to be sent notices via electronic means (The Firearms (Electronic Communications) Order 2011 SI 713/2011).

notice may also require that the dealer deliver up the certificate to the police within 21 days from the date of the notice for the purposes of amending the certificate.[30] An appeal to the Crown Court can be made against the imposition or variation by the police of a condition or against their refusal to vary or revoke it on the dealer's application.[31]

Failure to comply with any condition of registration is an offence,[32] and entitles the police to cancel a registration.[33]

REGISTRATION OF A NEW PLACE OF BUSINESS

16–06   If a person is registered as a firearms dealer in a police area and he proposes to carry on business as such a dealer at a place of business in that area which is not entered in the register kept by the police, he must notify the police of the fact and supply them with certain particulars; a form for this can be obtained from the police.[34] The police must register the new place of business unless satisfied that it is a place at which the applicant cannot be permitted to carry on business as a firearms dealer without danger to the public safety or to the peace.[35] Again, there is a right of appeal to the Crown Court against any police refusal to register.[36]

A registered firearms dealer[37] commits an offence if he has a place of business which is not entered in the register for the police area in which the place of business is situated and carries on business as a firearms dealer at that place.[38]

REMOVAL FROM REGISTER OF DEALER'S NAME OR PLACE OF BUSINESS BY THE POLICE

16–07   The name of a firearms dealer or his place of business is removable from the police register in the following circumstances:

(1)   The police **shall** remove the dealer's name if, after giving reasonable notice[39] to the dealer, they are satisfied that—

---

[30] FA 1968 s.36(2).

[31] FA 1968 ss.36(3) and 44. See further Ch.5.

[32] FA 1968 s.39(3). The maximum punishment upon summary conviction is six months' imprisonment, or a fine at level 5 on the standard scale (currently £5,000), or both (FA 1968 s.51(1) and Sch.6, Pt I).

[33] FA 1968 s.38(3). See also, item (2) at para.16–07.

[34] FA 1968 ss.37(1), 57(4). Firearms Rules 1998, Rule 10(2) and Sch.5 Pt II.

[35] FA 1968 s.37(1), (2).

[36] FA 1968 ss.37(3) and 44.

[37] A registered firearms dealer is defined as one who is either registered in Great Britain or is registered in Northern Ireland under the Firearms Act 1920 s.8 or any enactment of the Parliament of Northern Ireland amending or substituted for that section (FA 1968 s.57(4)).

[38] FA 1968 s.39(2). The maximum punishment on summary conviction is six months' imprisonment, or a fine at level 5 on the standard scale (currently £5000), or both (FA 1968 s.51(1) and Sch.6 Pt I).

[39] This notice may be sent by registered post or by recorded delivery service in a letter addressed to the dealer at his last or usual place of abode or at any place of business in respect of which he is registered (FA 1968 s.56). It may also, of course, be delivered to him personally. Notice can alternatively now be sent via email in certain circumstances, para.16–05 fn.29 and further see para.3–34.

(a)   he is no longer carrying on business as a firearms dealer; or

(b)   he has ceased to have a place of business in the police area; or

(c)   he cannot be permitted to continue to carry on business as a firearms dealer without danger to the public safety or to the peace.[40]

(2)   The police **may**, if satisfied that a dealer has failed to comply with any of the conditions of registration which have been imposed, remove from the register the dealer's name or any place of business of his to which the condition relates.[41]

(3)   The police **may** remove a dealer's place of business from the register if satisfied that it is one at which the dealer cannot be permitted to carry on business as such without danger to the public safety or to the peace.[42]

(4)   The police **shall** remove a dealer's name from the register if the dealer so desires.[43]

(5)   The police **shall** remove the dealer's name from the register if—

(a)   the dealer fails, on or before its expiration, to surrender his certificate of registration to the police or to apply for a new certificate; *and*

(b)   the police give written notice[44] to the dealer requiring him to do whatever he has failed to do under paragraph (a) above; *and*

(c)   the dealer fails to comply with the written notice within 21 days from its date or such further time as the police may in special circumstances allow.[45]

Again, there is a right of appeal to the Crown Court in any of these cases.[46]

On removal of a dealer's name (but not his place of business) from the register, the police will require the dealer by written notice[47] to surrender his certificate of registration and his register of transactions. Failure to do so within 21 days from the date of the notice is an offence.[48] If an appeal is made against the removal of the dealer's name from the register and is not successful, the period of 21 days will, instead, run from the date on which the appeal was abandoned or dismissed.[49]

16–08

---

[40] FA 1968 s.38(1). There can, however, be no removal under para.(c) where the dealer has been authorised by the Home Office to deal in prohibited weapons or ammunition, as to which see Ch.2 (FA 1968 ss.5, 38(2); Transfer of Functions (Prohibited Weapons) Order 1968, arts 2(a) and 3(1)).

[41] FA 1968 s.38(3).

[42] FA 1968 s.38(4).

[43] FA 1968 s.38(5).

[44] As to the methods by which such notice can be sent, see para.16–05 fn.29 and further para.3–34.

[45] FA 1968 s.38(6).

[46] FA 1968 ss.38(7) and 44. For appeals, see further Ch.5.

[47] This notice may be sent by registered post or by recorded delivery service in a letter addressed to the dealer at his last or usual place of abode or at any place of business in respect of which he is registered (FA 1968 s.56). It may also, of course, be delivered to him personally, or now by email, Firearms (Electronic Communications) Order 2011.

[48] FA 1968 s.38(8); F(A)A 1988 s.13(3). The maximum punishment upon summary conviction is a fine at level 3 on the standard scale (currently £1,000) (FA 1968 s.51(1) and Sch.6, Pt I).

[49] FA 1968 s.38(8) proviso.

THE REGISTER OF FIREARMS TRANSACTIONS

16–09   Every person who by way of trade or business manufactures sells or transfers[50] firearms[51] or ammunition[52] must provide and keep a register of transactions[53] and must enter, or cause to be entered, in it certain prescribed particulars.[54]

In the following cases, however, this requirement need not be complied with:

(1)   When the firearms are component parts of, or accessories to, shotguns or air weapons.[55]

(2)   When the ammunition is any of the types described in items (a), (b) and (c) at para.3–05.[56]

(3)   When firearms or ammunition are sold by auction in accordance with the terms of a police permit issued to the auctioneer.[57]

16–10   The rules about keeping a register may be relaxed in the following situation. If it appears to the police that—

(a)   a person required to be registered as a firearms dealer[58] carries on a trade or business in the course of which he manufactures, tests or repairs component parts or accessories for shot guns,[59] but not complete shot guns; *and*

(b)   it is impossible to assemble a shot gun from the parts likely to come into that person's possession in the course of that trade or business;

---

[50] "Transfer" is defined as including letting on hire, giving, lending and parting with possession (FA 1968 s.57(4)).

[51] As to the meaning of these words and for two general exceptions, see Ch.1. The register must now include sales of air weapons, VCRA s.31(2).

[52] This means s.1 ammunition, see Ch.3.

[53] For form of register and directions for keeping it, see Firearms Rules 1998 r.10(4) and Sch.5, Pt IV.

[54] FA 1968 s.40(1). Failure to do so constitutes an offence, the maximum punishment for which on summary conviction is.6 months' imprisonment, or a fine at level 5 on the standard scale (currently £5,000), or both (FA 1968 ss.40(5), 51(1), (2) and Sch.6, Pt I). The prescribed particulars, as amended by the Firearms Rules 1998 r.10(5), are reproduced in Appendix H at the end of the book. They may be further amended from time to time by rules made by the Home Office (FA 1968 ss.40(7), 53 and Sch.4).

[55] FA 1968 s.40(2). The Violent Crime Reduction Act 2006 prohibits anyone other than an RFD by way of trade or business, to sell, transfer, or expose for sale an air weapon, (s.31), and requires such transactions to be face to face, (s.32). It also amends the requirement to keep a register to include air weapons in the requirement (s.31(2)).

[56] FA 1968 s.40(2).

[57] FA 1968 ss.9(2), 40(6).

[58] As to the persons required to be so registered, see para.16–02.

[59] For the definition of "shot gun", see Ch.4.

the police may, if they think fit, by written notice[60] given to that person exempt his transactions in those parts and accessories from all or any of the requirements for keeping a register. This exemption lasts "so long as the notice is in force".[61]

Every entry required to be made in the register must be made within 24 hours after the transaction to which it relates. In the case of a sale or transfer[62] of firearms or ammunition, the dealer[63] must, at the time, require the purchaser or transferee, if not known to him, to furnish particulars sufficient for identification[64] and must immediately enter those particulars in the register.[65]

16–11

A person keeping a register shall, unless required to surrender it to the police, keep it for such period so that each entry shall be available for inspection for at least five years from the date of the entry. In the past dealers tended to maintain manual registers, entering each transaction by hand. The Firearms (Amendment) Act 1997 inserted new provisions in the 1968 Act enabling dealers to keep a computerised register, subject to the requirement that the register can be readily produced in a form in which it is visible and legible and can be taken away.[66]

A person keeping a register of firearms transactions must, if asked to do so by a constable[67] or a civilian officer[68] authorised in writing to make the demand by the chief officer of police, allow the constable or civilian officer to enter his premises to inspect all stock in hand. The register must be produced for inspection to any constable or civilian officer authorised in the same way and to any officer of customs and excise.[69] If asked to do so, the constable or civilian officer must produce their written authorisations.[70]

16–12

It is an offence if a person knowingly makes any false entry in a register of firearms transactions.[71]

A person may buy from a registered firearms dealer a firearm for export without holding a firearm or shot gun certificate. When this happens, the dealer must within 48 hours of the sale send[72] a notice of it to the chief officer of police

---

[60] This notice may be sent by registered post or by recorded delivery service in a letter addressed to the dealer at his last or usual place of abode or at any place of business in respect of which he is registered (FA 1968 s.56). It may also, of course, be delivered to him personally, or alternatively can now be sent by email, provided the dealer has given the police his consent to be sent notices via electronic means (The Firearms (Electronic Communications) Order 2011 SI 713/2011).

[61] FA 1968 s.41. It is not clear whether the notice should be given for a limited or unlimited time; if given for an unlimited time, it may presumably be cancelled by the police at any subsequent time by a further notice served in the same way as the original notice.

[62] "Transfer" is defined as including letting on hire, giving, lending and parting with possession (FA 1968 s.57(4)).

[63] Or his employee, or other person on his behalf (FA 1968 s.40(1), (3)).

[64] It is suggested that the full names and address of the person concerned will be sufficient.

[65] FA 1968 s.40(3). Failure to comply with any requirement in this paragraph is an offence (FA 1968 s.40(5)).

[66] FA 1968 s.40(4A); F(A)A 1997 Sch.2, para.8(b).

[67] As well as police constables, including special police constables, "constables" includes others holding that office, e.g. harbour constables. The hallmark of a constable is his attestation as such before, usually, a Magistrate.

[68] A civilian officer is, briefly, a person employed by the police. Full details are in FA 1968 s.57(4).

[69] Failure to do so is an offence (FA 1968 s.40(5)). The maximum punishment on summary conviction is six months' imprisonment, or a fine at level 5 on the standard scale (currently £5,000), or both (FA 1968 s.51(1) and Sch.6, Pt I).

[70] FA 1968 s.40(4).

[71] FA 1968 s.40(5).

[72] The notice is to be sent by registered post or recorded delivery.

in whose register the dealer's premises are entered.[73] The notice must contain the same particulars of the transaction as the dealer is required to enter in his register for other kinds of transaction.[74] The notice, and the particulars to be entered in the register, shall also include the number and place of issue of any passport held by the buyer of the firearm.[75]

CONSEQUENCES OF CONVICTION OF FIREARMS DEALERS

16–13   When a registered firearms dealer[76] is convicted of almost any offence[77] connected with firearms or ammunition, the convicting court has power to order—

(1)   that the name of the dealer be removed from the register; and
(2)   that neither the dealer nor any person who acquires his business, nor any person who took part in the management of the business and was knowingly a party to the offence, shall be registered as a firearms dealer; and
(3)   that any person who, after the date of the court's order, knowingly employs in the management of his business the dealer convicted of the offence, or any person who was knowingly a party to the offence, shall not be registered as a firearms dealer or, if so registered, shall be liable to be removed from the register[78]; and
(4)   that any stock-in-hand of the business shall be disposed of by sale or otherwise in accordance with such directions as may be contained in the order.[79]

---

[73] F(A)A 1988 s.18(2). Failure to comply is an offence with a maximum punishment on summary conviction of 6 months' imprisonment, or a fine at level 5 on the standard scale (currently £5,000), or both (F(A)A 1988 s.18(5)).

[74] For those particulars, see Appendix H at the end of the book.

[75] F(A)A 1988 s.18(3), (4).

[76] A registered firearms dealer is defined as one who is either registered in Great Britain or is registered in Northern Ireland under the Firearms Act 1920 s.8 or any enactment of the Parliament of Northern Ireland amending or substituted for that section (FA 1968 s.57(4)).

[77] More precisely, the offences are: (i) offences against the enactments relating to customs or excise in respect of the import or export of any firearms or ammunition, except any of the types described in items (1) and (2) at para.16–09; (ii) all offences under the Firearms Act 1968 except (briefly): (a) Obtaining or possessing a shot gun without a shot gun certificate and failing to comply with a condition of such a certificate (FA 1968 s.2). (b) A person under 15 handling a shot gun without an adult's supervision or whilst not covered with a gun cover (FA 1968 s.22(3)). (c) Giving a shot gun or ammunition for a shot gun to a person under 15 (FA 1968 s.24(3)). (d) An offence relating specifically to air weapons (FA 1968 s.45(2)). References above to a shot gun include references to component parts of a shot gun and to any accessories for diminishing its noise or flash (FA 1968 ss.45(2); 57(4)).

[78] The evident purpose of an order that a person shall be "liable to be removed from the register" is to enable a court subsequently, after proof of a conviction under this section, to remove from the register another dealer who chooses to employ the convicted dealer or any person who was knowingly a party to the convicted dealer's offence.

[79] FA 1968 s.45(1), (2).

A dealer against whom such an order is made may appeal against it in the same way as he may appeal against his conviction, and the court may, if it thinks fit, suspend the operation of the order pending the appeal.[80]

---

[80] FA 1968 s.45(3). As to an appeal, see, further Ch.5.

CHAPTER 17

Museums' Firearms Licences

The Firearms (Amendment) Act of 1988 introduced provisions enabling the **17–01**
Home Office to issue licences to certain museums authorising them to acquire
and possess firearms for exhibition.[1] The museums to which these arrangements
apply are set out in Appendix B at the end of the book.

An application for a museum licence should be made in writing to the
Operational Policing Policy Unit at the Home Office at 50 Queen Anne's Gate,
London SW1H 9AT. There are no rights of appeal against a refusal to grant a
licence. It is an offence knowingly or recklessly to make a statement which is
false in any material particular in order to obtain the grant, renewal or variation of
a licence.[2]

A licence will authorise the persons responsible for the management of the
museum[3] and their employees, without holding a firearm or shot gun certificate,
to possess, and purchase or acquire,[4] for the purposes of the museum, firearms
and ammunition which are, or are to be normally, exhibited or kept at the
museum or in particular parts of it which the licence may specify. A licence may
also, in similar terms, cover prohibited weapons and prohibited ammunition[5]
without the need to obtain the Home Office special authority which is normally
required.[6]

A licence will not be granted or renewed unless the Home Office is satisfied, **17–02**
after consulting the police for the area in which the museum lies, that the
arrangements for exhibiting and keeping the firearms and ammunition will not
endanger the public safety or the peace.[7]

A licence may contain conditions to secure the safe custody of the firearms
and ammunition.[8] The persons responsible for the management of the museum
commit an offence if they fail to comply with a condition, or if they cause or

---

[1] F(A)A 1988 s.19 and Sch.
[2] F(A)A 1988 Sch. para.4(1)(a). The maximum punishment on summary conviction is six months'
imprisonment, or a fine at level 5 on the standard scale (currently £5,000), or both (F(A)A 1988 Sch.,
para.4(2)).
[3] These persons are defined to mean the museum's board of trustees, governing body or other person
or persons (whether or not incorporated) exercising corresponding functions (F(A)A 1988 Sch.,
para.6).
[4] "Acquire" is defined to mean hire, accept as a gift or borrow (FA 1968 s.57(4), F(A)A 1988
s.25(1)).
[5] For the definitions of "prohibited weapons" and "prohibited ammunition", see Ch.2.
[6] F(A)A 1988 Sch., para.1(2). As to the special authority, see para.2–08.
[7] F(A)A 1988 Sch., para.1(3), (5). Whilst some of the matters reviewed at paras 5–11 to 5–14 in
relation to endangering the public safety or the peace may be relevant, the Home Office's primary
concern is likely to be the security arrangements for the firearms and ammunition.
[8] F(A)A 1988 Sch., para.1(4). There is evidently no power to impose other conditions.

permit another person to do so,[9] but it will be a defence for them to prove that they took all reasonable precautions and exercised due diligence to avoid commission of the offence.[10]

A licence will be granted for a five-year period and can be renewed for successive five-year periods.[11] It will continue in force for that time unless previously revoked or cancelled.[12] Revocation is effected by notice sent by the Home Office to the persons responsible for the management of the museum. A licence can be revoked if—

(a)   the Home Office are satisfied that the continuation of the exemption conferred by the licence[13] would result in danger to the public safety or to the peace[14]; *or*

(b)   the persons responsible for the management of the museum, or any of their employees, have been convicted of an offence under the licensing provisions[15]; *or*

(c)   the persons responsible for the management of the museum have failed to comply with a notice requiring them to surrender the licence on its variation by the Home Office,[16] as described below.

17–03   A notice of revocation will require those persons to surrender the licence to the Home Office.[17] Failure to comply is an offence.[18]

A licence may be varied by notice from the Home Office in two ways: by varying its conditions, or by varying the licence itself so as to extend or restrict the buildings to which it applies.[19] The notice may require the persons responsible for the management of the museum to send the licence to the Home Office for variation within 21 days of the date of the notice.[20]

There is no right of appeal against the revocation or variation of a licence.

The fee for the grant or renewal of a licence is £200, though the Home Office may reduce this in particular cases. When a licence is extended to cover additional premises, the fee will be £75.[21]

---

[9] F(A)A 1988 Sch., para.1(1)(b). For maximum punishments, see fn.2 above. Special provisions about offences by a body corporate may be found in para.4(5) and (6) of the 1988 Act Schedule.

[10] F(A)A 1988 Sch., para.4(4).

[11] The Home Office may by order substitute longer or shorter periods (F(A)A 1988 Sch., para.1(6)).

[12] F(A)A 1988 Sch., para.1(5). A court convicting the licence holders of any of the offences mentioned in this chapter may order the cancellation of the licence (FA 1968 s.52(1); F(A)A 1988 s.25(5)).

[13] i.e. exemption from the need for a firearm or shot gun certificate or for an authority to hold prohibited weapons or ammunition, as the case may be.

[14] F(A)A 1988 Sch., para.1(3), (5). Whilst some of the matters reviewed at paras 5–11 to 5–14 in relation to endangering the public safety or the peace may be relevant, the Home Office's primary concern is likely to be the security arrangements for the firearms and ammunition..

[15] i.e. any of the offences mentioned in this chapter.

[16] F(A)A 1988 Sch., para.2(2), (3).

[17] F(A)A 1988 Sch., para.2(4).

[18] The maximum punishment on summary conviction is a fine at level 3 on the standard scale (currently £1,000) (F(A)A 1988 Sch., para.4(3)).

[19] F(A)A 1988 Sch., para.2(1)

[20] F(A)A 1988 Sch., para.2(2). Failure to return the licence is not made an offence, but is one of the grounds on which the licence may be revoked..

[21] F(A)A 1988 Sch., para.3(1). The amounts of the fees may be varied, or abolished altogether, by Home Office order (FA 1968 s.43(1); F(A)A 1988 Sch., para.3(2)).

The purchase, acquisition[22] or possession of antique firearms by a museum as items of curiosity or ornament will not require a licence.[23]

---

[22] "Acquire" is defined to mean hire, accept as a gift or borrow (FA 1968 s.57(4), F(A)A 1988 s.25(1)).

[23] FA 1968 s.58(2); F(A)A 1988 s.25(6). See, further, para.1–26 and Appendix A where the difficulties of judging whether a firearm is an antique or not are considered.

APPENDIX A

Antique Firearms: Home Office Guidance to the Police

The below may be used as a *guide* in considering whether a firearm is to be **AppA–01** regarded as an antique, although bear in mind, it is always a question of fact for a court as to whether a particular gun is an antique, see para.1–26 for more details:—

Antique firearms

The following will *usually* be considered Antiques:—   **AppA–02**

(a) All muzzle-loading firearms
(b) Breech-loading firearms capable of discharging a rim-fire cartridge exceeding .23 inches calibre (or its metric equivalent), but not 9mm.
(c) Breech-loading firearms using ignition systems other than rim-fire or centre-fire. (These include pin-fire and needle-fire ignition systems.)
(d) Breech-loading centre-fire arms originally chambered for many obsolete cartridges, and which retain that original chambering.

Not antiques

(a) Shot guns and smooth-bored guns, including shot pistols, chambered for **AppA–03** standard shot gun cartridges, .22 inch and 9mm rim-fire cartridges.
(b) Rifles and hand guns chambered for .22 inch or 9mm rim-fire ammunition.
(c) Revolvers, single-shot pistols and self-loading pistols which are chambered for, or will accept, popular centre-fire cartridges of the type .25, .32, .38, .380, .44, .45, .450, .455 and .476 inch, or their metric equivalents including 6.35, 7.62, 7.63, 7.65, 8 and 9mm.
(d) Modern reproduction firearms or old firearms which have been modified to allow the use of shot gun cartridges or certain other cartridges.
(e) Extensively modified weapons (e.g. sawn-off guns).
(f) Verey signalling pistols chambered for 1 and 1½ inch cartridges or 26.5/27mm cartridges.
(g) Pump-action and self-loading centre fire rifles, except that examples originally chambered for certain obsolete cartridges and retaining that original chambering may qualify for exemption as antiques.

AppA–04 **Note (i)**   The exemption does not apply to ammunition, and the possession of ammunition suitable for use with an otherwise antique firearm will normally be taken to indicate that the firearm is not possessed as a curio or ornament.

Note (ii)   The exemption does not apply to firearms of modern manufacture which otherwise conform to the description above. Thus modern firing replicas of obsolete breech-loading or of muzzle-loading firearms will require to be held on certificate. "Modern manufacture" should be taken to mean "manufactured since (or during) the Second World War".

For Firearms of historic interest see Appendix I below.

APPENDIX B

Museums for which Firearms Licences may be issued

The Armouries, HM Tower of London   **AppB–01**
The National Army Museum
The National Museum of Wales
The Royal Air Force Museum
The Science Museum
The Victoria and Albert Museum
The Royal Marines Museum
The Fleet Air Arm Museum
The Royal Navy Museum
The Royal Navy Submarine Museum
The British Museum
The Imperial War Museum
The National Maritime Museum
The National Museums of Scotland
The National Museums and Galleries on Merseyside
The Wallace Collection

A museum or similar institution which is for the time being fully registered **AppB–02** with the Museums and Galleries Commission.[1]

Any other museum or similar institution in Great Britain[2] which has as its purpose, or one of its purposes, the preservation for the public benefit of a collection of historical, artistic or scientific interest which includes or is to include firearms and which is maintained wholly or mainly[3] out of money provided by Parliament or by a local authority.[4]

---

[1] F(A)A 1997 s.47; Firearms (Museums) Order 1997.
[2] "Great Britain" means England, Wales and Scotland, and excludes the Channel Islands and the Isle of Man.
[3] The word "mainly" probably means "more than half" (*Fawcett Properties Ltd v Buckingham CC* [1960] 3 All E.R. 503 at 512, HL).
[4] Other museums or similar institutions may be added to this list by Home Office order (F(A)A 1997 s.47).

APPENDIX C

Close seasons for shooting game and deer

Please note in the case of all the birds and animals in ss.1 and 2, shooting on **AppC–01** Sunday and Christmas Day is forbidden (GA 1831 s.3). All dates are inclusive. The close seasons are not operative in cases where the Ministry of Agriculture imposes a requirement that game be killed to prevent damage to crops, pasture, foodstuffs, livestock, trees, hedges, banks or any works on land (AA 1947 s.98(1), (2)). In the case of all the birds and animals in ss.1 and 2, shooting on Sunday and Christmas Day is forbidden (GA 1831 s.3). All dates are inclusive. The close seasons are not operative in cases where the Ministry of Agriculture imposes a requirement that game be killed to prevent damage to crops, pasture, foodstuffs, livestock, trees, hedges, banks or any works on land (AA 1947 s.98(1), (2)).

Section 1[1]

Black game	11th December to 19th August, except in Somerset, Devon and that part of the New Forest which lies in Hampshire where it is 11th December to 31st August.
Bustard or wild turkey	2nd March to 31st August.
Grouse or red game	11th December to 11th August.
Partridge	2nd February to 31st August.
Pheasant	2nd February to 30th September.

The seasons under s.2. **AppC–02**

---

[1] GA 1831 s.3.

Section 2

Hare	None.[2]

AppC–03 Please note for s.3 other species of deer and close seasons for them may be added by order of the Home Office who may also vary or delete such additions. For instances where deer may be shot out of season, see para.12–12.

Section 3[3]

Male red deer, fallow deer and sika deer	1st May to 31st July.
Female red deer, fallow deer, roe deer and sika deer	1st March to 31st October.
Male roe deer	1st November to 31st March.

---

[2] According to Oke's Game Laws, 5th edition, p.8, the period is March 1 to July 31. This book does not, however, indicate whether or not the dates are inclusive, nor quote any statutory authority for the period. On the other hand, Oke at p.118 takes the view, supported by Halsbury's Laws of England, 4th Edition Reissue, Vol.2, para.292, that there is no specified close season for hares, and this is thought to be the better view. Certainly, there is no period of the year during which it is an offence to kill hares, except for the restrictions on the rights of occupiers to shoot hares and rabbits on certain moorlands and unenclosed lands at certain times of the year, for which see para.13–04. However, in Scotland pursuant to the Wildlife and Natural Environment (Scotland) Act 2011 s.6(2) creates close seasons in respect of the mountain hare and the brown hare. In the case of the mountain hare the close season is the period in any year beginning with March 1 and ending with July 31. In the case of the brown hare the close season is the period in any year beginning with February 1 and ending with September 30. Such close seasons may be varied by Scottish Ministers by Order.

[3] DA 1991 Sch.1.

APPENDIX D

Wild Birds which are Protected by Special Penalties

Avocet
Bee-eater
Bittern
Bittern, Little
Bluethroat
Brambling
Bunting, Cirl
Bunting, Lapland
Bunting, Snow
Buzzard, Honey
Chough
Corncrake
Crake, Spotted
Crossbills (all species)
Curlew, Stone
Divers (all species)
Dotterel
Duck, Long-tailed
Eagle, Golden
Falcon, Gyr
Fieldfare
Firecrest
Garganey
Godwit, Black-tailed
[1]Goldeneye
[2]Goose, Greylag (in Outer Hebrides, Caithness, Sutherland and Wester Ross only)
Goshawk
Grebe, Black-necked
Grebe, Slavonian
Greenshank
Gull, Little
Gull, Mediterranean
Harriers (all species)

---

[1] The special penalties only apply to these birds during their close seasons, for which see App.E, Pt (2).

[2] The special penalties only apply to these birds during their close seasons, for which see App.E, Pt (2).

Heron, Purple
Hobby
Hoopoe
Kingfisher
Kite, Red
Merlin
Oriole, Golden
Osprey
Owl, Barn
Owl, Snowy
Peregrine
Petrel, Leach's
Phalarope, Red-necked
[3]Pintail
Plover, Kentish
Plover, Little-Ringed
Quail, Common
Redstart, Black
Redwing
Rosefinch, Scarlet
Ruff
Sandpiper, Green
Sandpiper, Purple
Sandpiper, Wood
Scaup
Scoter, Common
Scoter, Velvet
Serin
Shorelark
Shrike, Red-backed
Spoonbill
Stilt, Black-winged
Stint, Temminck's
Swan, Bewick's
Swan, Hooper
Tern, Black
Tern, Little
Tern, Roseate
Tit, Bearded
Tit, Crested
Treecreeper, Short-toed
Warbler, Cetti's
Warbler, Dartford
Warbler, Marsh
Warbler, Savi's
Whimbrel

---

[3] The special penalties only apply to these birds during their close seasons, for which see App.E, Pt (2).

APPENDIX E

Wild Birds and Close Seasons

(1) Wild birds which may be killed or taken outside the close
     season

WCA 1981 s.2(1), (3) and Sch.2, Pt I. Those marked with asterisks may no longer **AppE–01**
be killed or taken in Scotland on Sundays or Christmas Day pursuant to WCA
1981 Sch.1A as inserted by the Wildlife and Natural Environment (Scotland) Act
2011 s.3(8).

    Capercaillie
    Coot*
    Duck, Tufted*
    Gadwall*
    Goldeneye*
    Goose, Canada*
    Goose, Greylag*
    Goose, Pink-footed*
    Goose, White-fronted[1]
    Mallard*[2]
    Moorhen*[3]
    Pintail*
    Plover, Golden*
    Pochard*[4]
    Shoveler*
    Snipe, Common*
    Teal*
    Wigeon*
    Woodcock*

---

[1] In England and Wales only.

[2] Before the term Mallard, pursuant to the Wildlife and Natural Environment (Scotland) Act 2011 s.3(7)(a) Black Grouse and Red Grouse are added in respect of Scotland.

[3] After the term Moorhen, pursuant to the Wildlife and Natural Environment (Scotland) Act 2011 s.3(7)(b) Grey Partridge, Red-legged Partridge and Common Pheasant are added in respect of Scotland.

[4] After the term Pochard, pursuant to the Wildlife and Natural Environment (Scotland) Act 2011 s.3(7)(c) Ptarmigan is added in respect of Scotland.

(2)   Close seasons outside which wild birds listed at (1) above
       may be killed, injured or taken

AppE–02 WCA 1981 s.2(4). All dates are inclusive. These close seasons may be varied, and special protection for additional periods given, by Government order (WCA 1981 s.2(5), (6)).

Capercaillie and woodcock[5]	1st February to 30th September.
Snipe	1st February to 11th August.
Wild duck and wild geese in or over any area below high water mark of ordinary spring tides	21st February to 31st August.
In any other case	1st February to 31st August.

---

[5] This period does not apply to woodcock in Scotland which therefore in that country fall under the heading "In any other case".

APPENDIX F

Licences for Shooting Wild Birds and Wild Animals

In this context game birds are included. However, game birds will not be included in respect of Scotland pursuant to the Wildlife and Natural Environment (Scotland) Act 2011 s.2. See WCA 1981 ss.16(1)–(3), (9), 27(1). Licences may be: general or specific; granted to persons of a class or to a particular person; subject to compliance with specified conditions; modified or revoked at any time by the issuing authority. A licence will be valid for the period (not exceeding two years) stated in it (if not previously modified or revoked), and a reasonable charge may be made for it (WCA 1981 s.16(5), (6)(b)).

Purpose for which licence may be granted[1]	Type of wildlife to which it is applicable	Issuing Authority
1. Scientific research or educational	Both	English Nature[2] or the appropriate Secretary of State[3] for birds[4]; English Nature, in other cases
2. Conserving wild birds or wild animals	Both	English Nature[3] or the appropriate Secretary of State[4] for birds[5]; English Nature[3] in other cases
3. Protecting a collection of wild birds or a zoological collection	Both	The appropriate Secretary of State[4] for birds. English Nature[3] for wild animals

---

[1] In respect of Scotland, licenses may also be granted for any other social, economic or environmental purpose pursuant to the Wildlife and Natural Environment (Scotland) Act 2011 s.18.

[2] English Nature's address is Northminster House, Peterborough PE1 1UA.

[3] i.e. (1) in England, the Secretary of State for the Department of the Environment, Transport and the Regions at Tollgate House, Houlton Street, Bristol BS2 9DJ; (2) in Wales, the Secretary of State as above at Cathays Park, Cardiff CF1 3NQ.

[4] The Department of the Environment, Transport and the Regions advises that, in cases of licences which concern birds and where there is an alternative issuing authority, applicants should contact English Nature in the first instance.

4. Preserving public health or public safety and (for birds) air safety	Both	The Ministry of Agriculture or the appropriate Secretary of State[5]
5. Taxidermy	Wild birds	The appropriate Secretary of State[4]
6. Preventing the spread of disease	Both	The Ministry of Agriculture or the appropriate Secretary of State[4]
7. Preventing serious damage to livestock[6], foodstuffs for livestock, crops, vegetables, fruit, growing timber or any other form of property or to fisheries	Both	The Ministry of Agriculture or the appropriate Secretary of State[4]
8. Providing food for human consumption. Licences restricted to: (a) gulls' eggs (b) lapwings' eggs at any time before 15th April in any year	Wild birds	The appropriate Secretary of State

---

[5] Applications should be submitted as follows: in England, to the local Divisional Office of the Ministry of Agriculture; in Wales, to the Welsh Office, Crown Building, Cathays Park, Cardiff CF1 3NQ.

[6] Livestock includes any animal which is kept: for the provision of food, wool, skins or fur; for the purpose of its use in the carrying on of any agricultural activity; or for the provision or improvement of shooting or fishing (WCA 1981 s.27(1)).

APPENDIX G

Wild Animals Which May Not Be Killed or Taken By Certain Methods

WCA 1981 Sch.6. Those marked by an asterisk are repealed in respect of **AppG–01** Scotland pursuant to the Wildlife and Natural Environment (Scotland) Act 2011 s.19.

Badger
Bats, Horseshoe (all species)*
Bats, Typical (all species)*
Cat, Wild*
Dolphin, Bottle-nosed*
Dolphin, Common*
Dormice (all species)*
Hedgehog
Marten, Pine*
Otter, Common*
Polecat*
Porpoise, Harbour (otherwise known as Common porpoise)*
Shrews (all species)
Squirrel, Red

APPENDIX H

Particulars to be Entered by Firearms Dealer in Register of Transactions

1. The quantities and description of firearms and ammunition manufactured **AppH–01** and the dates thereof.
2. The quantities and description of firearms and ammunition purchased or acquired with the names and addresses of the sellers or transferors and the dates of the several transactions.
3. The quantities and description of firearms and ammunition accepted for sale, repair, test, proof, cleaning, storage, destruction or other purpose, with the names and addresses of the transferors and the dates of the several transactions.
4. The quantities and description of firearms and ammunition sold or transferred with the names and addresses of the purchasers or transferees and (except in cases where the purchaser or transferee is a registered dealer) the areas in which the firearm certificates were issued, and the dates of the several transactions.
5. The quantities and description of firearms and ammunition in possession for sale or transfer at the date of the last stocktaking or such other date in each year as may be specified in the register.[1]
6. In the case of a firearm sold for export to a buyer without a firearm or shot gun certificate, the number and place of issue of any passport held by the buyer.[2]

Note:— The Violent Crime Reduction Act 2006 and the Firearms Rules 2007 made provision for the same details to be recorded in a register in relation to sale, repair and possession of air weapons and their components, and of 'metallic primers'.[3]

---

[1] FA 1968 Sch.4; Firearms Rules 1998 r.10(5). See Chs 1 to 3 for further details and references to definitions of the words "transfers", "firearms" and "ammunition". The words "transferees" and "transferors" are to be construed according to the definition of "transfers". The word "acquire" means hire, accept as a gift or borrow (FA 1968 s.57(4)).

[2] F(A)A 1988 s.18(4).

[3] FA 1968 Sch.4, Pt 2.

APPENDIX I

Firearms of Historic Interest

Certain hand guns, which would otherwise be treated as prohibited weapons, may **AppI–01** be held under the authority of a conditional firearm certificate or a visitor's firearm permit[1] if fulfilling certain conditions. one condition is that these guns are not chambered for any of the following types of ammunition[2]:

.22" rim-fire
.25" ACP/6.35mm
.25" – 20
.32 ACP/7.65mm
.32" – 20
.32" Smith & Wesson Long
7.62mm Soviet Tokarev
.38" 40 Winchester
.380 ACP 9mm short
9mm Luger/Parabellum/9 x 19mm
.38 Smith & Wesson
.38" Special
.38" – 200
.44" Special
.44" – 40 Winchester
.45 ACP

---

[1] For visitors' firearm permits, see Ch.7.

[2] F(A)A 1997 s.7; F(A)A 1997 (Firearms of Historic Interest) Order 1997.

INDEX